WORD LIKE A BELL

JOHN A. MINAHAN

WORD
LIKE A
BELL

JOHN KEATS,
MUSIC AND
THE ROMANTIC POET

THE KENT STATE UNIVERSITY PRESS
KENT, OHIO, AND LONDON, ENGLAND

Library of Congress Catalog Card Number 91-29422
ISBN 0-87338-453-9
Manufactured in the United States of America

Library of Congress Cataloging-in-Publication Data
Minahan, John A., 1956–
    Word like a bell : John Keats, music and the romantic poet / John
A. Minahan.
        p.   cm.
    Includes bibliographical references and index.
    ISBN 0-87338-453-9 (cloth : alk.) ∞
    1. Keats, John, 1795–1821—Knowledge—Music. 2. Romanticism—
England. 3. Music and literature.   I. Title.
PR4838.M74M56   1992
821'.7—dc20   91-29422

British Library Cataloging-in-Publication data are available.

CONTENTS

PREFACE

In his verse epistle "To Charles Cowden Clarke," John Keats writes:

> But many days have passed since last my heart
> Was warm'd luxuriously by divine Mozart;
> By Arne delighted, or by Handel madden'd;
> Or by the song of Erin pierc'd and sadden'd:
> What time you were before the music sitting,
> And the rich notes to each sensation fitting;
> Since I have walk'd with you through shady lanes
> That freshly terminate in open plains,
> And revel'd in a chat that ceased not
> When at night-fall among your books we got . . .
>
> (109–18)[1]

It's an early poem and overall not a very good one, full of the stilted diction and indulgent imagery marring Keats's first efforts. But it's an important work for us to know. When he wrote it in the fall of 1816, Keats was trying to learn his craft (and to make a living) as a poet. This was a particularly unsettled time in an unsettled life. Keats often took comfort in visits to Clarke, an old friend and the son of his schoolmaster at Enfield, who introduced him to both poetry and music. To visit with Clarke was to read and discuss Spenser *and* to listen while Clarke played the works of the great composers on the piano.

From an early age, then, the two arts were associated in Keats's mind. In fact, he never stopped associating poetry with music, and he went on to achieve greatness as a poet largely by drawing upon the energy of that association. Consider these somewhat more well-known passages:

> Awakening up, he took her hollow lute,—
> Tumultuous,—and, in chords that tenderest be,
> He play'd an ancient ditty, long since mute,
> In Provence call'd, "La belle dame sans mercy":
> Close to her ear touching the melody;—
>
> The sedge has wither'd from the lake,
>   And no birds sing.
>
> Fled is that music:—do I wake or sleep?
>
> Where are the songs of spring? Ay, where are they?
>   Think not of them, thou hast thy music too,—
>
> A haunting music, sole perhaps and lone
> Supportress of the faery-roof, made moan
> Throughout, as fearful the whole charm might fade.

Music—sometimes deliberately employed imagery like the above examples, sometimes otherwise—is ever present in Keats's masterpieces. This is to a degree Clarke's legacy. But a devoted, simultaneous attention to poetry and music also typifies the age. As I'll argue, when we inquire into the relationship between poetry and music, we also inquire into the essence of Romanticism itself. Music and poetry meet in that region where Romantic poets can find, on conscious and intuitive levels, what they most need to find as Romantic poets: a vocabulary and a model for the interaction of time, mind, and language. To understand Romantic poetry, we must explore that region.

I can hardly claim to be the first to notice the importance of music to Romanticism. What's new about this study is that it offers both a more extensive treatment of the topic than it has yet received and a sense of *pattern*. The two are related. A comprehensive overview of Romantic poetry and critical thinking reveals that these artists, in giving voice to their central concerns, make use of music in consistent ways. The following pages will show how and why.

This study, therefore, is not a work of comparative aesthetics. Rather, it is an effort to illuminate the connections among differing but related modes of expression, the better to locate Romantic poetry in its historical and aesthetic context. Such an effort will also render more tractable certain issues in current theoretical debate. Using music as a critical resource, this study will explain what many Romantic texts, using music as a literary resource, suggest: neither formalist fixity nor radical indeterminacy can account for all interpretive acts, yet each of these responses, along with many others, can have a place in time's unfolding patterns. Today, when diversity and divisiveness are so often confused both within the academy and without, the Romantic understanding of temporality offers a particularly important lesson.

John Keats, in a brief and remarkable career, unblinkingly explored the complexities of temporal experience with music's help. His poems thus provide excellent source material. The following introduction will develop a method with which to examine the meeting ground of poetry and music, preparing the way for the discussion of Keats's work itself in parts 1, 2, and 3.

Before proceeding, however, I should acknowledge that any consideration of one art in tandem with another runs a couple of risks. On the one hand, it is tempting to make an argument that, to be admittedly reductive, often runs like this: poetry and music act similarly because the same forces shape all thought, thus all products of thought. This search for deep structure or archetype or cultural master code tends to trivialize the experience of the artwork per se, treating it as so much foreground clutter to be gotten past. More important, that approach offers little in terms of critical method. Any structure or code so vastly inclusive must also be nebulous, connected tenuously, if at all, to the artwork as artwork. To get *to* the archetype, you have to get *through* the poem and *through* the musical composition, and the archetype teaches you nothing about how to do that. To read or to listen, one needs to understand the ways in which artistic accomplishments are defined and valued. Such definitions and values can change; poetry and music belong to a time and a place. So, therefore, does whatever they share.[2] Art may show us something about the mind-in-itself; but it also shows us how the mind works under the pressure of particular circumstances, which is of equal if not greater interest.

How then, if not from some ur-pattern of culture or experience, can music inform poetry? Here we run into another vexing issue: influence. Though doubtless real, influence is often too tangled to be useful. We know, for instance, that Keats learned much from Clarke; we do not know precisely what he learned. And even if we did, we would still need to assess what Keats made of what he learned—which may not, in the end, have much to do with Clarke. As Marilyn Butler says, we're liable "to read the writer's mind as being more logical, coherent and academic than the human mind naturally is."[3]

Still, because we do not wish to ascribe to Keats notions impossible for him to have held, a discussion of something like influence is necessary. If we ask, What did the poet know and when did he know it? we're on the right track—more or less. Literary criticism must often be based on circumstantial evidence. We have to work with what we have: the poems themselves, of course, and any other records the poet left that seem useful in light of the poems (Keats's letters are especially relevant, as we'll see). The rest is a matter of motive and opportunity. We study the records of those who knew the poet, or of those who, at about the same time, explored issues that the poet explored, in order to ask a better, if more complicated, question: What can we know about what could have shaped this poetry? Hence, this study will examine not only Keats but also, when appropriate, other eighteenth- and nineteenth-century artists and thinkers—neither as a matter of influence nor of archetype but as a matter of context. Our goal is to determine where Keats might have gotten his ideas and attitudes so that we might better understand what he did with them.

Though pieces by other composers are discussed, I've mostly used Beethoven's work as the musical examples. Practicality informs my decision. This being a work of literary scholarship, I assume my readers will generally be more familiar with poetry than with music, hence they will appreciate my directing them toward some of Beethoven's best-known compositions. But I do have another motivation. Many readers may feel that, beyond the difficulties of comparing one art with another, a further issue presents itself—one having to do with temperament. Keats may not seem, at first, a Beethovenian poet (or Beethoven a Keatsian composer). I hope my work will offer some new perspectives—on Beethoven, and on Keats, and perhaps on even more. We ask about music to learn about Keats; we ask about Keats to learn about Romanticism; and we ask about Romanticism to speculate—with, one hopes, the proper mixture of daring and humility—about the essential meanings of human experience.

Which is, I think, the whole point.

My thanks to: Gordon Bok, Barb and Norman Brand, Jim Corcoran, Jon Hassler, David Jarroway, Mr. and Mrs. Daniel F. Minahan (senior and junior), Julia Morton and the staff at Kent State University Press, John Pfordresher, the staff of the Mount Pleasant branch of the Providence Public Library, and Robert and Rita Rinehart. I'd also like to thank Mutlu Blasing, Bill Keach, Elizabeth Kirk, Lorraine Mazza, Rick Russom, and my students at Brown University.

This book began as a way to bring together my interests as a musician, writer, teacher, and reader. "Five years have passed," full of ups and downs. My wife and children have made every moment something to be treasured. To them this work is dedicated.

WORD LIKE A BELL

INTRODUCTION

Poetry and Music:
The Search for a Meeting Ground

A CADEMIC disciplines exist for the convenience of academic analysis. Nothing wrong with that—as long as we remember that life is often messier than the existence of departmental boundaries might suggest. Granted, literary criticism can't afford to be so messy; critical thinking of any kind can be defined as an attempt to leave life a bit tidier than one finds it. But neither can criticism afford to overlook what Jean-Pierre Barricelli has pointed out: literature is interdisciplinary anyway.[1] Competent reading is necessarily informed by strictly literary concerns—you have to know a sonnet when you see one—but it also requires an awareness extending far beyond those concerns. I conceive my inquiry into John Keats, music, and the Romantic poet as an exercise in literary criticism; I also believe that literary criticism itself ought to be conceived as an exercise in a much larger endeavor. Writers, whether poets or critics, may live *for* art, but they live *in* a world—a world with a lot more in it than their writings, just as their writings have a lot more in them than ideas about writing. As Earl Wasserman says, only the most ascetic critic would scorn history and biography.[2] We use that information anyway, whether we admit doing so or not, just as we use psychology, linguistics, sociology, philosophy. Parallels and intersections between literature and the other arts may also tell us a great deal, especially in the case of the Romantics. Music was of special importance to them and to John Keats in particular.

The most valuable (and honest) criticism, then, has always been interdisciplinary to begin with. But I use the term advisedly. Interdisciplinary studies are often so general that they're generally of little value. Barricelli argues that such studies should be specific enough to contribute to the critical methodology of *all* the fields they draw on.[3] That may be a bit too ambitious for this study. But Barricelli's point is well taken. If we would better understand a literary work, we must try to understand not only what is in the work but also what conditions and is conditioned by the work. As Bernard Blackstone says, our concern should be with "affinities, with mental structures which here and there overlap, however widely they may proliferate in other directions."[4] In other words, the specific patterns of thought that we call music and poetry, though they differ in important ways, also interact in important ways. An understanding of their interaction will enable us to understand poetry better.

Lawrence Kramer, whose work has been indispensible to my own, offers a handful of readings that bear out this claim.[5] While we should emulate Kramer's ability to read closely, to see correspondences between this poem and that piece of music, we must also try to develop a deeply grounded, broadly applicable method. What causes the intuition that poetry and music may be related? More exactly, what allowed Keats, consciously or otherwise, to sense relations between poetry and music? What will allow *us* to perceive, to understand, and to explain those relations? Can those relations be applied to the reading of Romantic poetry in general?

Here we hit a snag. Within the broader domain of literary criticism, "Literature and Music" is still a fledgling. It has yet to prove its worth as an exact mode of inquiry, in spite of its not being exactly new. Nearly fifty years ago, Calvin Brown attempted to define the meeting ground between the two arts. He wanted to eliminate the simplistic impressionism that often characterized literary-musical discussions. Like René Wellek and Austin Warren before him, Brown argued against any real equation between the arts. Literary phenomena correspond only generally, if at all, with musical phenomena. An artist who tries to use in a literal way the means of another art is an artist who doesn't understand his or her own craft. Which is why, according to Brown, the study of music and literature must focus by and large on second-rate art.[6]

Brown's groundbreaking work remains a valuable corrective to overly eager leaps at intuition. But he based his judgments solely on surface events; for example, counterpoint, the simultaneous sounding of two melodic lines, can occur only in music, because in poetry you must read one thing at a time. Yes and no. Reading is a complex affair, as is the relation between consciousness and temporality. To "read one thing at a time" is not necessarily to *think about* one thing at a time. Might there be some connection between musical counterpoint and, say, the simultaneity of meaning in poetic metaphor? This seems a profitable way to go: looking not for literal translations or for shared "mood" but for correspondingly structured experiences.[7] In fact, many recent studies, by articulating such experiences, preserve Brown's standards yet go beyond his limitations. The field is growing rapidly, though not without resistance. Some of this resistance—the kind that can be ignored critically if not politically—is based on academic territoriality; the more productive kind senses a need for direction. If "Literature and the Other Arts" is to achieve precision, it must clarify its goals, its methods, and its grounds.

Again, we need to understand how music and poetry meet. Where to begin? The two arts converge in opera, song, musical drama, and the like. But these are secondary, not in terms of quality but in terms of number. Few composers have made their mark exclusively in opera; few poets have achieved greatness exclusively as lyricists; and those artists who write both music and lyrics, though often great, are also rare. More important, whether a contest or a synthesis, the sung word differs in effect from both spoken poetry and instrumental music, which, in Keats's day, were far more common. We don't want to restrict our scope from the beginning. Our interest is in seeing what poetry as poetry and music as music share.

We encounter a similar problem if we focus on poets who know something about music, or on composers who know something about poetry. Again, they are rare individuals, as often dilettantes as experts in both fields, who tempt us to talk about something we're trying to avoid: How did music influence the poet? But there is another possibility. Brown says that, in consolation for being forced to discuss the second-rate art that seeks literal translations between poetry and music, we can discover what little there is to know about poetry's relation with music by studying the musical allusions in first-rate literature. But poetry alluding to music represents a small body of verse, and even a great poet may say something about music that's just plain wrong; we may learn about that poet's idea of music but we learn nothing about the meeting ground of the two arts. Moreover, some poems and some aspects of poetry may have a relation to music without mentioning, or needing to mention, that art at all. So we sense with metaphor. We'd be foolish to overlook what poets themselves say about music; this is a good place to begin, as we'll see in part 1. But we'd be even more foolish not to ask, before we begin, why the poet would mention music. What grounds the use of music as an idea or allusion in the first place? How and why do the two arts meet?

Perhaps this meeting ground has something to do with sound. Music can be described as organized sound; so can poetry—at least, so can certain aspects of poetry such as rhythm and rhyme. Still, we have to be on guard. For one thing, as Northrop Frye argues, when we call poetry "musical" we usually mean that it "sounds nice." Different people have different ideas about what sounds "nice." Does German sound nicer than French? Does Swinburne sound nicer than Shakespeare? The answer is, of course, that it depends. Whose standards of niceness are we using? And what exactly have we learned about poetry's link with music if we do demonstrate that a poem sounds nice? According to Frye, not much; music itself sounds nice very little of the time: "Every piece of music is a disturbance of an underlying concord."[8] Music needs a reason for moving forward in time. To do so, it departs from and returns to consonance. Once this return is accomplished on a small scale, that section of the piece is resolved; once accomplished on a large scale, the piece itself is complete. Thus music must comprise for the most part either chordal dissonance or structural instability.

Because a lack of consonance motivates musical events, Frye goes on to argue that "musical" poetry is poetry that sounds rough. This doesn't necessarily follow—"rough" is as slippery a term as "nice"—but Frye's point is worthwhile: we should not confuse our ideas of pleasant poetic sound with the complexities of musical structure.[9]

Still, sound may have something to do with the meeting ground between poetry and music. Composers organize sound so that, with their art, they can convey meaning and emotion. Do poets organize sound in similar ways so that they can convey similar meanings, similar emotions? This question assumes, of course, a verbal performance of poetry—which is not unwarranted: whether read aloud or silently, poetry is that use of language where sound plays an unusually active role. The question also assumes that music does convey meaning and emotion, thereby acting like verbal language. Again, this is not unwarranted. According to Deryck Cooke, music is a language whose laws are within the unconscious mind—not as archetypes but as a system, a set of formulae (related to stylistic conventions but also to the physical characteristics of sound) that the listener must learn in order to make sense of music. We recognize notes and chords and rhythms as following or deviating from certain patterns.[10] For example, the dominant chord should resolve to the tonic; if not there, then to the submediant; if not there, then to the subdominant, but only as part of a move back to the dominant and from there to the tonic.

Fred Lerdahl and Ray Jackendoff, who have attempted to apply the principles of linguistics to music theory, argue that music does have a grammar, a way of putting its materials together to make coherent statements. But it has no grammatical functions like noun and verb, no semantic categories like synonymy, and, despite its basis in sound, no phonological patterns themselves productive of meaning like lip-rounding, tongue height, or intonation. As Leonard Meyer puts it, though "the overall emotional organization" in music often resembles what happens in language, music has nothing like linguistic syntax.[11]

On the other hand, verbal language has no equivalents for chord function or key systems; for textural hierarchies like harmony and melody; and, again despite its basis in sound, no real equivalents for music's systematic and structural use of dynamics, tone color, or tempo. Further, poetry, though highly organized speech, is made of the same stuff as ordinary speech. Thus, if it's read (or written) with the strictness of musical rhythms, or if its choice of words seems forced by the rhyme scheme, the poem is usually unsatisfying. The best poetry often treats sound as a subtext: rhyme and rhythm employed so unobtrusively that ordinary language acquires an attractiveness and complexity made all the more powerful because they float just beyond conscious attention.

We've described rhyme and meter as *aspects* of poetry. They contribute; they do not govern. As James Anderson Winn points out, though we might enjoy the sound, we can't get over the feeling that poetry must also say something; more precisely, that poetry can never not say something and still be poetry—or verbal language at all—whereas music needn't "say" anything.[12] Music and poetry, though both can be described as language, thus seem to share nothing that makes each a language to begin with.

We might conclude, then, that verbal language must refer to the world, whereas musical language refers to nothing except its own patterns of sound. Such a conclusion would be not only barren but unhistorical. The idea of "absolute" music—music needing nothing but itself to organize itself—is no older than the eighteenth century. Until then, music, lacking a clear and comprehensive sense of inherent structural necessity, had to be organized by some extramusical program—a story, a set of lyrics, a ritual, a dance figure—or it had to be very short. And even after large-scale instrumental music came on the scene, no composer would claim that an individual piece could stand on its own, independent of some system of relations extrinsic to the piece itself. Even Arnold Schoenberg, who in the early twentieth century abandoned all previous systems of relations, struggled mightily to set up, with the twelve-tone method, one of his own.

Music means system. A musical composition must have a relation to some system of sonic patterns beyond itself—the "tonal" system, for example, which mandates that chords follow particular progressions—in order to make sense of itself. Those patterns, Meyer argues, have a relation to something beyond themselves. Music conveys meaning because its "formal and emotional impact are one." Cooke argues similarly when he talks about "the naked feeling communicated directly" in music.[13] We are moving in a good direction here, though each position has problems. To assert the identity of emotion and form in music is to assert an opposition between them, a potential or prior not-one-ness needing to be negated, if not in the work, then in the consciousness that perceives the work; such a perception defeats Meyer's own point that structure and feeling are inextricable. As for Cooke, communication of feeling is neither naked nor direct, since communication *is* mediation. But Cooke's emphasis on feeling, and Meyer's emphasis on music need-ing emotion, or meaning, or something besides itself: these are on target. As Susanne Langer has argued, though music exists in sound and pat-tern, our interest in it is related to the life of feeling.[14]

All music is program music. I say this not because a musical compo-sition tells a story, though such may be a composer's intent, but because sound doesn't become music unless it follows certain patterns informing but not residing in the music. Leo Treitler has argued that the model of music as self-referent pattern perpetuates an ancient and useless sense of antagonism between reason and passion.[15] We listen not solely because we wish to understand chord progressions and the like; we listen be-cause, in so understanding, we are touched and moved. We perceive and make sense of patterns of sound. Those patterns are enabled to make sense because they direct our attention beyond themselves to ideas of re-lation, such as tonic and dominant or dissonance and consonance. And those patterns in turn direct our attention to emotional and intellectual relations like tension and release or loss and recovery.

Music looks outward from itself to the world, or at least to the pat-terns of experience. It refers. This referentiality, however, is hardly its link with poetry, and for several reasons. Although music must direct our attention to systems of sonic and emotional relations, it clearly does not refer to things and ideas and feelings the way words do: a C chord does not name a person, place, or thing; a dominant to tonic progression does not join a subject with a predicate. On the other hand, poststruc-turalist theory has shown us, if nothing else, that referentiality is itself a difficult issue. Because the word causes us to look (or try to look or fail to look) to a meaning, it must always stand at a distance from that mean-ing. No necessary relation exists between a word and the thing or idea or feeling with which we associate it. This is not to imply that any connec-tion between word and meaning is a fiction begging to be deconstructed. Roman Jakobsen says that though the relation of word and meaning is arbitrary (discounting special cases like onomatopoeia), it is necessary within a system. Once established, the word-as-idea-and-sound takes its place in a much larger complex of sound-meanings; change this one element and the entire system will experience a shift. Craig La Drière points out that connections between sounds and meanings, though they may lack inherent necessity, are products of social action; hence, they exist as literary, social, and aesthetic objects in themselves.[16]

It is an undeniable fact of empirical experience that those constructs of sound / meaning called words refer to the world. But if words *merely refer* to the world, how do we account for the ways that words seem to constitute our world, or at least to condition our perception of it? And if words refer merely *to the world,* how do we account for the ways in which words achieve different meanings in different contexts, how a word can mean something in, say, a particular poem that it means nowhere else? A poem refers and in some ways it is self-contained, yet its self-containment differs in type and degree from a musical composition's. Music is self-contained and in some ways it refers, though how it refers and what it refers to differ from the referentiality of verbal language. What the two kinds of language do seem to share, then, is that neither looks unequivocally to itself or outward from itself.

It is within this problem area that we may find a solution. What neither language possesses may be precisely what they share. Kramer points the way. Rather than two different *kinds* of language, he suggests two *dimensions.* One "invests significance in realities or fictions outside the work of art," whether in the world or in the self. The other looks inward toward the work itself. Verbal language's ability to mean derives primarily from the former, music's from the latter—primarily, but not exclusively. Words refer explicitly; yet any verbal utterance, especially one as self-consciously constructed as poetry, derives a portion of its effect from the ways in which the elements of the utterance are combined, the way they unfold in the reader's experience. Music reverses that balance. Its combinatory dimension is experienced explicitly; it is, in fact, all that can be experienced thus. Yet what Kramer calls music's "unique suggestiveness" derives from its ability to refer to meanings or ideas or emotions that gain power by being inexact, implicit, and tacit.[17]

Both words and music, then, convey meaning and emotion; both signify. In musical signification, combinatory meaning has priority; it is the first and the most important object of attention. The individual units of sense—notes, chords, rhythms—mean what they mean because they occur in this piece only. These units can mean because they also refer the listener to systems of musical relations without the piece, which relations in turn refer the listener to emotional and intellectual experiences. Yet to become aware of those relations and those experiences, we must first attend to, and let our attention be governed by, the piece or passage at hand.

In verbal signification, referentiality has priority. A word, to be a word at all, must refer to ideas, feelings, thoughts, or things. (At least it must *seem* to do so. If referentiality is an illusive construct, it is one without which we never function; hence, it is as real as any datum of awareness can be.) Meanings acquired in and by virtue of a particular arrangement are relevant, both to that arrangement and to our general sense of the word; yet to become aware of those meanings, we must first attend to, and let our attention be governed by, what the word means prior to that particular context.

Both aspects of signification—referential and combinatory—are needed to make sense of any statement, verbal or musical. We can use a global analogy: referential meaning at one pole, combinatory at the other pole. Much as all positions are to a greater or lesser degree north or south of the poles themselves, so all signification occurs in the variegated terrain between reference and combination. Some uses of language are closer to the poles, some to the equator. An owner's manual for a toaster or a piece of music composed according to rolls of dice are farther from the equator than the poetry we'll be examining in this study. Standing at the pole itself is impossible, since it disappears into a hypothetical point. Crossing the equator is likewise impossible, for then that mode of signification would cease to be itself. As Brown rightly says, poetry can't do what music does. But some uses of language, by steering into the equatorial zones, can draw more heavily than usual upon the energy flowing from the farther pole.

Verbal signification is primarily referential. But because it does not occur at the pole itself, it always draws to a greater or lesser degree on the energy of combination. The verbal sign, though it always points to a signified, also always points to itself as a signifier. When the act of pointing to itself approaches copriority with the act of pointing to the signified, then verbal language begins to act more like musical language. In fact, Walter Pater, whose work sometimes forms a link between Romantic thought and modern criticism, called this phenomenon "the condition of music."[18] What the sign stands for retains priority; referentiality cannot become tacit, as in music. But how the sign stands acquires priority; combination can become explicit, as in music.

We need to be more specific. Combination is always active in verbal language. In poetry, we are invited to attend to combination in special ways. Under what circumstances does this invitation occur, and how are those circumstances relevant to Romantic poetry? Poetry can approach music by virtue of explicit combinatory meaning. In the late eighteenth and early nineteenth centuries, poetry does approach music because the two arts share a particular kind of combinatory meaning. We can call this mode of combination "Romantic Time."

The distinction between reference and combination corresponds roughly to that between semantics and syntax.[19] The former is shaped by meanings in place prior to any particular context, the latter by meanings that develop within and by virtue of context, interplay, and patterning. To this rather static model (and here we break from structuralist or cognitive models) we can add the element of process. A combination requires time—to be perceived, to unfold its patterns, to form and deform, to build and unbuild. Of course, reference unfolds no less resolutely in time; any verbal signification requires duration. This adds little to our argument—nothing in human life does not unfold in time—though it does show that we need to forge a stronger connection between combinatory meaning, temporality, and Romanticism.

Usually, a verbal utterance is primarily referential, its semantical dimension being the object of primary attention. Combination, or its syntactical dimension, is usually an object of secondary attention: to know *how* a word means in a sentence or a poem, we need to know first *what* the word means. Though secondary, it is always active. Reference unfolds in time; combination is the way it unfolds as that way becomes productive of meaning. That is, combinatory meaning enables patterns of time themselves to be significant. A verbal utterance that not only points to a pattern of time but also, by the way it is structured, allows that pattern to contribute palpably to meaning is an utterance that acts in musical ways, because in music such palpable patterns of time are the objects of primary attention.

Romantic poetry seeks such time-saturated, musiclike utterances. Though they differed in many important respects, all the major Romantic poets make time integrally important in their work: Keats's wrestling with the opportunities and burdens of literary tradition, as well as his sense of the ineffability of all that is most desirable in life; Blake and the energy of dialectic, the ongoing process of contraries interacting; Byron's vision of how, in time, all things change, deteriorate, self-destruct; Wordsworth's, Coleridge's, and Shelley's sense of the ground of Being (whether nature or the imagination or God or the One) as a process, as well as their corresponding notion that duration must always intervene between experience and understanding of that experience.

Kramer calls Romanticism an *activity*.[20] A sense of dynamism and of possibility, a thankfulness, as in Wordsworth's ode on immortality, for misgivings, vanishings, unresolved and unresolvable issues: these help to define Romanticism. I say "help" deliberately. Barricelli says Romanticism can be defined by its undefinability, by its drive to experience "totality in all its contradictions." Susan Wolfson speaks of the "fundamentally interrogative character" of Romantic poetry, which is constituted on "perceptions that provoke inquiry, experiences that elude or thwart stable organization, events that challenge previous certainties and require new terms of interpretation."[21]

We'll examine Wordsworth, Coleridge, Shelley, and, of course, Keats in more detail presently. For now, we should note that this attention to and conception of time lines up with much in eighteenth- and nineteenth-century thought. As G. J. Whitrow points out, "Our intuition that time is something universal and absolute" is not necessarily correct. The Romantics have a very particular model of time. In their age, the duration rather than the instant becomes the characteristic quality of time.[22] Time is above all succession. Improvements in transportation and mechanization make duration urgently palpable (because we *can* hurry, we can also feel the present passing as never before); improvements in historical inquiry give the past both largeness and texture (we know what has been happening, and we know that it has been happening for a long time). The Romantics manifest this view of time as duration—as growth, change, dynamism, birth, decay. But they also reject, or try to reject, what they perceive to be the hollow confidence of this view. History can regularize causation too rigidly; and improvements in mechanization, transportation, and the like can compress experience too tightly.

In fact, time itself may be "a menace as much as a promise."[23] Thomas MacFarland has described the Romantic notion of time as "a simultaneity of nowness and passing away." In this moment there is life and food for future years; all things become more fully what they are as they grow and change. The sense of life as wholeness comes out of a sense of process, but so does a sense of life here and now as torn and broken.[24] Time builds and unbuilds. Growth, complexity, contradiction, vitality, organism: such is the condition (or, more accurately, the process) of Being itself. But the organic whole, be it plant or animal or poem, can exist only as and in duration—which is also what gives rise to fragmentation and decay. The entity as it is now will never be again what it has been, nor will it ever, as it is now, be what it will become; yet because it must contain and thus stand for and point to both past and future, it can never become fully present either.

Paul de Man has argued that Romantic poetry uses what he calls "the rhetoric of temporality." The Romantic self is endlessly caught in the impossibility of oneness with itself, because Romanticism is characterized by a sense of distance between the present and adequacy. What is here and now is not sufficient. Romantic poetry, then, is both allegorical and ironic: allegorical because meaning is always posterior, always related to its source by distance, difference, and falling-away; ironic because any sense of completeness that can be achieved in any present instant must belong in that instant to the past. Romanticism tends to locate meaning in a prior and essentially unavailable wholeness. Whatever is complete or attractive or meaningful is also gone.[25]

De Man's brilliant but confining argument shows some of the characteristics of Romantic time and its interplay with language. There are others. For one thing, the Romantic view of language, as we'll see in part 1, includes more than rhetoric. More important, Romantic time has a *pattern*. De Man grounds his argument on a metaphysics of absence; Romantic time grounds itself on the patterned process in which absence and presence become aspects of each other. Romanticism seeks to recover the past, but it also seeks to discover (or is surprised by) something new: not the past but the past-in-the-present.

Music is regularly found in the proximity of such a discovery. Recall the passage we examined in the preface:

> But many days have passed since last my heart
> Was warm'd luxuriously by divine Mozart; ...

One of the most delightful experiences available to the poet is gone. True, the passage could refer merely to a pleasant visit remembered fondly. But the act of fondly remembering itself characterizes this poet— and Romanticism in general. Fled is that (or any) music. The sedge has withered; no birds sing *now*. The fairy enchantment of music can fade. In Keats's poetry, music is associated either with the past or with the present's liability to become the past. This is crucial, insofar as we can read Keats as a poet of sensory immediacy and we can regard Romanticism as an urge toward spontaneity. To an extent, these are so. But they are themselves grounded on and enabled by a model of time in which the past plays a tremendously important role. De Man is partially right; so is the perception of immediacy and spontaneity. Romantic time is, for the same reason and in the same moment, nowness and passing away. It is the process of turning the past over in one's mind to discover now what was not (and perhaps could not) be discovered then, a process that saves the past from loss and the present from anomie—a process much like what is involved in listening to music. The visit with Clarke, though past, has become a recollection, with its own value and its own dynamics.

It's arguable that the poem's closed couplet form is itself an attempt to recover the past. The act of employing a device belonging in 1816 more to literary history than to contemporary poetry is possibly emblematic of the act of returning, or of trying to return, to those warm and luxurious yet vanished moments spent with Clarke. Notice, though, how Keats uses the form:

> What time you were before the music sitting,
> And the rich notes to each sensation fitting;
> Since I have walk'd with you through shady lanes
> That freshly terminate in open plains,
> And revel'd in a chat that ceased not
> When at night-fall among your books we got . . .

The couplets stretch at their own limits; the poet's thoughts run beyond the rhyme boundaries. Tension within the poem results; but out of this tension comes a fresh approach to the closed couplet, whose use had long since grown stale. In attempting to recover the past, the poet finds something new—which is a fairly accurate description of Keats's career, and of Romanticism in general. Again, as in music, the sound of the poem as it unfolds in time makes its own suggestions toward the meaning of the experience of time.

Music can interact with poetry in other ways as well. In the late eighteenth and early nineteenth centuries, the musical organization most frequently employed was "rounded binary," often formulated as A-B-A'. One group of materials gives way to another, then the original group returns, usually altered (e.g., a change of texture or harmony, an added or deleted passage here and there). These changes heighten interest by adding variety to measures already heard; more important, they articulate the difference between first and second hearings. Even when material reappears exactly as before, our perception of it differs. We now hear the first section as lost-and-then-recovered. Thus, the material itself is often made different: not A but A prime. The rounded binary shape can organize pieces small and large: minuet / trio / minuet, melody / bridge / melody, rondo (theme, departure, return of theme), sonata (exposition, development, recapitulation). The pattern is both progressive and regressive: from stability through instability to stability recovered though changed.

A parallel between music and poetry can be seen in the paradigm of "the Greater Romantic lyric" as formulated by M. H. Abrams. Typically the poetic speaker will begin by describing a landscape. Something in that landscape, usually some change, will initiate a response bound up in memory or feeling or anticipation. This response in turn will lead the speaker to an insight, a decision, a way of confronting loss. The poem will then return to where it began, but with a vital difference: both landscape and poet are renewed by virtue of what Abrams calls "the intervening meditation."[26] This dynamic informs many important Romantic poems, among them "Frost at Midnight," "Ode: Intimations of Immortality," "Tintern Abbey," "Ode to the West Wind," and "Ode to a

Nightingale." But why? What motivates the artwork to round on itself thus, and what enables this rounding to provide closure?

To address these issues, we should turn again to the meeting ground between poetry and music. Music can interact with poetry as an idea or allusion, or as ways of manipulating sound, or (as we've just seen) as a formal shape. But all these, I will argue, are at the least manifestations or symptoms, at the most enactments, of a model of time shared by literary and musical artists in the late eighteenth and early nineteenth centuries. Beethoven is quoted as saying of his working methods:

> I carry my thoughts about with me for a long time, sometimes a very long time, before I set them down. At the same time my memory is so faithful to me that I am sure not to forget a theme which I have once conceived, even after years have passed. I make many changes, reject and reattempt until I am satisfied. Then the working out in breadth, length, height and depth begins in my head, and since I am conscious of what I want, the basic idea never leaves me. It rises, grows upward, and I hear and see the picture as a whole take shape and stand forth before me as though cast in a single piece . . . .[27]

The process of composing music is an establishment of some initial conception, then a departure from and, finally, a return to that conception with the realization that it has changed somehow. Duration must intervene between the idea in itself and the fulfillment of that idea in a work of art. The pattern of time in Beethoven's music—most frequently one variant or another of the rounded binary form—is also the pattern of time in which Beethoven composed his music: establishment, departure, return with a difference.

A similar pattern informs the Romantic model of poetic composition. Wordsworth argued that

> poetry is the spontaneous overflow of powerful feelings: it takes its origin from emotion recollected in tranquillity: the emotion is contemplated till, by a species of re-action, the tranquillity gradually disappears, and an emotion, kindred to that which was before the subject of contemplation, is gradually produced, and does itself actually exist in the mind. In this mood successful composition generally begins . . . [28]

Poetry is secondary. It comes *after*—its emotions are "kindred to" but not the same as those in—the patterned duration preceding the moment in which writing begins. Composition is impossible until the original conception or experience that underlies the poem becomes the past, because in the process of becoming the past it acquires something. The poet, though losing the immediacy of what was once present, gains its meaning. Between establishment and return grows difference, whose essence, Wordsworth hoped and believed, is wisdom.

Only when the poet is "without immediate external excitement" can poetry occur. He is affected "by absent things as if they were present."[29] Note: as if. They remain absent. Thus they can be contemplated and then written about—made present again and differently:

> That time is past,
> And all its aching joys are now no more,
> And all its dizzy raptures. Not for this
> Faint I, nor mourn nor murmur: other gifts
> Have followed, for such loss, I would believe,
> Abundant recompense . . . And I have felt
> A presence that disturbs me with the joy
> Of elevated thoughts . . . [30]

Poet and poem are "composed." When tranquil, the poet recollects emotion in order to find its true meaning, thus building both self and artwork. According to Wordsworth, What is poetry? cannot be asked without also asking, What is a poet? Poetry is the utterance of the individual who

> has acquired a greater readiness and power in expressing what he thinks and feels, and especially those thoughts and feelings which, by his own choice or from the structure of his own mind, arise in him without immediate external excitement.[31]

The poem itself is nothing more and nothing less than that use of language documenting the poet's experience. Poetry depends upon a particular kind of consciousness—more specifically, upon the perception of a pattern of time that shapes and is shaped by this consciousness: establishment, departure, return with a difference. After this return is accomplished in the poet's experience, composition begins. Once composed, as Abrams suggests, the poem establishes, departs from, and returns differently to its initial materials. That is, it can most effectively document experience by unfolding according to the dynamic of experience, thus in effect enacting experience. As was the case with Beethoven, the pattern of the Romantic artwork is also the pattern of Romantic time.

Shelley gives a similar account. He argues that the "poetical faculty" is limited by time, meaning that

> the mind in creation is as a fading coal, which some invisible influence, like an inconstant wind, awakens to transitory brightness . . . when composi-

tion begins, inspiration is already on the decline, and the most glorious poetry that has ever been communicated to the world is probably a feeble shadow of the original conception of the Poet . . . The toil and the delay recommended by critics, can be justly interpreted to mean no more than a careful observation of the inspired moments . . . "[32]

Poetry re-presents. Coming after a departure from uninspired, ordinary experience, and after a departure from inspired experience, it is a return to a different, postinspired experience. The rounded binary pattern of the Romantic lyric (and of the musical compositions of the day) is the rounded binary pattern of the poet's (and the composer's) experience.

Shelley says that "the conscious portions of our natures" can but watch and wait for this pattern to unfold.[33] "Toil and delay" are inseparable from "careful observation." We'd be inclined today to call these ideas that grow unbidden the work of the unconscious. The Romantics called it the imagination, the process by which the artist recovers the past, re-creates it, gives it meaning in and for the present. Wordsworth tends to focus on "the philosophic mind" that the years bring, whereas Shelley tends to focus on the loss of immediate contact with what is most vital in life. But for both, the act of composing—the "spontaneous" overflow—is the irruption into conscious attention of an ongoing and patterned interpretation of memory. Memory as creation and creation as memory—the same "species of re-action" Beethoven spoke of, the reattempting and "working out" of "the basic idea [that] never leaves" yet "rises [and] grows upward" over the course of "a very long time."

As Christopher Salvesen has pointed out, where the eighteenth century tends to see imagination as decayed memory, the Romantics tend to see imagination as memory reactivated and renewed. Paul Robinson says eighteenth-century thought centers around reason, nineteenth-century thought around history.[34] Though these positions are perhaps not sufficiently complex, clearly the Romantics do see time as history, as a patterned duration, whose pattern includes more than reasonable notions of succession. The idea of return with a difference, though it may unreasonably suggest that time runs both forward and backward, is also an undoubted fact of Romantic experience, as well as a necessary dynamic in Romantic composition. The child is father to the man; the past is parent to the artwork. To create art is to use the imagination to recover the past and to discover the difference between the past and the present.

This pattern is not confined to artists and artworks. The phenomenal success of "serious" music, particularly Beethoven's, in the Romantics' day merits mention here. Economic, political, and social conditions had a lot to do with it, of course. Beethoven's career coincided with (and, in fact, helped to make possible) an increasingly educated and affluent listener, an expanding audience, the rise of the concert hall, and the end of royal and religious patronage and the artistic limitations they imposed. But Beethoven's works were not just widely available; they were widely popular. His flamboyant personality and performances helped. More important, though, listeners seemed to perceive in his work an emotional accuracy. E. T. A. Hoffmann described Beethoven's music as

> a many-voiced consonance of all the passions, that we live on, enchanted beholders of the supernatural . . . [it] sets in motion the level of fear, of awe, of horror, of suffering, and wakes just that infinite longing which is the essence of Romanticism . . . the soul of each thoughtful listener is assuredly stirred, deeply and intimately . . . [35]

Beethoven's works tended to be massive; and they tended to be instrumental rather than vocal, thus suggestive in ways neither words nor music could be before (which is what Hoffmann means by "Romantic": music's newfound ability to be organized by solely musical means, thus its newfound freedom to be fully itself).[36] His music offered powerful and detailed accounts of time as experienced. The pattern that this experience most often assumed in Beethoven's music was rounded binary: meaning as memory. If Being itself were music, most listeners seemed to feel, it would sound like this. Life moves forward by rediscovering (thus changing) its origins. Beethoven's art is but life intensified. What is true for the artist and the artwork is true in essence for all.

Similarly, Wordsworth says that the poet, "endowed with more lively sensibility, more enthusiasm and tenderness," feels more deeply, more intensely, what we all feel. His experiences differ from the experiences of others by degree, not by type. The poet uses memory and imagination to conjure

> in himself passions, which are indeed far from being the same as those produced by real events, yet . . . do more nearly resemble the passions produced by real events, than anything which, from the motions of their own minds merely, other men are accustomed to feel in themselves . . . [37]

Like Beethoven's music, poetry approaches what life really feels like when life is really felt.

This feeling is bound up in return with a difference. Wordsworth says in *The Prelude:*

> There are in our existence spots of time,
> Which with distinct preeminence retain

A renovating virtue, whence . . . our minds
Are nourished and invisibly repaired . . .
Such moments, worthy of all gratitude,
Are scattered everywhere, taking their date
From our first childhood—in our childhood even
Perhaps are most conspicuous. Life with me,
As far as memory can look back, is full
Of this beneficent influence.[38]

Following this passage are three distinct descriptions of a scene where occurred an event in the poet's childhood—actually two events conflated into one.[39] Poem and person share a pattern of time: the poem returns with a difference to itself no less than the person returns with a difference to the past. We tend to be more forgiving of novelists than of poets when they fiddle thus with "the truth." But in Romantic time, truth is less what "really" happened than how the past really feels now. Moving back and moving forward become inextricable. The artwork itself is an enactment of the dynamic that organizes the artist's experience, and the poet's experience is a more deeply felt version of all experience.

Coleridge argues similarly. He holds the primary imagination, the faculty responsible for consciousness, as

the living Power and prime Agent of all human Perception, and as a repetition in the finite mind of the eternal act of creation in the infinite I AM.[40]

Consciousness repeats, with a difference, what God does. As God on an infinite scale is the process that creates creatures in all their unity and difference, so the imagination on a finite scale is the process that creates consciousness by re-creating (dissolving, diffusing, dissipating) experience, in order to achieve "the balance or reconciliation of opposite or discordant qualities. . . . "[41] Any thought that comes to consciousness has already acquired a history and a pattern. The moment of perception and the instant of thought are themselves durations in which experience is established, departed from, and returned to with a difference. The secondary imagination—the faculty that creates art—is but a more active and consciously willful version of the primary imagination. It is a louder echo, as it were, a repetition with a difference, of the basic relation between time and mind.

There is a certain resemblance between Romantic time and the Hegelian dialectic of thesis / antithesis / synthesis. Given that Hegel,

Wordsworth, and Beethoven were all born in the same year, similarities in their ideas of time's patterns are not surprising. But in Romantic time (and in the Romantic artwork) both thesis and antithesis tend to be located in the establishment region, with the synthesis—the fracturing and recombining of moods, themes, ideas, feelings, memories—coming in the departure region. A new kind of relation, a deeper understanding of time and of the interaction between past and present, tends to be explored, or at least asserted, in the return. At its best, Romantic art seeks to ground temporal experience in temporality itself. This is in contrast to Hegelian dialectic, where the synthesis becomes a new thesis that calls forth a new antithesis, a process that ends only in the ultimate synthesis of Absolute Spirit, or God. In Romantic art, an appeal to an atemporal ground like Absolute Spirit, though it may happen distressingly often, happens usually as a last resort, the poet looking to heaven because earth seems, after a thorough exploration, to offer no more.

The Romantic poet always returns *to* time *in* time. Abrams has written of the "circuitous journey" of Romanticism: a paradigm of unity-separation-reunification.[42] As we've noted, reunification, by virtue of having passed through separation, bears the mark of that passage; some residue of disunity remains, a sense of difference between then and now. Recent, more clinical studies suggest much the same about memory and consciousness. Which means either that the Romantics were right, or—what is perhaps indistinguishable from this—that we are still returning to their way of thinking, with the difference that we rely more on critical proof than powerful feeling. After surveying those clinical studies, Claude Blair Bolles concludes that any "storehouse" model of memory cannot stand. It is impossible in the end to distinguish consciousness from memory, in that we are always guided by an awareness of past experience; but it is likewise impossible in the end to distinguish memory from consciousness. Due to the ever-changing circumstances that cause it to arise, a memory is different, literally re-membered, on each occasion that it comes to attention. Memory is as closely related to the present as to the past.[43]

Romantic time, then, is both linear and circular; its essence is return with a difference. For the artwork, for the artist, for consciousness itself, meaning means both gain and loss. An origin, to be an origin, must be moved away from in time and returned to in memory. The sense of meaning never appears without the sense of loss; but—so the Romantic hopes—the sense of loss never appears without the sense of meaning. Though we may sometimes feel that Wordsworth dwells on "abundant recompense" as a way of glossing over "such loss," we should also acknowledge that the best art of this age aims for what Robert K. Wallace calls "Romantic equilibrium": an infusion of vitality into old forms, a balance of the new and the given.[44] Romantic time is patterned duration, and that pattern brings loss as much as growth. With memory, we can regain all we have lost. The emotion itself exists again in the mind—or one "akin" to it: the recollected emotion involves a sense of time having passed. In fact, because even the instant of thought or feeling is a duration in and of Romantic time, the original emotion was itself a memory. Awareness is recognition: to be aware is to re-cognize, to learn again and differently, to recover the past and to discover the gap between the past and the present. Out of this gap can emerge regret, disillusionment, a sense of the burden of passed and passing time. Also from this gap can emerge meaning, value, insight—indeed consciousness itself.

Thus the question to ask of, say, Wordsworth's ode on immortality is not, Did he really believe in reincarnation? but rather, Do we ever *not* recollect when we think? Knowing is remembering. To the Romantic, life is life in time, and time has a pattern: we move from what we have to what we lose, and then from what we lose to what we can, though changed, recover. Consciousness is consciousness of the past as we choose to remember, or find that we must remember, that past. I wish to adapt a term from Wordsworth for this process: re-collection. At the risk of trendiness I hyphenate it thus to emphasize that I mean not only what the term usually means but also more. To re-collect is to bring again to attention, and, necessarily, to put together differently. The artist is the individual keenly aware of this process; the artwork is the record and the enactment of that awareness.

Ideas about time and about language and about their relation change, of course. But in all language, says Whitrow, the principle underlying syntax in speech and language "is essentially rhythmical in nature." That is, language, "man's most outstanding feature, [is] concerned with the regulation of *sequences* of sounds." Language means duration. As Whitrow also points out, the acquisition of language occurs alongside the child's acquisition of both a sense of self and a sense of time: what I am is what I want, and what I want is what I've had in an experience called "before" and therefore want to have again in an experience called "now," not in an experience called "later."[45] A crucial reason, perhaps, why Wordsworth should find the image of the child so attractive: as we grow older, we grow more concerned with using language in as utilitarian a fashion as possible. We emphasize its referential aspects in order to conduct the business of communication expeditiously. We thus lose touch with its combinatory aspects, with the intimacy of time and language—an intimacy all the major Romantic poets tried to make explicit. In their work, time enters the foreground; as in the child's sense of language, reference shares priority with combination.

Again, we want to avoid reifying the referential / combinatory distinction. Both aspects are always present in verbal language. Reference unfolds in time no less than combination does, and points to meanings in place prior to any particular context. Combination allows the pattern of that unfolding itself to be significant. Such signification is an object of primary attention in music. Romantic poetry seeks this status for verbal signification, thus turns to music for a model and a vocabulary. We cannot understand Romanticism unless we understand the Romantic attitude to time, and we cannot understand that attitude without also understanding the Romantic attitude to music.

In a gesture emblematic of reaching toward wholeness, toward a deepened understanding of time and a heightened ability to express such an understanding with verbal language, Romantic poetry reaches out to music. Part of the fragmentation of life-in-time is a fixed, confining, and isolating relation between poetry and the other arts. Such fragmentation can be healed by asking what those arts can do that poetry does not do but could. Paradoxically, poetry was aiming for music's level of explicit combinatory meaning at a time when, as John Neubauer points out, music had "liberated" itself from words. In the eighteenth century, music became an "absolute" art needing solely musical means to organize itself.[46] The powers of combinatory meaning were being fully felt for the first time. Music could finally do what words could not. But this is to the point. *Because* music had become so different from words, artists who used words found it that much more attractive, both as an experience and as a literary resource. The result was not an appropriation of musical effects, which poetry can't do without ceasing to be poetry, or at least good poetry; rather, poets discovered within the means of poetry (ideas, prosodic practices, organizational principles) numerous ways of allowing the combinatory meaning inherent but subordinate in verbal language to cogovern with reference.

Hence, it is no surprise that poetry reaches out to music, or that poetry is the art reaching out thus. As we've seen, Romantic poetry and the music of the age share a model of time as well as ways of unfolding time that are themselves productive of meaning. Our examination of Beethoven, Wordsworth, Shelley, and Coleridge suggests that both composers and poets not only attend to time assiduously but also see much the same things when they regard time—as experienced in the artwork, by the artist, and by the mind in general. As a way of organizing a composition, as a way of understanding the act of composition, and as a way of perceiving and conceiving the basic relation of time and mind, Romantic re-collection informs poetry no less than it informs music. That is, music's combinatory patterns are present, though usually tacit, in verbal language. The characteristic feature of Romantic poetry is an attempt to make re-collection explicit, to make palpable with words the particular relation between language, time, and consciousness that we've described as return with a difference. This Romantic poetry does with the help of music.

The independence of the arts; the exploration of possible mergings for the arts because of this independence; the attention to the patterns of time: all these occur, of course, at other points in literary and musical history. But seldom do they occur so consistently and so intensively. It's arguable that nowhere else does the relation of poetry and music so characterize the age and the age's art. Like all the major Romantic poets, Keats paid very careful attention to time's patterns; he was also unusually resistant to appealing to an atemporal ground when trying to understand time's complexities. Hence, he paid particularly close attention to music, the art made primarily of unfolding time.

We should do likewise. "Critics, no less than poets," MacFarland writes, "proceed from subliminal awareness of concrete shapes."[47] We began by noticing the "symptoms" of poetry's relation with music: musical allusions, sound, and structure. Now that we have explored the cause of these symptoms, we can examine the symptoms themselves in depth. To serve as an orientation to the Romantic ideas of music, part 1 will discuss Keats's use of those ideas. Part 2 will explore parallels between music and the sound of Keats's poetry, and part 3 will inquire into whether Keats's poems are organized in ways similar to music. Discussion of the great odes will be saved until then, since they culminate Keats's use of music as idea, as prosodic model, and as formal principle. They also culminate Keats's artistic career and his coming to terms with what Andrew Cooper calls "intervening temporal difference."[48] As I'll argue, this twin culmination is no coincidence.

PART ONE

The Trumpet and the Lute:
Music as Idea in Keats's Poetry

"I Am . . . Writing at Random"

I N a letter to his sister, John Keats says, "If I could play upon the Guitar I might make my fortune with an old song—and get t[w]o blessings at once—a Lady's heart and the Rheumatism" (L265). This was July of 1819. Keats was twenty-three and in the middle of his most productive period. He had already completed "La Belle Dame sans Merci," "The Eve of St. Agnes," and some of the great odes. Before the year was over, he would have written the rest of the odes, *The Fall of Hyperion,* and *Lamia.* Plagued as always by financial worry, however, he was only half-joking when he spoke of looking for some way to make money besides writing. While the humor of his letters rarely enters his poetry, the movement here between fanciful images and worldly troubles is characteristic of his verse, as is the guiding, if multivalent, role music plays in that move. You stand out in the cold and the rain to play guitar beneath a lady's window, and you have as much of a chance of becoming sick as of being transported by love.

I've argued that to understand Romanticism, we need to understand its relation to music; and to understand that relation, we should begin by examining what a Romantic poet actually says about music. In Keats's case, this task presents great frustrations, but holds out the hope of great rewards as well. Keats had both a very wide-ranging intelligence and a very short career. He wanted to make his work as full as life itself. To that end, he embraced richness, variety, contradiction. He experimented and explored, producing a wealth of fragments, apprentice work, outright failures, even doggerel—and a handful of poems that not only succeed but are among the finest in the language.

All are relevant. As we'll see, what Keats learned in the lesser work often made possible the greater; in fact, his achievement becomes all the more remarkable when we consider where he started, what he had to build up, what he had to burn away. His letters, too, are worth examining. They provide us with invaluable commentaries on his work, much as they apparently provided Keats himself with a forum for working out many ideas in advance of their appearance in his verse.

To read Keats is to see a poet trying to find his way. He often uses music as a guide. The difficulty, as I've suggested, is that throughout his career, Keats seems to have held no consistent attitude toward music. He writes in another letter of having attended a party at the home of Vincent Novello, a famed organist with a circle of literary and musical friends:

> [T]here was a complete set to of Mozart and punning—I was so completely tired of it that if I were to follow my own inclinations I should never meet any one of that set again, not even [Leigh] Hunt—who is certainly a pleasant fellow in the main when you are with him—but in reallity he is vain, egotistical and disgusting in matters of taste and in morals . . . (L180–81)

The letter writer, no less than the poet, is alive to language. Keats heightens the contrast between the company and himself by ironically echoing their "complete set to" (or involving activity) in his being "completely tired of" that "set" (or group). Keats is also alive to many possible ways of experiencing and thinking about music. Here, instead of the "divine Mozart" of the early epistle to Clarke, we find a Mozart who is merely a diversion, entertainment at a party.

Perhaps Keats's annoyance is more at the company than at the use of music as entertainment. Such annoyance comes and goes in Keats's life. His dislike of Hunt would alternate with affection. Similarly, he would later write that with "a little chance music," he could pass a summer quietly without caring much about any problems whatsoever (L284). Music needn't be divine; it can also provide delight, a pleasant evening, or a much-needed diversion, each of which seems to have a place. In the late "To Fanny" (1820), music breathes voluptuous visions (25–26). They are hardly the crux of the poet's concerns. But those concerns are at once so important and so troubling that, quite understandably, the poet is torn between the need to face them and the desire to escape them. Music provides just such an escape.

But this may not always be enough. Other kinds of music can be found in other poems, both early and late. "Sleep and Poetry" (1816) speaks of harmony as a dynamic force, a mighty self that makes the ordinary world special by turning noise into music (173ff.). The world of troubles and the much-needed diversions from that world both disappear into music's "dizzy void" (177). In "On Leaving Some Friends at an

Early Hour" (1816), the poet wishes for a mind "full of many wonders of the spheres," which are brought to him by music that wanders around his ears. Keats's rhyme, by the way, in linking "ears" and "spheres," also links the poet himself with those wonders, and thus shows him participating actively, both in his experience and in his poem. Much later, *Lamia* (1819) speaks of "a song of love, too sweet for earthly lyres" (1.299), of music being the sole support of a fairy castle's roof (2.122–23); even the "fluent Greek" spoken by the poem's characters is wondrous, "a vowel'd undersong" (2.199–200). Not a diversion only, music can also be special: unearthly, wonder-full, magical, mystical, mythical, void of ordinary meaning yet full of opportunity for imaginative participation.

Again, though, in both early and late works, music can be something besides diversion or magic. "On the Grasshopper and the Cricket" (1816) makes an attempt at defining this other kind of music.

> The poetry of earth is ceasing never:
>   On a lone winter evening, when the frost
>   Has wrought a silence, from the stove there shrills
> The Cricket's song, in warmth increasing ever,
>   And seems to one in drowsiness half lost,
>   The Grasshopper's among some grassy hills.
>
>   (9–14)

The cricket, singing on the hearth in winter, returns the poet to summer, though neither he nor that season are quite what they were before. Winter and summer, ordinarily exclusive of each other, come together in the experience of one *half* lost: neither waking nor dreaming but something else, some form of awareness open to (and perhaps at least partially responsible for) the never-ceasing poetry of earth. Music and poetry are linked somehow. Like the "music of that vision pale" (392) that breathes despondingly (434) in "Isabella" (1819), like the "song concerning dying" (43) in "Fragment of Castle-builder" (1818), the ordinary cricket's song can lead, via the poet's imagination, to the insight that life can be found in the midst of death. Music preserves yet transforms mortality— the ongoingness of time that is the basic human circumstance.

Later poems likewise seek in music this quality of insight. The cricket's song becomes in *Hyperion* (1818) a sterner music of the landscape:

> There is a roaring in the bleak-grown pines
> When Winter lifts his voice; there is a noise
> Among immortals when a God gives sign,

With hushing finger, how he means to load
His tongue with the full weight of utterless thought,
With thunder, and with music, and with pomp . . .

(2.116–21)

The gods speak of "songs of misery, music of our woes" (2.269). Music can provide the insights that come from "mournful" Memnon's harp (2.376), revised in the later *Fall of Hyperion* (1819) as "dolorous accent from a tragic harp" (1.444). This music, special yet linked with ordinary life, is a fitting image for Keats's effort in that poem to link a mythic vision with something besides the dreaming of fanatics and savages—and poets. But again, skepticism: it is the gods, after all, who experience music thus, and even they can find these thoughts "utterless."

"I am however young writing at random," Keats warned his brother when trying to explain his ambivalence toward religion (L230). He might have said the same about his attitudes toward music. The preliminary and fairly random examination of Keats's work conducted in the last few pages has suggested that music can be found in plenty from first to last. Apparently, what can also be found from first to last is a bewildering variety of ideas about that art, each of which the poet treats with varying degrees of acceptance or skepticism.

This should not prove overly distressing. For one thing, a great artist ought to have great range. For another, a more thorough examination of Keats's writings will show that his attitudes toward music, though they range widely, tend to fall into well-delineated categories.

2

The Varieties of Musical Experience

$\mathbf{A}$ LLUSION as articulation: Keats's use of music as an idea, although it tells us a great deal about the poet's attitude toward music, also tells us much more. We might re-collect—bring to attention again and differently—the passage from the verse epistle "To Charles Cowden Clarke" that we examined in the preface.

> ... my heart
> Was warm'd luxuriously by divine Mozart,
> By Arne delighted or by Handel madden'd,
> Or by the song of Erin pierc'd and sadden'd
> . . . .
> And the rich notes to each sensation fitting;

We've already noted how the passage manifests that attention to both time and music characteristic of Romanticism. We should note now that we also encounter here attitudes we've just seen scattered throughout Keats's work or across his larger poems: music can cause simple delight; it can warm so luxuriously that it seems divine; it can cause madness; or it can pierce and sadden so strongly that one feels the pain of another as if it were one's own, thus perhaps receiving an insight into what is essential and common in all human experience. The idea of the "notes to each sensation fitting" is crucial. Music can be many kinds of experiences: this music, this effect. Each of those notes / sensations has its own value to Keats; each has a place as a moment in a patterned duration.

That patterned duration could be life or a poem—*could* be: Keats was ever searching for the exact link between the two. He wrote his brother George that, as was the case with Shakespeare, "a Man's life of any worth is a continual allegory . . . like the scriptures, figurative . . .

his works are the comments on it" (L218). This seems in accord with Wordsworth's notion that poetry in essence records the poet's experience. But rather than fleshing out this speculation, Keats goes on to give quotidian details about what he's been doing lately. Such a move, of course, is endemic to the form of the personal letter (insofar as it has a "form" at all). Yet the way Keats handles the remark explains the remark: life is an allegory because the quotidian and the speculative, the ordinary and the special, summon each other—and do so according to a certain order in time.

I've asserted that the Romantic finds ongoing meaning by recollecting prior meaning. Keats's work bears out this assertion. Jack Stillinger sees a basic structure in many of Keats's poems: the poet begins in the actual world, crosses a boundary into the ideal, then moves back to the actual. Upon returning, the poet discovers that he "has acquired something—a new understanding of a situation, a change in attitude toward it—from the experience of the [imaginative] flight, and for better or worse he is never the same afterward."[1]

Keats's many and varied ideas about music conform with Stillinger's model—in fact, with what is central to Romantic poetry. The basic Keatsian pattern suggests the pattern of Romantic time, which applies to the artwork, the artist, and experience in general. The uses of music as an idea provide a vocabulary for discussing Romantic time, and, more important, a way of boosting the combinatory power of verbal language. With music, Keats's poetry enacts Romantic time. The work becomes the commentary on the life; the life becomes the origin for the work. Each justifies the other; each provides the other with a reason for being.

Before proceeding, however, we should note a potential difficulty with the Romantic idea of music. As M. H. Abrams has documented, music came to be seen in the Romantic era as a model for all the arts.[2] By the late-eighteenth century, music had become "the art frequently pointed to as having a profound affinity with poetry" because, like music, the best poetry could directly express spirit and emotion. Poetry, then, should act like music: a "melody of ideas and images, a thematic organization, a harmony of moods," free from the tyranny of the real, at least from the real as narrowly defined.[3] But we should consider exactly whose music the Romantics would have been listening to. Interestingly, musicology being in its infancy, this history-conscious age tended to know only recent or contemporary music: Haydn, Mozart, Beethoven, and others composing in the Viennese classicist style. Today we're little inclined to view this highly rule-governed idiom as an example of direct expression. In fact, these musicians themselves were resistant to the idea of music as unpremeditated art. Music's newly acquired power and independence came from uniquely musical procedures—for example, dominant resolves most logically to tonic—which were universally observed by professional composers in Western Europe. A loosening of these procedures would hardly make for more powerful and freer expression; in fact, it would weaken music's ability to make sense at all *as* music.

James Anderson Winn argues that when Romantic poets tried for what they perceived to be music's unmediated expression, one of two things resulted: a general loosening of syntax that made poetry less musical than what was "arguably the most syntactical music in Western history"; or a *faux naïveté,* a restricted, monotonous, premeditated simplicity in form and syntax far removed from the structural exigencies of even the simplest composition.[4] According to Winn, the Romantics saw in music something it did not become until much later. Taking their cue from Romantic poets' statements about music, later nineteenth-century composers moved away from the rules of Viennese classicism in search of greater freedom. Procedures like dominant-to-tonic were loosened and finally discarded. Reluctant to put any new rules in place, yet needing to organize their typically massive works somehow, composers often turned to extramusical programs, rationalizing that they were effecting a fusion of the arts.[5] Arguably, serious music today is still recovering from this loss of power and independence.

Were the Romantic poets and those later composers (and Abrams) wrong about music? One way to address this issue is to distinguish, as John Neubauer suggests, between music and ideas about music. Those ideas, though they do not necessarily accord with actual music, can still forge some link between actual music and the world of thought. They tell us how music has been perceived.[6] From the Romantic poet's position, music, though highly rule-governed, isn't word-governed. As Peter Conrad puts it, music for a poet like Keats is more a literary paradox than a sonic actuality: a language, but one free of the constraints of verbal language.[7] It lacks the restrictions I face; therefore it lacks restrictions.

Neubauer's suggestion is both accurate and useful: Western thought has traditionally distinguished between *musica speculativa* and *musica practica;* and, in fact, we will focus throughout part 1 on the former, whereas parts 2 and 3 will examine the latter more closely. But theory and practice never quite achieve the divorce that would make our analytical lives so much simpler. One wonders, then, whether the Romantic poets could have heard what they said they heard in Mozart et al. and not need us to plead, aesthetic hat in hand, that their ideas, though basically wrong, are still interesting. In Winn's objections, and no less in our countering with Conrad and Neubauer, much depends on an insufficiently examined polarization between "freedom" and "rules," as well as on a corollary proceeding from this polarization that the Romantic, unlike the classicist, really shouldn't like Mozart—not if the Romantic really understands Mozart.

According to Gary Schmidgall, Mozart as an opera composer was unbiased, open-minded, accepting of human nature with all its contradictions (he didn't write his libretti, but he did choose them). This attitude would have appealed to a poet like Keats.[8] Yet Keats found Mozart's instrumental music "divine" as well. Why? Perhaps because Mozart, then being new, may have seemed considerably more free to the Romantics than to us: rule-governed but "modern," too, with a tonal idiom architecturally strong yet remarkably chromatic and flexible. Or perhaps music can seem wizardry to one largely ignorant, as most of the Romantic poets were, of the technical requirements that enable it to achieve its "divine" effects. But these explanations still smack of apology. We should inquire more thoroughly into what conditioned the Romantic perception of Mozart. Doing so will reveal where Keats got his ideas about music.

Linda Kay Barlow, in her study of Keats's musical imagery, suggests that we should look to Shakespeare and Milton. Barlow bases her argument on an observation of a multivalent attitude in all three writers.[9] That much is indisputable. But the particular content of each author's multivalence is of greater concern. Though we cannot deny that Shakespeare and Milton influenced Keats, neither can we deny that Keats's *particular* ideas about music correspond closely with those of more recent thinkers. Keats may have been familiar with the writings of these thinkers—though not in any systematic or scholarly way, his higher education extending only to his apprenticeship as an apothecary-surgeon. Still, he would have had many opportunities to become aware of their attitudes. His letters and poems prove that he found music to be a crucially important experience. He was a shrewd observer of his own responses to such experiences, and of the responses of persons he knew or met—among whom were some of the most important artistic figures of the day: Hunt, Hazlitt, Wordsworth, Coleridge, Shelley, the painter Haydon, the organist Novello. We cannot prove that they ever discussed the age's various ideas about music. Nor need we. Such ideas were elements of the intellectual atmosphere that they all breathed.

I say "ideas"—plural not singular—deliberately. Mozart could be "divine"; he could be other things, too, things that Abrams and Winn, in their otherwise excellent accounts of Romanticism and music, miss. Though Abrams is careful to differentiate between species of Romanticism (the German brand insisting more on music's pure expressiveness than the English, possibly because of the relative achievements of composers in each country), and though Winn gives numerous examples from a wide range of poets and poems, both critics suggest that Romanticism's idea of music is essentially univocal.[10] Evidence suggests otherwise. When philosophers wrote about music, when Romantic poets such as Keats used the image of music, they could mean any or all of at least three different experiences.

It should be less of a conundrum, then, why the Romantics saw the freedom they did in the Viennese classicists: the backgrounds of Romantic thought allow for various perceptions and conceptions of that art, none of which opposes freedom and system. Music is free because it is free to be what it is, and it is free to be what it is because it is systematic. To the Romantic, music means systematic time: pleasing sequences of sounds, or pure beauty as it unfolds, or the interpretation of memory. Music, that is, permits various understandings of temporal experience. These conceptions of music can be called, respectively, rhetorical, Pythagorean, and affective.[11] Further, the Romantic use of these three ideas of music, thus of the three kinds of temporal understanding they involve, has its own well-ordered syntax. Each type of music has its place in a system. We will examine each as it is relevant to Keats's work.

In the mid-eighteenth century, D'Alembert called music imperfect, inherently vague—too vague and indeterminate, in fact, to signify by itself at all. One way around this vagueness—the solution long in use—was to seek a broad mimetic base: to imitate "real" things, to tell stories, to accompany dance, or to be linked with words as in song or opera.[12] But, since music could, at least on a small scale, order itself in consistent patterns, some composers and philosophers felt that it should seek to establish a grammar such that a listener could feel that a statement had been made, a coherent experience undergone. Music should make sense as music.

The most important spokesperson for this "rhetorical" point of view was Jean-Phillipe Rameau. It can be said without much exaggeration that his attempt to "define all musical possibilities as natural and rational" made possible all the music the Romantics knew. This music was either instrumental or, if vocal, organized by the principles of instrumental music. That is, it achieved coherence by using solely musical means. Partly because of his own music, more so because of his tremendously influential *Treatise on Harmony* (1722), Rameau established what "musical means" were. Studying the physics of sound—Rameau was called in his day the "Newton of Music"[13]—he concluded two things. First, when a group of notes is sounded simultaneously, one note is heard as the most important one—the "root" of the chord. Second, because certain musical intervals involve simpler acoustical relations than others (e.g., the upper note of a perfect fifth vibrates three times for every two times the lower note vibrates, whereas an augmented fourth is much more complex), certain root progressions are simpler than others. Hence, they sound more logical, more inevitable. The chord sequence G-C makes sense more easily, understandably, and pleasantly than the chord sequence G-C-sharp. This is not to say that such a difficult progression has no place in music. Quite the contrary. Music finds its reason for being by positing the need for resolution. Music is organized time, and time becomes organized when simpler relations are able to provide a sense of consonance (or closure or stability) *because* they follow more complex relations that have provided a sense of dissonance (or tension or instability).

Rameau established the system we call harmony: music makes sense because of the way one root leads to another over time. This system can be applied locally in order to make a coherent passage; or it can be applied globally in order to organize large-scale regions. Just as the phrase moves from dissonance to consonance, so the entire piece can move from dissonant or unstable regions to consonant or stable regions. Music is a rhetoric, a set of materials and conventions with which meaning and emotion can be signified in predictable ways. In its own way, music is an ordinary language. According to the rhetorical point of view, though music differs from verbal language in how and what it signifies, it does not differ from verbal language in *that* it signifies.

We've seen Keats making use of this viewpoint: music as an unusual but essentially ordinary experience, an image of the establishment region of Romantic time. Unique in the circumstances of ordinary life, it is not removed from those circumstances; in fact, it exists largely because of them. Mozart can be entertainment at a party, diversion from the cares of life. Music pleases. This it does by setting up and fulfilling expectations, by making sense according to certain conventions.

One of the many things that makes Keats's poetry so rich is the notion that anything—even conventionality—can have value. Part of living a full life (and of writing poetry informing and informed by that fullness) is realizing that leisure is important. And music, when viewed as rhetoric, can be leisurely. It need inspire no great insight, no ardent following of artistic vision. It need be no more than fun—and need represent to the poet nothing more than a source of fanciful, albeit ordinary, poeticisms. The early "Calidore" (1816) speaks of "the song from Philomel's far bower" and "the nightingale's first under-song" (154, 61)—phrases that, though hardly comparable to what Keats would later do with the song of the nightingale, do provide a certain attraction, one that resides largely in the ease with which the poet can find and use such conventional phrases. Sometimes verse, like music, should be no more than easy and pleasant.

This idea of music fits in with, and helps gives voice to an aspect of, Keats's overall model of experience. We should note how very much ordinary life was of concern to Keats. A glance at his letters reveals much attention to the details of ordinary life:

> This morning I received a letter from George by which it appears that Money Troubles are to follow us up for some time to come perhaps for always ... (L12)

> And here I could go on complaining of my Misery, but I will keep myself cheerful for your Sakes. (L167)

> I do believe if I could be a hatter I might be one. (L311)

Certainly, we expect to find such ordinariness and mundanities in anybody's letters. We should be no less surprised to find, as we do, that Keats's letters also discuss at length various diversions from the cares of ordinary life:

> The other night I went to the Play with Rice, Reynolds, and Martin—we saw a new dull and half damned opera call'd 'the heart of Mid Lothian' that was on Saturday— (L242–43)

> —when we get in of an evening and I have perhaps taken my rest on a couple of Chairs [Charles Brown] affronts my indolence and Luxury by pulling out of his knapsack 1st his paper—2ndy his pens and last his ink. (L138)

> [At dinner] then there was Wordsworth, Lamb, Monkhouse, Landseer, Kingston, and your humble Sarvant. Lamb got tipsey and blew up Kingston ... (L45)

Keats apparently spent more time getting drunk than talking poetry when he met Wordsworth, at least on this occasion. And he wanted to rest, not compose, after a long day of walking through Scotland with his friend Charles Brown. The poet needs relaxation and fun as much as he needs poems.

Again, we expect this sort of thing in letters. What's interesting is that his verse likewise makes a bow towards the value of both ordinary experience and diversions from it. At the end of "I stood tip-toe upon a little hill," Keats cuts off his mythical and spiritual speculations as if reminded that the pleasant country scene—"Nature's gentle doings" (63)—with which the poem had begun has its own worth. The ordinary world is a place of cares, but also potentially of happiness. "Give me women wine and snuff," the poet cries in the title line of an early effort (1815), projecting what we'd call today "an attitude." A line like this reminds us, as do so many of his letters, that part of what makes Keats's work so remarkable is that he was so young when he wrote it.

In Stillinger's model, we remain in that phase of Keatsian experience that we can term ordinary time. For Keats, ordinary time has two phases: usual and unusual. Where one is, the other cannot be. Usually, I must face life squarely; to get through the average day, my wandering spirit must not soar. But sometimes I need to take a drink or enjoy myself at the theater in order to get relief from the struggles of life. By definition these activities are unusual; if they occurred all the time, they would lose their status and effectiveness as vacations, festivals, enjoyments, escapes. Music viewed as rhetoric is attractive precisely because it is *not* usual. Rhetorical music is Keats's emblem for these much-needed diversions.

Some philosophers sought more for music. Few disagreed with Rameau that music should be able to make sense as music. Rhetoric was necessary, though not necessarily sufficient. Around the same time as Rameau, Diderot said that music should not seek its ultimate and unique meaning either in its own internal relations or in the depiction of objects and events. A musical statement makes sense and therefore pleases; but music is defined by its "ability to conjure up an infinity of thoughts, none of which is adequate to the generating aesthetic idea." That is, the generating aesthetic of music is patterned sound; but music can be much more. Diderot anticipated Kant, who described music as the "free beauty" of pure form, containing no concepts, only its own "inwardness."[14]

This is the Pythagorean view: music as neither the expression of something definite and "real," nor merely pleasing patterns, but a realm in which unfolding patterns themselves are felt to have tremendous power. Novalis described this as the "creative combination of non-referential signs." We established in the introduction that the combinatory dimension of music's language is explicit, its referential dimension tacit. Pythagorean thinking makes much of such tacitness. According to this viewpoint, music moves us *because* we cannot know precisely what it points to. Hence, it is almost mystical—what Kant called a direct expression of the will.[15] It uses temporal organization (rhythms, melodies, chord progressions) to create its own special time, which seems apart from and emptied of ordinary, worldly time.

For Kant, music was morally ambiguous. Its numerical relations induce emotions whose power derives from, and is amplified by, their inability to point to right and wrong. Where Kant was wary of such power, others embraced it. Wackenroder viewed music as a "magical transformation of matter into pure form by means of mathematical structure." Schopenhauer called music "an unconscious exercise in metaphysics," and welcomed its ability to allow us to think and feel without the mediation of ideas,[16] meaning not that music is "unmediated," but that mathematical patterns of sound, music's particular kind of mediation, are more powerful than words or ideas or concepts.

The Keats of "Sleep and Poetry" and *Lamia* regards music from the Pythagorean viewpoint—music as magical, a dizzy void. "The excellence of every Art," Keats writes to his brothers, "is its intensity" (L42). Granted, neither the poet nor poetry can be on fire every moment; even *Endymion* (1817), often marred by the poet's attempting to do just that, speaks of regarding dance and song as simple celebration (1.136, 3.933), of needing sometimes to be lulled by a "velvet summer song" that refreshes the "o'er-sweeten'd soul" (4.297, 3.445). As Keats well knew, problems arise when such escapism is all one strives for (Keats seems to have had difficulties from time to time with alcohol).[17] More to the point, and skirting those dangers, art can also offer something besides escapism and shallow pleasures. The mind needs ordinary experience in both its usual and unusual forms. But it can also have a richer kind of experience—the departure region of Romantic time—when the usual and the unusual are not so rigidly opposed.

The sonnet "On Sitting Down to Read King Lear Once Again" (1818) suggests that Keats has come to believe, even while still revising *Endymion,* that his early epic is itself "o'er-sweeten'd," thus more annoying than refreshing, at best a serene lute capable only of simple melodizing (1, 3). Music as entertainment, diversion, sensual indulgence, mental indolence, conventionality: none of these is necessarily low or undesirable. They provide relief and enjoyment. Yet they cannot fully satisfy the poet. Another kind of art exists, a "bittersweet fruit" found in Shakespeare, whose work accomplishes something besides what Keats calls in "Isabella" "the simple plaining of a minstrel's song" (388).

Note the copresence in "bittersweet" of terms that ordinarily exclude each other. Like Shakespeare's drama, music could be a special experience fundamentally removed from both usual and unusual experience. Neither bitter nor sweet but both—and neither. In the epistle "To My Brother George" (1816), Keats longs for "the still murmur of the honey bee" to teach him a rural song, a song the poet closely associates with Apollo's "golden lyre," with an "enchanting" lay, and with the unfolding of "some tale of love and arms in time of old" (9–18). The present becomes distant from itself; the world becomes special when the pleasant but ordinary countryside, as imaged by the music of the bees, joins via the poet's imagination with myth and magic, also imaged by music.

In an 1818 letter to his brother George and his wife (written, interestingly, at almost the same time as the "complete set to of Mozart" letter), Keats states that he has met a very special woman. "I forget myself entirely because I live in her . . . she kept me awake one night as a tune of Mozart's might do" (L162). Her exotic beauty and rich eastern look allow Keats to step out of himself. His ordinary identity becomes empty, full of otherness, which Keats compares to the effect Mozart has on him. Mozart can be more than one of the unpleasant pleasantries at Novello's. What this woman provides the poet is imaged by what Mozart's music (sometimes) provides him: not mere fancy, but an imaginative taking leave of ordinary life.

We can term this phase of Keatsian experience Special time. Now the mind attempts not a diversion from life but a deepening of experience. In Stillinger's model, the poet crosses into the ideal, as is the case in "On First Looking into Chapman's Homer" (1816). This sonnet is arguably Keats's first completely successful poem, largely because here Keats works out much of what would become the characteristic pattern of his poetry. The poet says that he had long been acquainted with Greek myth ("Much have I travell'd in the realms of gold"). Yet there was nothing terribly special about this. It was pleasant reading, no more: unusual but ordinary experience. Then he came across Chapman's translation of Homer. Now he has access to a "pure serene" not restricted to Greek myth. The experience of reading Chapman leads to other imaginative experiences. The poet enters the figurative realm, where imagination attempts to loosen, perhaps even to empty, ordinary referential meaning in order to seek new combinations, new connections. Then I was not myself: "Then felt I like some watcher of the skies . . . Or like stout Cortez." Special experience dwells in "like" or "as if": neither opposition nor identity but something else, a not-really-thereness, a void filling the imagination.

This new and more deeply imaginative experience, not exclusive of but beyond ordinary experience, has a strong resemblance with Keats's notion of

> what quality went to form a Man of Achievement especially in Literature & which Shakespeare posessed so enormously—I mean *Negative Capability*, that is when man is capable of being in uncertainties, Mysteries, doubts, without any irritable reaching after fact & reason . . . with a great poet the sense of Beauty overcomes every other consideration, or rather obliterates all consideration. (L43)

Special time is both full and empty—full of intensity and possibility, empty of all that is ordinary. In Special time, the mind can have fundamentally different, or opposed, or contradictory ideas and feelings. This is, perhaps, the real gold, a very precious kind of experience, for which the poet seeks an image with his reference to the search for plunder that Cortez made (or more correctly Balboa; being largely self-educated, Keats was prone to this sort of mistake, which makes the poetic plunder he found all the more extraordinary). The exclusivity between usual and unusual ceases to have force. In fact, the characteristic quality of Special time is the breakdown of exclusivity itself. Beauty obliterates every other consideration. Now the mind experiences the real richness and complexity of life: not many-made-one but many-at-once. "Welcome joy and welcome sorrow," Keats says in a poem of that name (1818), "I do love you both together!" (1, 4). The emblem of this Special time in Keats's work is Pythagorean music: "Dancing music, music sad, / Both together, sane and mad" (18–19).

Again, this was not always enough for Keats. As we'll see, Negative Capability, though important, is hardly the key to his thought in its entirety. It was one of many attempts Keats made at voicing one of many ideas, some of which came to be even more important. Similarly, some philosophers argued that music had to mean something more than pleasing patterns of sound and more than the powerful but unspecified emotions inspired by free beauty. Morally empty, music is richly irrational. Like Kant, Goethe was wary of that richness.[18] Goethe called music "the art furthest removed from nature, the most highly structured according to abstract principles." As such, it has the greatest "demonic potential."[19] Music can move us in extremely powerful ways. Each may be valuable. But a context is needed in which to assess that value.

We see, then, a third strand in musical philosophy, based on what Neubauer calls the "subtle psychological realism of the late eighteenth century." Even Kant found himself unable to fully explain music by an appeal to pure form. The imagination always works within certain limits; consciousness is consciousness-of. Music must express *something:* what Kant calls "the harmony of the mind's faculties." Music is representative, not of external events and things but of mental and emotional events. According to A. W. Schlegel, music is "a language of feeling independent of all external objects."[20] As distinguished from both rhetorical and Pythagorean thought, affective philosophy believed that music should indeed be mimetic but that mimesis should be internalized.[21]

The affect involved in this internalized mimesis goes far beyond the pleasure Rameau spoke of. Dugald Stewart argued in the early nineteenth century that the inadequacy of the signs in music, or "their mode of *suggestion,* is the occasion and evidence of activity and energy of the mind"; music is seen as an art that emphasizes "the interpretive process as an unstable but decisive source of meaning."[22] Music makes sense, it leads us beyond sense, and it invites us to make sense again differently. In the rhetorical point of view, we recognize the signs of music as signs. In the Pythagorean point of view, we also recognize that these signs point toward we-know-not-where; in the affective point of view, we attempt to find out where and, in so doing, learn as much about ourselves as about whatever meaning music has. More than any other art, music makes palpable to the mind the simultaneity of nowness and passing-away, the emergence of meaning and loss from each other, that is the essence of Romantic time. The content of awareness and the form of temporality cannot be distinguished.

As we've seen, "On the Grasshopper and the Cricket" suggested that Keats had room in his poetry for this other kind of music, neither ordinary nor Special but somehow connected to each without being limited by either. Likewise, *Endymion* speaks of a "wild and harmonized tune / My spirit struck from all the beautiful" (3.170–71), and of "a noise of harmony" which reanimates all life (3.791). *Endymion* calls "Truth the best music" (4.773). More than diversion, more even than imagination, music can be truth, no matter how hard. Even despair can be sung, can become a "war-song of defiance 'gainst all hell" (3.603). "Who lov'd— and music slew not?" (2.365). Music slays the lover: it causes a swoon or imaginative taking-leave of self; yet it also kills the lover *as* a lover and thus returns the lover to a post-Special ordinary experience.

We enter the third phase of Stillinger's Keatsian experience and of Romantic time. The mind returns to where it began, and discovers, for good or ill, that its move through imagination has changed everything. I long for a life untrammeled by narrow logic. "I have never yet been able to perceive," Keats writes in a letter to his friend Benjamin Bailey, "how any thing can be known for truth by consequitive reasoning . . . O for a life of Sensations rather than of Thoughts!" (L37). But I also want to have sensations informed by knowledge. "I have been hovering for some time," he writes to his publisher John Taylor, "between an exquisite sense of the luxurious and a love for Philosophy"—by which Keats means less a formal academic discipline than knowledge that becomes systematic by virtue of much reading, thinking, and living (L88). At best, the third phase of time returns us to ordinary time with the difference that imaginative luxury and knowledge inform each other. "The difference of high Sensations with and without knowledge," he writes to J. H. Reynolds,

> appears to me this—in the latter case we are falling continually ten thousand fathoms deep and being blown up again without wings and with all

[the] horror of a bare shouldered Creature—in the former case, our shoulders are fledge, and we go thro' the same air and space without fear. (L92)

Ordinary time, in both its usual and unusual form, has its own value; but being ordinary, it cannot fully satisfy the poet. Richly imaginative or Special time has even greater value; but being Special, it cannot sustain itself. Most valuable is the richly imaginative experience that provides insight into the ordinary, because, as Stillinger points out, that is where, for better or worse, the mind will end up. If poetry never moves beyond flights of imagination, Keats writes his brother, then, though fine, it is also "erroneous . . . [and] not so fine a thing as philosophy—For the same reason that an eagle is not so fine a thing as a truth" (L230). Unlike philosophy, which seeks only truth, poetry seeks beauty for its own sake. But the best poetry seeks both beauty and truth, even as it explores the relation between the two (which exploration helps to make the great odes great). The best poetry speaks, in a voice made attractive by imaginative experience, of and to ordinary human joy and suffering. This poetry allows access to another kind of time, which loses itself neither in what is called in "Sleep and Poetry" the realm of Flora and old Pan nor in the "sense of real things . . . [which] like a muddy stream, would bear along / My soul to nothingness." It leads, rather, to "a nobler life" that takes from and adds to both ordinary and Special experience (155–62).

"I find that I can have no enjoyment in the World but continual drinking of Knowledge," Keats wrote Taylor. "I find there is no worthy pursuit but the idea of doing some good for the world" (L88). Not to oversimplify Keats's personality, but we should never forget that he was trained in medicine. The poet as healer: to know and to act cannot, or ought not, be separated; poems "are the comments on" life. "Let me not wander in a barren dream," the poet says at the end of the *King Lear* sonnet: let my poetry be, like Shakespeare's, a way both to transcend and to live with ordinary life. "Give me new phoenix wings to fly at my desire": let my desires take off into the imaginative, figurative realm, where "like" breaks down the distance between who I am and what I want. More important, let those wings somehow come out of the dream and into my life as lived.

In a letter to his brother George, Keats points out that the ordinary world, as defined by the "little circumscribe[d] straightened" notions of common religion, is a "vale of tears." He offers another, less "misguided and superstitious" notion:

Call the world if you Please "The Vale of Soul-making." Then you will find out the use of the world . . . There may be intelligences or sparks of the divinity in millions—but they are not Souls till they acquire identities,

till each one is personally itself . . . Do you not see how necessary a World
of Pains and troubles is to school an intelligence and make a soul? A Place
where the heart must suffer and feel in a thousand diverse ways! (L249–
250)

The ability to remain in doubts and mysteries was important to Keats.
Yet he would come to feel—this letter was written a year and a half after
the Negative Capability letter—that the making of an identity was at
least as important, and perhaps even more so. Reaching after fact and
reason, though irritable under some circumstances, had its place. We
must go forth from and return to ordinary identity. "If a Sparrow come
before my Window I take part in its existence and pick about the Gravel"
(L38). This is the writer of *Endymion* speaking: the poet suspends his
own ordinary identity for the sake of experiencing life's richness. While
the writer of the greater poems continued to believe this, he also empha-
sized that for "intelligences or sparks of divinity" to become souls, they
must also build upon ordinary identity,

so as ever to possess a bliss peculiar to each ones individual existence . . .
This appears to me a faint sketch of a system of Salvation which does not
affront our reason and our humanity. (L250)

All experience is preserved yet transformed. Time passes, yet is saved:
recovered with a difference.

Affective music is the emblem of this process. In this viewpoint, music
becomes a Special insight into ordinary experience. Music is understood
to act much like the mind as it posits and is posited by Romantic time: an
experience of memory, loss, suspension, anticipation, hope. Its affect is
full of time already passed or time passing now. Its meaning and value
arise directly out of the individual's experience of temporality.

Which presents a dilemma. Linked to time, meaning and value can be
as transient as they are powerful. Precisely because of the inextricability
of value and transience, of meaning and loss, the attempt to define this
affect exactly and discover how to employ its emblem would constitute,
from first to last, the central drama of Keats's career. Like Goethe, he
suspected that music was a daimonic (or at least irrelevant) disruption
of ordinary time. Unlike Goethe, he wanted it to be more—as he hints
early on:

So [Endymion] inwardly began
On things for which no wording can be found;
Deeper and deeper sinking, until drown'd
Beyond the reach of music: for the choir

Of Cynthia he heard not, though rough briar
Nor muffling thicket interpos'd to dull
The vesper hymn . . .
                    (4.961–67)

Of what use finally is music? Indeed of what use is poetry if "no wording can be found" for the deepest things? Here Keats shows again what he tried to show in the sonnet on the grasshopper and cricket, and what he will show in far more detail as he goes on: poetry and music operate similarly and, therefore, can be questioned similarly. In relation to the Pythagorean, how desirable is the rhetorical state? In relation to the affective, how desirable is the Pythagorean state? Most important, is either poetry or music really capable of achieving the affective state? How can work be a comment on life?

If Keats can grope toward such questions in *Endymion*, then he may have judged himself too harshly in the *King Lear* sonnet—although not much too harshly: *Endymion* sometimes reaches beyond simple melodizing and "o'er-sweeten'd," overimaginative lulling, but it's still tough going. Yet if an appreciation and acceptance of life's variety enriches (and occasionally overenriches) Keats's poetry, so does an all-pervading and no less characteristic skepticism. The questioning of music in *Endymion* can also be found in the late *Lamia*. Here, the music that holds up the fairy roof during a time of celebration ceases when the beautiful bride is exposed as the serpent of the poem's title (2.263). Precisely because the music is magical, it is unable to survive when reality, as seems inevitable, reasserts itself. Music can be diversion. Here it was more. But does this special music have anything to offer in any but the special circumstances in which it occurs? Besides diversion and magic, what else is there?

We've attempted to establish that Keats's many ideas about music not only correspond with the major strands of musical philosophy in his day but also give voice to Keats's major concerns. If we have smoothed over certain differences, it should be borne in mind that Keats himself was struggling to forge his many and often-contradictory ideas into a coherent philosophy of art and experience. Certainly we cannot prove, for instance, that Negative Capability and Pythagorean music emblematize each other in every respect, much less that Keats was thinking about one when the other came to mind. But the point is this: Though his emphasis and images may have shifted, his range of concerns tended to remain constant. In Keats's work, particular issues consistently involve particular images of and ideas about music.

Since experience can be described as the interplay of time and mind, and since music can be described as the artistic experience where the patterns of time are most palpable and most productive of meaning, it's not surprising that Keats uses music to articulate his most important ideas about time, experience, and meaning. As there is an ordinary kind of music, so there is an unusual yet ordinary kind of time, a diversion from the problems of real life that provides refreshment but is always understood to be opposed to those problems. As there is a deeper kind of music, at once more mysterious and more meaningful, so there is a special kind of time. But here one runs the risk of becoming lost in the dizzy void of sound, the sheer luxuriance of the imagination. The mind needs yet another kind of experience, a way to save whatever value Special time has when the mind returns, inevitably and inevitably changed, to ordinary time. Music provides Keats a vocabulary for discussing time, mind, and meaning. More important, as the next chapter will show, it provides him a method, hence, a poetic structure.

3

Image as Structure

A XIOMS in philosophy are not axioms," Keats wrote, "until they are proved upon our pulses" (L93). He was ever anxious to incorporate his speculations into his poetry and into his life. But it was seldom easy. As we've seen, his ideas about experience, like his ideas about music, tend to be widely diverse—and widely scattered. In a handful of letters and poems, among which we can find his greatest poems, Keats brings together all his ideas about music. Indeed, those ideas themselves provide the very structure that enables him to discover a way of accomplishing the inevitable return to ordinary time without losing the value of Special time. Herein, I think, lies the essence of Keats's genius and the power of his work, even while accepting that art can be an escape from reality or a reality unto itself, he seeks more. His greatest poems bring together all the moments—establishment, departure, return with a difference—of Romantic time.

Without music, Keats can get only so far in doing so. We've already seen in *Endymion* the first two moments. The return moment is also present there. It begins as a step beyond dreaming: the dream within a dream, which leads to a new kind of wakefulness. Endymion awakes to see more clearly than ever the love he's sought, then finds that this image was itself a dream. Yet it was no ordinary dream, no mere illusion or unreality; it was a vision of truth, of the love he would eventually find after being inspired and guided by this dream within a dream (4.398ff.).

Such is the case again in *The Fall of Hyperion*. The poet falls asleep and dreams the poem, then experiences a dream within a dream: a vision of the fall of the Titans, which Keats hoped would be a vision of truth. But the goddess who guides the poet's dreamed vision also says that

> The poet and the dreamer are distinct,
> Diverse, sheer opposite, antipodes.

45

> The one pours out a balm upon the world,
> The other vexes it.
>   (1.199–202)

The poet needs dreams—and something else. How to get to that something else without concluding that poetry is merely the reinstatement of exclusivity, the sheer opposite, that is, of that ordinary state in which reality and dreams are opposed?

In a letter to his friend J. H. Reynolds, Keats compares life to "a large Mansion of Many Apartments" (L95ff.). Characteristically, Keats renews a well-worn Biblical parable about eternity (in John 14:2 Jesus describes Heaven as a mansion of many chambers) by transforming it into a speculation about earthly experience. First comes the "infant or thoughtless chamber, in which we remain as long as we do not think." Yet the awakening of "the thinking principle" impels us to see and to be drawn toward the doorways leading from this chamber. We then enter "the Chamber of Maiden-Thought" and "become intoxicated with the light and the atmosphere." After a time, this atmosphere sharpens our vision into "the heart and nature of Man." A newly acquired imaginative life leads us less toward sheer delight and wonder and more toward pain, suffering, oppression. "To this point was Wordsworth come ... when he wrote 'Tintern Abbey.' " Wordsworth's genius, Keats says, lay in exploring some of those dark passages; many more remain. We must continue searching.

In ordinary consciousness, we are aware not only of the usual but of its opposite, the unusual, which tempts us away. The infant chamber is a delight as long as we don't think; if we do—and we must, since the thinking principle awakens in time, indeed is awakened by time—we see that there are doors, always open, leading away. It is an unstable state. We see the other doors, get a taste of Special experience, and finally enter the realm of delight and wonder. But this itself proves unstable. The many-at-once quality of Special time makes us more aware at once of everything, which includes the sufferings of humanity. Again, we long for something else, some way of using the imagination in daily life to confront those sufferings. Keats suggests in his letter that this dynamic—from ordinary to Special to a new sense of the ordinary—applies both to personal growth and to the "grand march of intellect" that he felt could be observed in European history (L96). As we develop both individually and socially, we should learn to preserve and transform the ordinary and the extraordinary. The innermost chambers, the dream within the dream, must lead elsewhere. The imagination, Keats says in a letter to Bailey, must like Adam in *Paradise Lost* awake and find its dream to be the truth (L37).

But how? Keats abandoned the first draft of *Hyperion* because he wished "to give [him]self up to other sensations" (L292). The careful working out of myth, like the careful working out of the poem's Miltonic diction, was too distracting, took too much time away from living life to the fullest. He tried to make use of the abandoned material in *The Fall of Hyperion* by making lines from the earlier poem a dream within a dream. But this attempt was even less successful. His attention as a poet was now focused on humanity, not divinity, on the difficulties and possibilities of life-in-time. Such a focus has two inherent and related difficulties. First, time passes; how to find abiding value? Second, how to find it in art? "Even if there is a structural similarity between reading, writing, and feeling," Andrew Cooper argues, "there is also a qualitative difference between them."[1] This is an especially important point to bear in mind as we go about the practice of criticism in our postmodern, all-the-world's-a-text age. A poem that does manage to say something about life is still a poem—usually unusual, sometimes Special, seldom more. If we fail to consider this, we fail to understand one of the central anxieties of Romantic poetry: the desire, often frustrated, to connect the poet's consciousness with that of "ordinary" persons. Even if reality is a fiction, it presents particular cases called "art" and "the artist" within itself. How to make Special time something besides an interruption of ordinary time? How to move from poetry to life?

Since, as I argued in the introduction, the Romantic artist believes that re-collection informs the basic workings of the mind no less than it informs the composing of art, this process may provide a clue. In Romantic time, consciousness is a simultaneous awareness of present and past. Truth resides in the relation between what was and what is. Keats tries to work with this idea. He says in a letter to Taylor that poetry "should strike the Reader as a wording of his own highest thoughts, and appear almost a Remembrance" (L69–70). Similarly, in the *Fall of Hyperion*, the poet receives a vision that he hopes will lead somehow out of myth toward truth—a vision he receives from Moneta, goddess of memory. To be aware is to establish a relation with meanings available through re-collection: a bringing again to attention and a putting together differently. The mind is the difference between time-then and time-now (more exactly, an awareness of time-now-as-then and time-then-as-now). A mind aware of itself as such is in that state where successful composition generally begins.

Then again, sometimes not so. Why does re-collection work when it does? Why doesn't it work when it doesn't? Keats's career is the search for a way to address these issues. He did so most successfully with music. As we've seen, most thinkers regarded music in one or at most two ways.

Keats finds room for many responses—given a pattern. By discussing music in certain ways, the poem acts like music. Its pattern or combinatory model enables the poem's unfolding to produce itself what the Romantic poet most needs to find—an enactment, thus an understanding, of the vicissitudes of temporal experience.

In the first quatrain of the sonnet "How many bards gild the lapses of time" (1816), the poet discusses the poetry that is "the food / Of my delighted fancy"—a kind of art that, though it contains beauties both earthly and sublime, exists specifically in opposition to a life beyond and without books. In the second quatrain, the poet mentions the "pleasing chime" in which all poets mingle in the life of the imagination. The mind can have usual, unusual, and Special experiences. But, as the sestet details, another kind of experience is available too, in which these poets' works, together with the sounds of nature, "make pleasing music, and not wild uproar." With imagination, the poet finds insight in and for the ordinary world. The poem enacts this dynamic in the way it arranges its utterances. It discusses experience in its unusual and, by implication, usual forms, then discusses Special experience, then returns to a different kind of ordinary experience. Thus it enacts its own insight: that the highest art leads from life to dreams and back to life.

From fancy through imagination to some other state, a state as attractive as it is difficult to define: even the doggerel "Song About Myself" (1818) shows this pattern. The naughty boy who is the poet's persona here runs away to Scotland and finds there that "fourscore was as eighty." After flight comes recognition; after departure, return. What then? Can after-Special time be anything but a reinstatement of ordinary time? Must Special time exist only as the antithesis of ordinary time? Worse, what if the passage through Special time changes the mind so much that functioning in ordinary time becomes impossible? Hegel solved the dialectical dilemma—that any synthesis will become a new thesis, calling forth a new antithesis—by arguing that eventually all oppositions and exclusivities collapse into the final synthesis of God. Keats, too, speaks of holiness; but his was "a holiness of the Heart's affections" (L36–37). Holy because of fundamental importance, this is still a human path through the problem—human and thus temporal. Linking truth with time, it gives voice and shape to this truth with music.

In that letter to Benjamin Bailey mentioning both Adam's dream and the "Heart's affections," Keats discusses "another favorite Speculation of mine":

> the simple imaginative Mind may have its rewards in the repeti[ti]on of its own silent Working coming continually on the spirit with a fine suddenness—to compare great things with small—have you never by being

surprised with an old Melody—in a delicious place—by a delicious voice, fe[l]t over again your very speculations and surmises at the time it first operated on your soul—do you not remember forming to yourself the singer's face more beautiful that [*for* than] it was possible and yet with the elevation of the Moment you did not think so—even then were you mounted on the Wings of Imagination so high . . . (L37)

Music is what you hear *and* what you imagine. The experience of having already heard the melody makes this hearing that much more meaningful. "Memory [i.e., mere habitual thought] should not be called knowledge," Keats says in another letter (L66). Something else must be added—what Keats calls the "silent Working" of the imagination. Like Wordsworth's "tranquillity," this is a time when the imagination goes to work on some experience. When repeated, as when one hears the melody again, the experience is in "a finer tone." This is the best that consciousness can strive for: memory that is neither sheer repetition nor sheer difference, but both and more. Ordinary and Special meet. The singer, by virtue of the song's being found, then lost (and worked on silently), then found again, becomes more beautiful; so, therefore, does the song.

Music is a path to insight. Even so, Keats has difficulty grounding that insight. Perhaps because he is working out his thoughts and is thus willing to at least experiment with religion, and perhaps because Bailey is a divinity student, Keats feels compelled to bring in a quasi-theological warrant: the after-Special time is a taste of immortal life. "[W]e shall enjoy ourselves here after by having what we called happiness on Earth repeated in a finer tone and so repeated" (L37). What happens with music

cannot be exactly the case with a complex Mind—one that is imaginative and at the same time careful of its fruits—who would exist partly on sensation and partly on thought—to whom it is necessary that years should bring the philosophic Mind—such an one I consider your's and therefore it is necessary to your eternal Happiness that you not only drink this old Wine of Heaven which I shall call the redigestion of our most ethereal Musings on Earth; but also increase in knowledge and know all things. (L38)

Though Keats's emphasis on the importance of here and now shows where his ideas would take him, he still maintains in this letter that what we do here and now is shaped and justified by something like God or Heaven. In comparison, what we do with music is a "small" thing: an example, not an end in itself. On other occasions, Keats might group such talk with what he called "the pious frauds of Religion" (L230).

Here, the finer tone is linked more with eternity than with the temporal patterns in which he would eventually have more success finding it.

Keats's "Ode to Apollo" (1815) makes a similar bow to the eternal and atemporal. It contains a catalogue of musical instruments— adamantine lyres, twanging harps of war, the far-sounding trumpet— that Keats compares to qualities of writers whom he admires. Such cataloguing, reminiscent of Dryden's St. Cecilia odes, had become by Keats's day a set of readily available equations between poetry and music: Milton's tuneful thunders, Shakespeare's Passions vibrating like strings, Spenser's martial trumpet, Tasso's ardent numbers.[2] Keats deliberates little here on what music can mean to the literary artist. Much as it can be a pleasant sensation to be indulged in by the poet, so it can be a pleasant image to be used but not examined too closely in the poem. Like this ode's "wild warblings from the Aeolian lyre," the poet and his poems are played upon by whatever happens to be in the air.

A "small thing" indeed. The Aeolian lyre needn't detain us long. If the major Romantic poets all used this image, they did so almost invariably as a cliché, or a convention, or, at best, something to be questioned. One has only to imagine poetry written about wind chimes, the modern descendent of this eighteenth-century toy, to see why. The instrument responding to the various breezes: here was a handy image of another cliché in weak Romantic poetry, that of the poet's sensitive soul swayed hither and thither by experience, whether from without or from within. Coleridge comes to reject the image of the Aeolian harp in the poem of that name (unfortunately, the religiosity he rejects it for is no less conventional and far more preachy), reviving it in "Dejection: An Ode" as an emblem of personal helplessness. The best poetry of the age, though it may use the Aeolian harp, also searches, with varying degrees of success, for not only fresher imagery but a more active role for consciousness to play in the shaping of its experience—"as if," says Shelley, "the [Aeolian] lyre could accommodate its chords to the motion of that which strikes them, in a determined proportion of sound."[3] Passive inspiration becomes active in-spiring.

The last stanza of the "Ode to Apollo" tries to find those more important roles. Again, note how the use of music as an idea provides a shape for the poem: from a conventional, ordinary sense of music, through imagination and myth, and toward—what?

> But when *Thou* joinest with the Nine,
> And all the powers of song combine,
>   We listen here on earth:
> The dying tones that fill the air,

And charm the ear of evening fair,
From thee, great God of Bards, receive their heavenly birth.

(42–47)

The finer tone: dying tones remain what they are but also become something else. Music becomes an image of how time passes yet, in passing,
leaves something of value that remains. Trying to define that something,
the poet falls not only into images of passive listening but also into passive writing: warmed-over Platonisms about earth being heaven's echo,
with appropriately stale allusions to the Muses and the god of song.

The later sonnet "On the Sea" (1817) also makes an attempt at the
finer tone. The poet advises "ye whose ears are dinned with uproar
rude, / Or fed too much with cloying melody" to listen to the "mighty
swell" of the ocean "[u]ntil ye start, as if the sea nymphs quired." By pay-
ing careful but imaginative attention to the given, we start: we are surprised, and we begin, finding something altogether new. Time renews
itself. The sea gluts the empty caverns much as the mind fills imaginative
experience with reality and reality with imagination, preserving and
transforming the sounds of the sea as well as both ordinary melody and
the imaginary sea nymphs' choir. Ordinary music, a diversion from the
uproar of usual experience, can become cloying. With the Special music
of the imaginative, "as if" realm, the mind can find amid spectacular but
ordinary nature an extraordinary sense of beauty, which the poem preserves. In a finer tone, the poem repeats the experiences of hearing the
sea and of thinking about both ordinary and Special music.

But "On the Sea" is both too specific as to where insight occurs and
too vague as to how. Elsewhere Keats is more precise. Again, the key to
this precision lies in the poetry's pattern, specifically in its pattern of musical imagery, which allows the verse to preserve and enact the duration
out of which the finer tone arises. Poetry and music *can* meet when verbal language's combinatory dimension becomes more explicit; they *do*
meet when poetry and music share a particular unfolding. In the sonnet
"Written in Disgust of Vulgar Superstition" (1816), Keats deploys his
ideas about music in such a way that the poem, like music, becomes that
patterned duration we're calling Romantic time. In the first quatrain,

The church bells toll a melancholy round,
    Calling the people to some other prayers,
    Some other gloominess, more dreadful cares,
More heark'ning to the sermon's horrid sound.

(1–4)

The music of vulgar superstition—the melancholy tolling, the sermon's horrid sound—is unusual but ordinary; it exists specifically as an other thing, exclusive of the usual form of ordinary life outside the church. By repeating "some other" and "more," Keats hammers home that sense of not-this-ness. He also demonstrates thereby that this music involves repetition but no finer tone: again and again the bells toll, but they lead only to "more dreadful cares." This music is the basest rhetoric: like the horrid sermon, the bells are organized sounds calculated to have a particular effect. In this case the effect is not pleasure but its opposite, which perhaps becomes, for those who heed the tolling of the bells, a perverse kind of pleasure.

The poet departs in the second quatrain from this "black spell" binding "the mind of humanity." Now the focus becomes "fireside joys" such as "Lydian airs," a phrase Keats probably got from Milton's "L'Allegro" to indicate relaxing and delightful music.[4] This music is not a diversion but, rather, a Pythagorean experience. The effect the airs are calculated to produce is the sensation of no particular effect. That is, they provide a deepened appreciation of life, a heightened sense of the fullness of outer and inner reality, of our atmosphere and our spirit ("air" can mean both of these as well as "melody"). Those airs are associated with a lofty discussion of all that is best in humanity ("converse high of those with glory crown'd"), which gives access to one's own highest thoughts as well as those of others, both present and absent (it is "one" who sits at home having such "converse"), both now and past (the crowning with glory has already taken place). The many-at-once quality of Special time: self and not-self, here and not-here combine.

In the sestet, Special time presents its essential problem: departure involves return. "Still, still, [the bells] toll." The poet is reminded that, though in contact with wonderful music and great minds, he is isolated from ordinary life. Can Special consciousness survive in some form when Special time ends?

Return is inevitable; but so is difference. Though the poet again hears the bells, he also sees now that the church is dying—dying because it never finds the finer tone, indeed never even seeks it. Meanwhile, a new age is being born in which "fresh flowers will grow, / And many glories of immortal stamp." The poem enacts its meaning by returning to itself with a difference. Note the echo, the repetition in a finer tone, of previous language: the past's "glory crown'd" becomes the glory of the future.

But also note the lack of musical imagery, except for those horrid bells, in the sestet. Keats seems skeptical about music being the way to that time beyond Special time. Though it can be rhetorical and

Pythagorean, its affective possibilities remain unclear. Perhaps, though, he was skeptical not of music's ability to lead there, but of his own ability as a poet to find it, not just in music, but at all. The sestet lacks music; it also lacks a program. Failing to address exactly how the new world will be born, the ending of this sonnet seems incompletely thought out. Nevertheless, it shows that Keats, even early on, was seeking both the finer tone and a way for poetry to enact the move from fancy through imagination that would, he hoped, lead there.

He didn't always succeed. In fact, he wasn't always trying. Sometimes he chose not to: pure diversion and pure otherworldliness have their places. Sometimes, as in "Lines on Seeing a Lock of Milton's Hair" (1818), he admits that it lies beyond his ability. These "Lines" were written quickly, probably within a matter of minutes (CP 436)—which makes this poem valuable: the artist lacking time to act in any but a characteristic way:

> Chief of organic numbers!
>   Old scholar of the spheres!
> Thy spirit never slumbers,
>   But rolls about our ears
> For ever, and for ever:
> O, what a mad endeavour
>   Worketh he,
> Who, to thy sacred and ennobled hearse,
> Would offer a burnt sacrifice of verse
>   And melody.
> How heavenward thou soundedst,
>   Live temple of sweet noise;
> And discord unconfoundest,—
>   Giving delight new joys,
> And pleasure nobler pinions—
>   (1–15)

Milton's poetry, like music, is both as empty as mathematics and as full as a living thing. Like music, it provides rhetorical, Pythagorean, and affective experiences. Each is unique; all are intertwined. Sensual pleasure is made nobler by spirit, which has access to the "forever" of the "temple." Yet the temple is "live," not eternal but temporal. Milton's verse gives ordinary "delight new joys"; it is also a Special, quasi-religious experience, a temple that is resonant or "live" because of its hollow spaces; and it provides an experience relevant to life-in-time: the unconfounding of discord (15).

In acknowledging Milton's accomplishment, the poet becomes aware of how far below that accomplishment he is: it would be a "mad

endeavor" to offer up to Milton "a burnt sacrifice of verse / And melody"—
mad because the poet's verse and melody fall short of Milton's level. But
that level is itself a level of verse and melody. Milton's art is a form of
madness, a Special consciousness where apparent opposites like words
and music meet. Any poet who would achieve that level must follow in
that madness. Thus the poet asks Milton to listen to his oath to Apollo
(18), god of music and poetry—and of healing. The poet-physician: art
must renew life. It must dedicate itself to finding the finer tone, even if it
cannot do so now. (Note that the poet's oath is described not as "Del-
phian" but as "Delian"; Apollo's major oracle was at Delphi, but he was
born at Delos and had a minor oracle there.[5] Perhaps the poet is reminding us that even a god doesn't begin mature, and can be responsible for
utterances of lesser importance.) The poet will wait and work for the day
when "every childish fashion" (22) will have vanished from his poetry.
Then, "grey-gone in passion," he will

> Leave to an after-time
> Hymning and harmony
> Of thee, and of thy works, and of thy life;
> (25–27)

Hymning—the madness of combined verse and melody—leads to a
higher sanity. The poet hopes to become "mad with glimpses of futu-
rity" (31), to become, by means of artworks, ecstatically aware of life's
possibilities.

The poet realizes that such a mad sense of the future can come only
from a firmly rooted sense of the past. The best art is associated not only
with music but also with memory: the poet says he will someday look
back on "this hour" (33), transforming the passion he feels now into
something new, more sober, more "high-rife / With old philosophy"
(29–30). Much as his poem moves through Romantic time by discussing
various kinds of music, so the poet must establish passion, then depart
from it, then return to it with a difference. Only then will his poetry be
like the music that fulfills all the possibilities of music, providing pleasure, and a dizzy void, and the finer tone that, in turning loss into meaning, teaches both how to write and how to live.

For now, though, the poet says that his "offerings must be hush'd"
(32): not mute but muted; not exactly poetic silence—he did write this
poem—but rather a poetry that, by admitting its own inadequacy, strives
for higher achievement. The end of the poem becomes a beginning, a
glimpse of this higher achievement:

> A lock of thy bright hair—
> Sudden it came,
> And I was startled, when I caught thy name
> Coupled so unaware;
> Yet at the moment, temperate was my blood—
> Methought I had beheld it from the flood.
>
> (36–41)

The poet remembers that he felt passion when he saw the lock of Milton's hair, and then, by writing this poem ("the moment" of line 40 refers to line 33's "this hour" in which the poem was composed), transformed all past time into the present. The primeval Flood becomes part of this day. All time becomes now. The past is repeated in a finer tone.

So is his passion, and—not surprisingly, given the link between the finer tone and music—in a format much like a musical composition: this is an ode, the lyric shape most closely associated with music (that association, as we'll see, will become increasingly important for Keats). The act of shaping a sounded utterance creates higher forms of awareness by providing opportunities for re-collection. Like music, the poem becomes a re-collective act. Combinatory meaning—time made significant—becomes explicit. As such, this ode succeeds as an ode, as a musical poem, though perhaps not in the best sense. With frequent short lines and infrequent delay of rhyme, the free ode shape Keats uses here unfolds too breathlessly. It is reminiscent of the hot and flushed forehead the poet wants to move away from (34). He seems to realize this, not allowing himself to call this work an ode—or even a poem. These are lines: directions, pointings-toward. He is now not Milton's heir but a viewer of Milton's hair, not an initiate of artistic mysteries unlocked by greater discipline but an outsider looking at a lock.

Too much discipline keeps the poet in ordinary time. At least with the free ode he's making an attempt at Special consciousness, if not at what lies beyond. We'll see in part 2 how Keats's working out, in the year following the "Milton's hair" ode, of a unique ode form played a crucial role in his discovering how to move from rhetorical through Pythagorean to affective music, thus how to move from ordinary to Special to re-collected ordinary. But he was ever skeptical. We can see this skepticism in one of his greatest poems, which was written around the same time as the great odes, in which music and mind are linked once again.

Keats included "La Belle Dame sans Merci: A Ballad" in that letter to his brother George where he defined the world as the "Vale of Soul-making" (L243–44). A search for salvation similar to the one he describes in the letter goes on in this remarkable, and remarkably hermetic, little poem. How do we "save" our experience? Must we detach ourselves from "reality" to find such salvation? If so, will salvation survive the inevitable journey back to reality? How extensive a role can music play in addressing these issues?

A knight at arms, alone, pale, and fevered, says that he met a lady in the meads. She was "beautiful, a fairy's child," who "made sweet moan" for him (14, 20). That is, she appeared to have sung, or at least to have provided something like music in its rhetorical mode. Her utterance, though nonverbal, was not just noise; it was, in fact, comprehensible as something sweet. So far, hers seems ordinary music, a nice diversion. Yet the combining of opposites in "sweet moan"—what's normally an indication of pain becomes pleasurable—suggests that the lady's music is potentially something more, something able to lead toward Special time.

Singing a fairy's song, the lady leads the knight away (21ff.). He enters a Special realm, not exclusive of the usual world but utterly beyond both usual and unusual. Music becomes the "language strange" (27) of the lady's elfin grot. Again we find the many-at-once-ness emblematic of Special time: this language can include her saying "I love thee true" as well as her singing, weeping, sighing, lulling. The knight shuts her eyes "with kisses four" (32), then appears to fall asleep himself. He enters a dream, the farthest remove from ordinary reality. All at once, the knight sees pale kings and warriors and princes, who warn him that "La belle dame sans merci" has him in thrall (35ff.). But who is she? The lady he met in the meads who now sleeps beside him? Someone else? Did the lady cry because she loves him *and* has him in a thrall that will effectively kill him? Is it worth noting that all those who warn the knight are, like him, male? The poem leaves these issues open. This Special realm—dreams, wonders, strange language, fairy songs—seems beyond all definition.

When the knight awakens, he is alone. He has returned to the ordinary world. This is why, he says, he remains here on the cold hill's side. Not much of an explanation: *what* is why? Is he waiting for the lady to return? Could this be a dream within a dream? What use was the trip to fairyland if this is the state the knight is left in—whatever that state is? Paralyzed with desire? With magic? With sadness or loneliness?

But the knight is not exactly alone, or rather his aloneness is complex. Because the poem refuses to attribute speech, the speaker who questions the knight is never clearly distinguished from the knight. Especially given the lack of quotation marks in Keats's text, we can never really be sure who's speaking. Granted, Keats's dispensing with devices of attribution like "he said" typifies the folk ballads he is more or less imitating here (more on this poem's relation to the folk ballad in part 2). But it also serves a purpose specific to the poem: the poet's insight depends upon having an experience similar to the knight's. Enthrallment to imagination is necessary, because the move from ordinary to Special and finally back to ordinary consciousness makes for meaning, whether in poetry or in music—or in life. The reader, too, is invited to join in the process that leads (so runs the hope) through Special time to insight: much as the lyric voice never distinguishes itself from the knight's, so it never sets itself up as a commentator or guide over and against the reader's experience of that voice.

That experience is not without its dangers—for knight, poet, and reader. According to Robert Pack, "Keats considered it a living death to awake from such a dream, know that it is a dream, and also know that the dream can never be forgotten."[6] What if you get stuck in Special time—or, rather, since Special time must end, what if your experience of it survives only as regret, paralysis, confusion, longing? Even if this is not the case, what if you discover that you can't use what you discovered in Special time? The harvest's done; what do you have to show for it?

Keats says in his letter to his brother that he decided the knight should bestow four kisses because the only other possible rhyme—a score—would have been too many (L244). Keats wants passion and restraint. In Special time they do not seem exclusive of each other. What about in ordinary time? As Cooper says, if Keats is afraid of anything, it is of "illusions risked when you try to cheat the normal economy of the emotions."[7] Keats himself wrote in that same letter that "[n]othing ever becomes real till it is experienced—Even a Proverb is no proverb to you till your Life has illustrated it" (L230). Which makes for a familiar dilemma of British empiricism: if nothing is real until experienced, then reality tends eventually to get located, if not in the mind, then at least in the mind's perception of it. In Keats's terms, we remain enthralled by Special time, unsure where to locate "reality." Like the knight, we feel in retrospect the intensity of our imaginative visions, but are unable to move and breathe and function otherwise. Those visions seemed so intensely and undeniably real at the time, yet now we have returned to another reality that is as unappealing as it is inescapable. We are back in a world of troubles. Remaining in uncertainty and doubt seems an unattractive prospect. Can we do any soul making?

Note how the deployment of music as an idea within the poem conditions the unfolding of the poem, and how that unfolding in turn becomes an enactment for the reader of both the poet's and the knight's experience. Music begins in the ordinary world. Then it becomes a fairy's song that leads away to a Special realm, which leads in turn to many more questions than answers: of what use is a fairy's song in a world where no birds sing? Music, or the specific and named lack of it, locates us again in the ordinary world, now utterly changed.

The poem acts musically in another way: its narrative shape enacts its effect. How it means over time largely governs what it means. The poem begins with the speaker asking what ails the knight; the knight replies by telling the story of his fairy enthrallment; then we are all back on the hillside, repeating, not quite verbatim, the poem's opening words: from present to past to the return of the present with a difference. As Susan Wolfson points out, we begin to see "now" as located in an anterior event, [8] as a re-collection of the past. Whether this leads to new freedom or renewed enthrallment, and the ways in which these two are and are not opposites, will become more and more an issue for Keats, an issue his greatest poems will attempt to clarify.

Perhaps Keats is not clear here because the issues are so difficult. Or perhaps the poem's uncertainties are one source of its power—a power that is fundamentally musical. To explain how, we need to address a related issue: If music provides such an effective model for poetry, why not aim more directly for its power and be a composer?

4

Words, Music, and Interpretation

TIME —the simultaneity of nowness and passing-away—is the essential fact of Romantic experience. Music is time organized in such a way as to make palpable this simultaneity. Hence, music is the paradigm of all the arts to the Romantic. How then does Romanticism justify to itself composing poetry rather than music?

Charles Lamb had one perspective on this issue:

> To music [the ear] cannot be passive. It will strive—mine at least will—spite of its inaptitude, to thrid the maze; like an unskilled eye painfully poring over hieroglyphics. . . . Words are something; but to be exposed to an endless battery of mere sounds; to be long a dying; to lie stretched upon a rack of roses . . . to fill up sound with feeling, and strain ideas to keep pace with it; to gaze on empty frames and be forced to make all the pictures for yourself; to read a book, *all stops,* and be obliged to supply the verbal matter . . . these are faint shadows of what I have undergone from a series of the ablest-executed pieces of this empty *instrumental music.*[1]

Writing in the persona of Elia, Lamb may not be completely sincere. But he does remind us that not all Romantics thought alike. What is for others an important experience is for Lamb "the distracting torment of endless, fruitless, barren attention."[2] Lamb prefers words, or at least seeks some verbal mediation between words and music. Note how his simile of written symbols (hieroglyphics) helps make music less baffling to him, and how his metaphors, both outrageous and copious, try to compensate for music's emptiness.

E. T. A. Hoffmann provides another perspective: though music is untranslatable into words, an author can and should seek ways of talking about how it works.[3] Explaining its effects is itself a valuable literary activity. Doing so lends greater comprehension to an experience often difficult to comprehend. Language with primarily referential meaning can be used to explain language with primarily combinatory meaning.

Hoffmann assumes here that music needs to be explained. Perhaps this is not, or at least ought not to be, the case. Music in the late eighteenth and early nineteenth centuries was instrumental. It was supposed to speak for itself as music. Hoffmann himself was one of the chief promulgators of that notion. Words may only get in the way. So why bother with them? Because, according to Shelley,

> language is arbitrarily produced by the imagination, and has relation to thoughts alone; but all other materials, instruments, and conditions of art, have relations among each other, which limit and interpose between conception and expression. The former is as a mirror which reflects, the latter as a cloud which enfeebles, the light of which both are mediums of communication. Hence the fame of sculptors, painters, and musicians, although the intrinsic powers of the great masters of these arts may yield in no degree to that of those who have employed language as the hieroglyphic of their thoughts, has never equalled that of poets in the restricted sense of the term; as two performers of equal skill will produce unequal effects from a guitar and a harp.[4]

Painting must imitate actual shapes and colors; music must follow the rules of tonal logic. Like Hegel, Shelley argues that music has relations only among its own parts and none to ideas; it must remain inferior to language.[5] In Shelley's conception, verbal language, though constrained to an extent by syntax and semantics, is also free to imitate the patterns of thought.

Or some language is. According to Shelley, certain uses of verbal language are truer than others to its arbitrariness in relation to the world, thus its necessary-ness in relation to ideas:

> [A] story is a catalogue of detached facts, which have no other bond of connexion than time, place, circumstance, cause and effect; [a poem] is the creation of actions according to the unchangeable forms of human nature, as existing in the mind of the creator, which is itself the image of all other minds.[6]

Where fiction must imitate accidental relations among events, poetry, "the expression of the imagination," imitates Being—more exactly, those relations that Being comprises. Thoughts and ideas, "have relation both between each other and towards that which they represent." Ideas are connected; what is *here* recurs *there*. Meter and rhyme are useful but not necessary enactments of such recurrences. More necessary is the quality of thought in poetry (so Shelley asserts here; elsewhere, as we'll see in part 2, he argues differently). In the act of perceiving recurrences, the human mind can adjust here and there. Present and past, self and world are seen as vitally related to each other—"as if," so we've noted Shelley saying, "the [Aeolian] lyre could accommodate its chords to the motions of that which strikes them."[7]

Which, of course, it can't. This "as if," like the simile of the guitar and the harp, typifies Shelley's use of music as an idea: it is a model for poetry, though a limited one. Having rhythm and harmony, music helps to remind us of the vital connectedness of all things and thoughts, thus to weaken the hold of dead ways of apprehending them. For Shelley, there is a lower form of music:

> When the lute is broken
> Sweet tones are remembered not;
> . . . .
> As music and splendour
> Survive not the lamp and the lute,
> The heart's echoes render
> No song when the spirit is mute . . .

And a higher:

> Music, when soft voices die,
> Vibrates in the memory—
> Odours, when sweet violets sicken,
> Live within the sense they quicken.[8]

Music is a useful idea for articulating various understandings of temporal experience. In the one case, all is lost to passing-away-ness; the lower music cannot survive the shattering of the lute. In the other case, all passes away, yet something remains behind; the higher music vibrates in the memory long after the notes are silent.

This higher music—like, but in the end superior to, a fine musician playing a fine instrument—is poetry. Both poetry and music enable us to perceive rhythm and harmony. Music may do it more obviously; poetry does it better, being the rhythm and harmony of the mind, the music of "as if." Like Keats, Shelley posits lower and higher forms of music; unlike Keats, he seems persuaded that the highest kind of music is poetry and poetry alone. In this he has something in common with Lamb. And, like Lamb, Shelley sees finally in terms of hieroglyphics: art as a written symbol for the rhythms and harmonies of ideas. "Poetry," Shelley insists, "is connate with the origin of man."[9] This particular act of writing entails the very principle that makes us human: we are able to adjust internally, to participate actively in our experiences, because we can perceive and preserve vital relations. Poetry *is* such perceptions and preservations.

As I've hinted, there are inconsistencies in Shelley's notions of language, poetry, music, and time. The important thing to note here is that there may be other approaches to the issue of why music should be a model but not a career. For example, though music can't do all that poetry can do, why not use it for what it *can* do? If music is useful to the poetic mind, should that mind create sung words, in which music and poetry exchange energies more directly? Such was seldom the case with the Romantics. Thomas Moore wrote lyrics for already-existing melodies, but his was a minor if charming talent. William Blake is reported to have sung some of his poems to improvised melodies, but these have not survived.[10] By and large, Romantic poets elect to create music *in* poetry, not to create music *and* poetry. They use the image of song frequently when speaking about the highest poetry. But they do so almost by default, as if there were really no other way of talking about that highest art: poetry so musical that it has no need of music.

We'll see Keats doing something like this in "The Eve of St. Agnes." Being also the man who advised Shelley, "curb your magnaminity and be more of an artist, and 'load every rift' of your subject with ore" (L390), Keats might have rejected songwriting for reasons that have more to do with craft. Sung words can provide an experience utterly unlike music or words alone. Song lyrics as song lyrics can be great art. But as poetry, they tend to be frail, or sparse, or rigid. Vocal music that tries to be otherwise (e.g., operatic recitative) tends to be highly specialized and relatively rare. As Susanne Langer points out, "A perfect poem doesn't readily give itself up to musical form."[11] Schubert's settings of Goethe, or Schumann's of Heine, are exceptions that prove the rule. A great songwriter writes great songs; a great poet writes great poetry.

And, of course, the poet may have no musical talent. But that needn't stop him or her from being drawn to music, from wanting to take advantage in poetry of what music has to offer. It may, in fact, give that desire a fine edge of envy and thus make it stronger, in much the same way that music's newfound independence made it more attractive and important to Romantic poets.

How can poetry take such advantage? One possibility lies in the notion of *Ursprache*. Rousseau, Herder, Chabanon, and A. W. Schlegel argued for "the original union of the arts."[12] According to this view, music and poetry are "tragically separated twins," fragments of a preverbal

language, of a direct and natural mode of expression connecting humanity's psychic depths and the world.[13] Shelley says:

> A child at play by itself will express its delight by its voice and motions;
> and every inflexion of tone and every gesture will bear exact relation to a
> corresponding antitype in the pleasurable impressions which awakened
> it . . . The savage (for the savage is to ages what the child is to years) ex-
> presses the emotions produced in him by surrounding objects in a similar
> manner . . . [14]

Ursprache, so the argument goes, is the expression of that primitive state
before verbal and nonverbal became distinct modes of signification, and
before self and world became distinct categories of perception.

As with his use of music, Shelley employs this notion (itself more
wishful conceit than linguistic or anthropological fact) yet distances himself from it. Poetry, he says, has a very different function. The language
of poets

> is vitally metaphorical; that is, it marks the before unapprehended rela-
> tions of things and perpetuates their apprehension . . . if no new poets
> should arise to create afresh the associations . . . language will be dead to
> all the nobler purposes of human intercourse . . . Time . . . for ever devel-
> ops new and wonderful applications of the eternal truth which [poetry]
> contains. . . . The frequent recurrence of the poetical power, it is obvious
> to suppose, may produce in the mind an habit of order and harmony cor-
> relative with its own nature and with its effects upon other minds.[15]

Our perception of eternal truths, of "a certain rhythm or order" and of
"a harmony in thoughts,"[16] can become stale over time. We need "the
frequent recurrence of the poetical power." We must constantly go forth
from what seem truths and certainties and vital metaphors, to enter into
a way of thinking distant from certainties, then return with a set of "before unapprehended relations," a new sense of old certainties, which allows us to "perpetuate their apprehension" with revitalized, "vitally
metaphorical" language. Times takes away the freshness of language;
but, in so doing, time creates the opportunity for its renewal.

According to the primitivist argument, *Ursprache* is how the savage or
the child performs this renewal. Sound vitally connects outer and inner
reality. But the renewal can't last. The new metaphor becomes an old
certainty. Moderns and adults need a more sophisticated approach,
which is what poetry provides. Words and music may be tragically separated twins. But each nonetheless has relevance and power now. Poetry
(according to Shelley) has more power than music. Still, that power is

based on a quality shared by both poetry and music. The notion of *Ursprache* can hint, but only hint, at that quality.

We get another hint from music. The highest form of poetry, Novalis argued, provides "associations, like dreams ... a broad allegorical meaning and an indirect effect like music." Similarly, Rousseau argued that music gives rise to feelings by virtue of the absence of a correlative object. Music is not an expression or a representation; rather, it tells us that we are approaching the limits of expression and representation, thus arousing emotions like fear and hope[17]—emotions intensely strong because they are intensely temporal and intimately connected with the patterned duration that is the fundamental fact of Romantic existence. Music is re-collection enacted. In music, presence falls into, and emerges out of, not-there-ness. The present falls into the past, and only when it does so can meaning emerge, because meaning can unfold only in time.

Two mid–eighteenth century aesthetic statements are relevant here. In James Usher's words,

> the most elevated sensation of music arises from a confused perception of ideal or visionary beauty and rapture, which is sufficiently perceivable to fire the imagination, but not clear enough to become an object of knowledge. This shadowy beauty the mind attempts, with a languishing curiosity, to collect into a distinct object of view and comprehension; but it sinks and escapes, like the dissolving ideas of a delightful dream, that are neither within the reach of memory, nor yet totally fled. The charms of music then, though real and affecting, seem yet too confused and fluid to be collected into a distinct idea.[18]

And, according to Kevin Barry, Thomas Twining argued that "the pleasure and signification of music depend upon an inadequacy or imprecision in the very material of its sound." Barry goes on to point out that Twining demonstrates a preference for instrumental music, because it involves a certain inadequacy: its meaning is not given except by the act of listening to it. Perception and signification become inextricable. In Twining's view, then, musical signs do not so much imitate or express as they turn a listener's attention to what Barry calls the listener's "own inventive subjectivity."[19]

"Subjectivity" is perhaps an unfortunate choice of words, implying as it does that music rejects an otherwise available objectivity. But I think Barry's point is that, according to Twining, music points less toward any particular meaning than toward the process of meaning making itself. That process is neither objective nor subjective as such; rather, in that process subject and object come into being by virtue of each other. Barry has suggested we adopt the concept of "the empty sign" to understand and explain such a view of signification. We might ask how "the empty sign" can be known as a sign at all if it is empty. By "empty," Barry means something like empty of explicit referential content. Music appears "to be outside the principle of mimesis and to imitate nothing." Music thus "directs attention towards the process of response."[20]

To Barry's model of the empty sign we can add the more Keatsian dimension of many-at-once-ness. Music seems empty not only because it lacks an overt referential aspect but also because it is so full of interpretive possibility as to defy clear and rational understanding. Music moves us because it always moves away from us. Call it an overpoweringly blank plenitude. In music, we recognize the sign as a sign insofar as we encounter it as part of a specifically musical utterance. Its appearance in a harmonic/rhythmic structure allows us to understand it as significant. We have encountered such a sign previously in other instances that we recognize as musical compositions, and in previous moments of the composition at hand. Such appearances tell us only that this is a musical sign; they tell us nothing about this appearance. The sign is empty—previously and potentially but not actually significant—until, by living through the music, we understand the sign as, say, a tonic chord, which in turn signals that we have arrived at a moment of repose or closure.

Musical structure, by giving coherence and context to notes and chords and rhythms, allows us to feel unmistakably that something is being signified. We cannot know what until we live through it, and even then our understanding is resolutely unlocatable. Lacking an explicit set of referential directions, we must then proceed to interpret, not so much the signs as our experience of them. Musical signification feels both powerful and ineffable; in fact, ineffability is a large part of its power. As Twining argued, "there is no kind of investigation so tempting & pleasant, as that *which can never be found*."[21] Sublime or mystical or numinous experiences are often described as similarly powerful and mysterious and tempting (though not always pleasant, as Lamb would attest). This helps explain further why Keats waxes theological when discussing the finer tone he associates with music. Like music, the finer tone has something of the numinous about it. Empty and full, absent and present, offering time-as-gone and time-as-abiding, it signifies nothing—nothing except our response to its organization of time. We let go of apparent fullness and of the powerful unknowable that takes its place, in order to proceed into interpretation. We move from a rhetorical through a Pythagorean to an affective understanding of experience.

To hear echoes in this description and in the ideas of Twining and Usher of Shelley's "like memory of music fled" or Wordsworth's

"affected by absent things as if they were present" would be correct—
sort of. It would be more correct to hear Shelley and Wordsworth
themselves as echoes with variations (repetition involves difference).
When Romantic poets describe what poetry should do, they tend to use
terms already used by previous aestheticians to describe what music
does. But they also assert that poetry can have a similar effect—more
precisely, that poetry produces certain effects similar to those produced
by music yet valuable in themselves. Music then is central to Romantic
poetry because it is a familiar and palpable model of what poetry should
strive to do. Poetry, like music, can use language in such a way as to be
suggestive, imperfect, demonstrative of how the mind works. Like music,
poetry should not be a sincere expression of what is *there* but, rather, as
Barry puts it, a "conjuring up of the sensation of what is *not* there."[22]
Barry points out that such an activity, fundamental to Romantic poetry,
was first described in musical aesthetics—an aesthetics of a consciousness that participates actively in the interpretation of empty and indeterminate signs.[23]

Wordsworth stated that the poet, keenly aware of how we thus "half-
create" our experience, is susceptible to "that blessed mood"

> In which the burthen of the mystery,
> In which the heavy and the weary weight
> Of all this unintelligible world
> Is lighten'd:—that serene and blessed mood,
> In which the affections gently lead us on,
> Until, the breath of this corporeal frame,
> And even the motion of our human blood
> Almost suspended, we are laid asleep
> In body, and become a living soul:
> While with an eye made quiet by the power
> Of harmony, and the deep power of joy,
> We see into the life of things.[24]

The affections lead us on. The drive toward the affective leads us from
fullness through emptiness to a new kind of fullness. Present becomes
absent and absence becomes presence. The Romantic landscape is the
landscape of a moment, empty save for uncertainty and time-
boundedness.[25] To find meaning, the mind must first recognize that what
was once "now" is gone, then find a way to make this absence and emptiness somehow present and full again. Fittingly, Wordsworth's *Prelude*
is full of emptinesses in nature—a dark cliff that blots out the stars, the
face of Mount Blanc, a chasm on Mount Snowden—which the poet later
tries to fill with imagination, or at least tries to write imaginatively

about.[26] Such not-there-nesses become emblems of re-collecting itself: something was signified; the mind could not know exactly what, therefore, it has been actively interpreting its experience of not-knowing. Return with a difference: the poet moves from a recognition of signification, through an awareness of that signification as radically indeterminate, to an attempt to refill the sign with interpretation. I begin by knowing *that* it means because I know it *has meant;* yet I do not know what it means now, so I must imagine over time. Such is the pattern of the poet's experience; such, therefore, should be the pattern of the poem itself, because poetry is in essence a record of that experience. Like music, a poem should be a duration whose pattern creates an opportunity for active recollection. It is secondary, an emptying and a filling, a language that follows.[27]

This idea of poetry does not constitute any attempt to borrow from music. Rather, it is the discovery of parallelism. As we've seen, the aesthetic philosophy of the day made available three approaches to music: rhetorical, Pythagorean, and affective. The first two tend to suggest contradictory functions for music: an alternative to reality versus a reality in itself. The third becomes attractive when it offers itself not as yet another alternative but as the culminating moment toward which the other two lead in a patterned duration—not as yet another way of regarding music but as a way of interpreting all musical experience. Music moves us from certainty through mystery to a renewed understanding of temporality. Romantic theory posits similar functions in verbal language, encounters similar problems, and discovers similar solutions. As Barry shows, the kinds of meaning that the late eighteenth and early nineteenth centuries held to be available to verbal language were: rhetorical (words are arbitrary signs performing the necessary task of communication), structural (context takes priority over words and names), and symbolic (language as the translucence of the eternal in the temporal). Again, the first two, names versus structure, tend to offer contradictory accounts of where verbal meaning originates. The third offers no solution; instead it becomes just one more way of naming, until verbal language looks beyond itself for a way to understand itself.[28] This it does by turning to music, where it finds a new kind of symbolic function: not naming but interpretation enacted, the ability to see in vitally metaphorical ways. Presence and absence, present and past become aspects of each other.

Parallelism shades into convergence. Referential and combinatory achieve copriority; name and structure lead equally to re-collection. Poetry discovers ways to allow verbal language to act like music: signs are recognized as meaningful yet arbitrary. The perception of arbitrariness is boosted by the placing of a name in a temporal structure, which helps empty the sign of its necessary meaning prior to this particular unfolding. This creates the opportunity for interpretation, for a return with a difference to the sign's prior meaning. Arbitrary becomes necessary when the poem, like music, like the mind itself, re-collects, thereby enacting the natural pattern of Romantic time. The sign is emptied to be filled again and differently.

Keats described something like this in his sonnet "On the Sea." The ocean is able to resonate with its own music because it fills the empty caverns; similarly, the mind is able to function because it empties and fills itself, departing from and returning with a difference to its experiences. In this light, "La Belle Dame sans Merci" becomes an even more musical poem. It is a deliberate journey through ineffability. Along with the knight, we move from reality to fairyland and back, wondering what to make of the journey. Returned from both the rhetorical and the Pythagorean, we struggle to locate and understand our affect. The poem does not provide answers; rather, it is an occasion for interpretation—*an occasion created specifically by the way it unfolds as that unfolding is governed by the deployment of musical imagery.* The poem becomes itself an empty sign: we recognize *that* it means. We cannot say what it means; therefore, we must re-collect our experience of it, and of poetry, verbal language, and life.

Barry's notion of the empty sign, to which both poetry and music have access, answers Wellek and Warren's charge that Romantic attempts at musicality usually turn out to be little more than a loosening of syntax and logic; and vagueness does not musicality make, since music has its own definite syntax and logic.[29] Granted, each art has its own unique ways of governing meaning: reference can never have exclusive priority in music, any more than combination can in poetry. But both poetry and music can enact the pattern of Romantic time, and can do so in a way that allows not just a parallelism but a convergence between their respective ways of meaning. Both move us through a shaped duration. Both begin by communicating rhetorically. Then both put us into a "pure serene" or "dizzy void"—be it distance, hollowness, absence, mystery, mysticism, the past, the "live temple," the sea's caves, the "intoxication" of "Maiden-Thought," or any of the other images of emptiness Keats uses for Special time. Both arts then ask, demand, and enable us to come back to a different present, a present removed from certainty, full of a distance now past yet present, and therefore charged with the need for interpretation. Poetry has "the power of harmony."

A Romantic artist, then, may be a poet rather than a composer because poetry has its own value. Its particular effect (and affect) is to move away from the certainties that referential priority ordinarily allows, to dance on the edge of the nonverbal by making its pattern of unfolding, as governed by ideas of music, point finally toward our need to interpret our experience of the poem. The way that passing time feels, as enacted by the artwork, becomes the source of the artwork's meaning and power. What Lamb shuns, Keats openly courts. To read is to "supply the matter" for the "empty frame." Poetry should strike the reader almost as a remembrance—almost: it uses words whose meaning we know before reading the poem. After the poem, all's changed. What now?

This dynamic organizes poetry because it also organizes all experience as Romanticism understands experience. The mind is as a fading coal; to be conscious is to have lost an origin and to have recovered that origin in a different form by means of interpretation. Poetry records and enacts that process. The need for interpretation in and of Romantic time becomes the all-important link between art and consciousness. Works are the comments on life. We've seen Keats struggling to coordinate and employ this dynamic in his work. It finds one fulfillment in "Belle Dame": we move from the rhetorical through the Pythagorean, with the finding of affect up to us. "The Eve of St. Agnes" moves similarly, but offers a discussion at once more detailed and more suggestive. Proceeding from fancy through imagination, it provides a chance to seek the finer tone. The next chapter will detail how this approach in that poem does (and does not) allow Keats to find what he was looking for.

5

"The Eve of St. Agnes"

JOHN Keats had what Brian Bartlett calls "an intense historical imagination."[1] Equal emphasis ought to be placed on all three terms in that description. Like the other major Romantic poets, Keats possessed a keen sense of the intimacy between consciousness, time, and interpretation. What makes him unique is his belief that each kind of experience, given certain circumstances, can have a place in that imagination. In Keats's view, the task of the poet is to live through and with them all: not to choose one over the others, but to understand what each has to offer, to experience in full the circumstances under which each becomes valuable.

Keats's determination to live out the poet's task—to move from recreation through imagination to the re-creation of life—makes for his greatest poems. One of these is "The Eve of St. Agnes." Written early in 1819, this is his first successful extended poem. Here Keats tells a good story well.[2] But this does not fully account for the poem's success. Keats's handling of the narrative, his choice and arrangement of detail: these proceed from the pattern of Romantic time and the musical emblems of its moments. Music provides a vocabulary and a method. In the Romantic age, music was highly syntactical; the Romantic poet's use of music is no less so. Music-as-idea is a system, from rhetorical through Pythagorean to affective. That system gives the poet freedom to explore Romanticism's central concerns, as the following discussion will show.

In the poem's opening, all nature is numb: the owl, the hare, the "flock in woolly fold," and an old Beadsman. As opposed to the others, however, the Beadsman is not *all* "a-cold." There is more to his experience than winter's "bitter chill." His "frosted breath [is] / Like pious incense from a censer old" (6–7). The words of the poet refer, but in a way that combines ideas usually exclusive of each other: frozen breath and burning incense, frost and fire. With figurative language, oppositions begin to break down—not into a synthesis, but into a multiplicity, usually impossible, of ideas and feelings.

But oppositions only begin to break down. Dwelling amid fixity—accustomed prayers, pictures of the Virgin, the dead in their sculptured caskets—the Beadsman possesses what Clifford Adelman calls "lifeless religiosity."[3] When he tries to imagine life after death, the Beadsman can only think that the dead, in their icy hoods and mails, must be as cold this night as the living. To him, they "seem to freeze." At least some imagination is needed for an awareness of how things seem; but this is imagination of a low order. And even this effort makes his "weak spirit" fail (17).

Ordinary consciousness can be described as the sense of opposition between its own usual and unusual modes. Other oppositions then may follow. Such is the case with the Beadsman's experience. Likening his frosty breath to the smoke of burning incense, the poet opposes him to nature; but the Beadsman himself remains as chilled as the rest of nature because he is still part of the ordinary, "natural" world, a world founded on opposition: hot and cold, summer and winter, life and death, earth and heaven. Similarly, the language the poet uses to describe him is rhetoric and rhetoric only: unusual but ordinary language. A simile can break down oppositions, but only in language. This particular kind of combinatory meaning is of limited use. The Beadsman's breath only *seems* to be taking flight to heaven without a death (8). Ordinary consciousness, though it seeks to go beyond its bounds, cannot: no Special time without leaving behind ordinary time, no heaven without death, no summer in winter—except in figures of speech. The Beadsman's experience is not the poet's; the poet's experience is not reality. The opposition between "seems" and "is" remains in place. And, Keats appears to ask, if insight and vitality exist only in the Special language and time of poetry, then of what use are they to the ordinary or "natural" time where, by definition, we spend most our lives?

> Northward [the Beadsman] turneth through a little door,
> And scarce three steps, ere Music's golden tongue
> Flatter'd to tears this aged man and poor;
> But no—already had his deathbell rung:
> The joys of all his life were said and sung;
> His was harsh penance on St. Agnes' Eve:
> Another way he went, and soon among
> Rough ashes sat he for his soul's reprieve,
> And all night kept awake, for sinners' sake to grieve.
>
> (st. 3)

From a distance, from the far side of a door, the Beadsman hears the "golden tongue"—the unusual language—of music (20). But this is a cold comfort: he's facing north in a European setting, away from the warm south. Though the music moves him to tears, all the joys of his life are behind him. "Another way he went" (25): the Beadsman returns to usual consciousness, but with the difference that he no longer gazes toward unusual experience. Like the dead in their "black, purgatorial rails" (15), he settles down among rough ashes to do penance for sinners, which leads only to more penance: it's his job not to save sinners, but to pray for their salvation. The past is real and present but lifelessly repeated: re-collection without the finer tone.

Given the important role music plays in this stanza, it's fitting that Keats should use the poetry's unfolding sound—a feature verbal and musical language share—to boost the potential of words to make meaning. Rhyme schemes tend to suggest syntactical boundaries. Thus in the Spenserian stanza, which Keats uses in "The Eve of St. Agnes," the end of the fourth (or sometimes the fifth) line generally satisfies the ear as a logical place to conclude the stanza's opening thought. But here, a radical turn occurs at the end of the third line. The Beadsman's attraction to music and the faint sense of hope it inspires seem to be presented almost too quickly. This is to the point: the thought of death is so strong that it creates a back pressure, which makes the poem's recounting of music's vitality as foreshortened as the Beadsman's experience of it. His forward motion is but an encounter with what is gone.

> Bŭt nó/ / ălréad- / -ў hăd / hĭs déath- / -béll rúng
> Thĕ jóys / ŏf áll / hĭs lífe / wĕre sáid / ănd súng

The dead past's power is enacted by that "But no" in the first line above, falling squarely on the iambic stress with a full medial stop following, and also by the fast weak stresses (-y had his) slamming into the hammered accents of "deathbell rung." The dead past's persistence is enacted by rhyme, which carries the thought of death over from the first to the second line. That line's long, rhythmically regular phrase, monosyllabic crawl, alliterative turning-back, and coinciding foot, word, and grammatical divisions provide a strong sense of closure, thus an inescapable sense of things ending. Desolation, magnificently accomplished: forward momentum encounters the past; but rhyme and meter, unlike the Beadsman's mind, allow for repetition with a finer tone.

Since the present is a re-collection of the past, all the makings of the future must be contained in the present. "Now" is not only a repetition with a difference of the past; it is also that which will be repeated with a difference later. By detailing the Beadsman's re-collective experience and its link with music, Keats enacts this phenomenon in these first few stanzas: from a bitter chill, through music, and back again. Moreover, Keats lays out here all that will become important later. The rest of the poem will re-collect the Beadsman's experience: bringing again to attention his establishment, departure from, and return to ordinary consciousness, but putting these together differently such that the finer tone becomes possible.

The music the Beadsman heard is itself but an unusual form of ordinary experience, though of a slightly higher order than his own. Associated not with the deadness of the past but with life and celebration, it grows and changes like a living thing. The "prelude soft" gives way to "the silver, snarling trumpets" as the "thousand guests" burst in and begin a grand celebration (37ff.). But this is still rhetorical music: unusual but very much part of the ordinary world. The revelers have set aside this time, which is valuable precisely because it is not usual, not what they spend most of their time doing. Barring a too-bad hangover, they'll afterward be refreshed and ready to return to their daily routine. But feast time remains rigidly opposed to ordinary time. In fact, throughout these stanzas, oppositions—the marks of ordinary time—are made proximate not by the simultaneity of Special time but only by succession, as in stanza 4 where soft music leads to loud. Or they are broken down rhetorically but not actually, as in stanza 5 where the bright array of the revelers is likened to "shadows" in the same way that the Beadsman's breath was likened to burning incense. Those shadows themselves are the images that haunt a youthful brain stuffed with old romance (39–41). Such a young mind re-collects the aged legends of the past, but only to understand them *as* legends of the past: pleasant but essentially distant or gone, therefore irrelevant. Presence and absence remain presence and absence; where one is, the other cannot be. This is fancy, not imagination. That Keats, unlike Coleridge, sometimes uses these two terms interchangeably demonstrates that he always retained a skeptical attitude. Sometimes unusual time becomes confounded with Special because both can seem irrelevant to ordinary life. Keats's greatest poetry puts this confusion to work.

"These let us wish away," the poet says of the partygoers (41). Let us act as if the present were absent and the absent were present, as if there were no distance between desire and fulfillment. An act of imagination moves us closer to Special time—not surprisingly, the imagination being the realm of Special experience. We focus now on a more imaginative consciousness. Beautiful, young, lost in thought and prayer, Madeline dreams about how this night, as legend has it, she may get a glimpse of her true love.

> . . . upon St. Agnes' Eve,
> Young virgins might have visions of delight,
> And soft adorings from their loves receive
> Upon the honey'd middle of the night,
> If ceremonies due they did aright; . . .
>
> (46–50)

Again, the past, as imaged in the oft-declared legends of old dames, is re-collected: now it's the youthful Madeline's turn to feel their full and renewed vitality. But Madeline still dwells in and among opposition. Hers is an experience of dreams as opposed to the reality of her loveless, unhappy life. And, though she herself is lost in fantasy—"[h]oodwink'd with faery fancy" (70)—and cannot hear the loud music around her, it nevertheless continues to blare, "yearning like a god in pain" (56). Another rhetorical, not actual, breakdown of opposition: the human ear finds something like divine agony pleasing; the myth and the music remain a background for the very human "throng'd resort / Of whisperers in anger or in sport" (67–68); and the whole moment remains a figure of speech. The music may be *like* a god; but it *is,* in fact, just pleasant noise. The Beadsman's is a feeble imagination; that of the revelers is slightly stronger; Madeline's is stronger still. Yet for her as for them, the exclusivity between "is" and "seems" weakens only in fancy—by virtue of fanciful music, as expressed by fanciful language.

Then comes Porphyro. His heart is on fire for Madeline (75–76): a more real ardency than the Beadsman's breath. He arrives at the castle, whose residents are to Porphyro

> barbarian hordes,
> Hyena foemen, and hot-blooded lords,
> Whose very dogs would execrations howl
> Against his lineage . . .
>
> (85–88)

Keats doesn't say why they are enemies. Perhaps it has something to do with a family quarrel ("his lineage"). Again, repetition but no finer tone. Perhaps Keats is unspecific for a reason: what's more important is not *why* but *that* Porphyro's love resides among those who have long hated him. Like the poet, who should be a lover of life, lovers must enter Special time, break down oppositions, embrace life in all its contradictory fullness, make new the past.

Angela, an old beldame, helps Porphyro. Note the many-at-once-ness, the tremendous compression of imagery when these two meet: old and young, female and male, enemy and friend. Exclusivity weakens further. Angela tells Porphyro that Madeline is "asleep in lap of legends old" and waiting for a vision of her true love (135). After much thought and debate, Porphyro concocts a "stratagem": with Angela's assistance, he will hide in Madeline's closet, wait for her to go to bed, and then appear to her as if he is that vision she's awaiting (st. 12-21). Is Porphyro a lover or a cad, the old woman an angel or an accomplice? Can they be both (more combined oppositions)? Jack Stillinger has argued persuasively for an ironic reading of this poem, with Madeline being duped by Porphyro. Similarly, Wolfson has suggested that the poem helps us to see "romance as an engaging but patent fiction."[4] These insights keep us from reading the poem as a legend entertaining because unreal—the very activity of the mind in unusual but ordinary time. But whether the poem is *only* ironic, whether Keats allows no truth to fiction: these are open to debate. Certainly irony, no less than an awareness of fiction as fiction, plays a large role in the poem, because these are means of detachment. Keats asks us to see the Beadsman, Madeline, Angela, and Porphyro all in a somewhat ironic light, to feel a certain distance from, perhaps even a certain distaste for, each one. And for a reason: in characteristic fashion, Keats will detach us from ordinary time—even from the unusual ordinary time of prayers, festive music, legends old, ardent lovers—to move us into Special time. But in equally characteristic fashion, Keats will demonstrate a profound distrust of that Special time. As Harold Bloom and Calvin Trilling suggest, Keats seems skeptical about St. Agnes's influence.[5] Porphyro's stratagem calls our attention to the need for helping old legends along a bit. Consciousness must actively participate in its imaginative experiences. A detachment from detachment, which, like the dream within a dream, may or may not be a means of reattachment: this dynamic makes for the most magnificent passages in the other great poetry Keats wrote in 1819—"La Belle Dame sans Merci," the odes, *The Fall of Hyperion*—and it makes for the most satisfying moments in "The Eve of St. Agnes" as well.

Leaving behind the music of the feast hall, Madeline rises "like a mission'd spirit, unaware" (193). Unaware, yet not exactly unconscious. She makes her way to her chamber. There, she hopes and believes she will enter the realm of the spirit: imagination, dreams, visions. But, as she will learn, love needs both spirit and body, no less than it needs male and female. Though Madeline is "all akin / To spirits of the air," her heart also pains "with eloquence her balmy side" (201–02, 205). What moves her spirit moves her body too. Special consciousness needs both terms of an opposition—not to synthesize them into a single entity and thus to banish opposition altogether, but rather to change the ground of their relation. Opposition is a necessary energizing force, but it ordinarily mandates exclusivity between its terms: X and not-X cannot occupy the same moment. Under Special circumstances, both can be experienced fully and simultaneously, as Keats goes on to detail.

"Out went the taper as she hurried in" (199). The light of ordinary consciousness is extinguished in the realm of Special consciousness—in and by a line of poetry anchored with the words "out" and "in." One needs the other; both work together, each one as itself, for a single effect. This effect does not occur, as with the Beadsman, only in the poet's language, since Madeline, like the poet, strives to enter Special time, not to regard it from afar. Here in her chamber, the site of her imaginative life, the materials of ordinary consciousness are transmuted by the alchemy of Special time. The precious metals and music of ordinary consciousness, as imaged by the "silver snarling trumpets," become a different kind of precious material. The silver light of Madeline's taper had guided her to her chamber. Then even this light goes out, replaced by silver moonshine, which joins with other, richer colors as it shines through her casement window, "innumerable of stains and splendid dyes" (212). Watching from the closet, "Porphyro grew faint" at the sight of "so pure a thing" (Keats's phrasing clearly implies that this is how Porphyro now thinks of Madeline, again at least suggesting disdain for the ardent lover, at least at this point). The poet details how the light falls on Madeline's hair and on her silver cross (221–25). As in a cross, directions combine at this crucial point. Colors blend. Pureness and lust, sacred and sensual, the woman likened to a saint and the man described almost as a sinner: all approach each other.

Note again the many-at-once-ness of the imagery and language, the density, simultaneity, and intensity of Special time: Madeline finds in "her soft and *chilly* nest" the "poppied *warmth* of sleep" which "*oppress'd* / Her *soothed* limbs (235–38, emphasis added). She then is

> Blissfully haven'd both from joy and pain;
> Clasp'd like a missal where swart Paynims pray;
> Blinded alike from sunshine and from rain,
> As though a rose should shut, and be a bud again.
>
> (240–43)

Ordinary experience—which is consciousness of joy as opposed to pain, Christianity as opposed to paganism, sunshine as opposed to rain, a grown rose as opposed to a bud—is fading. Re-collection: time continues to move forward, yet does so for the purpose of circling back on itself, of making the future by re-making what has been. The process of re-collection is more Special than it had been for the revelers—and for

Madeline, too, when she was among them. Now all the elements of her experience and hopes are brought again to attention but put together differently. Note how the rhyme scheme links *pain* with the joy of the rose becoming a bud *again* in spite of the *rain* that would make it grow and mature. But, at last, the poet's language is more than rhetoric. An intermingling of essences is enacted by, but does not occur only within, the poet's Special language. Unlike the Beadsman, Madeline is entering that Special state herself.

As Adelman points out, the variety and richness of Madeline's chamber—the stained glass, the triple casement "All garlanded with carven imag'ries / Of fruits and flowers" (209–10)—suggest a combining of sensual and spiritual riches.[6] Art can both preserve and transform ordinary material; compare the vitality of the sculptures here with those that surround the Beadsman. Similarly, poetry's rhymes both preserve and transform ordinary language. And likewise, in Madeline's chamber, heavenly and earthly concerns will be re-collected by the sexual act that will soon occur—an act precipitated by music.

Given that the quality of experience here is shared by both poet and character, it's interesting to note that, like Madeline, Keats himself went through a re-collective experience when writing these lines. In Keats's original draft of stanza 26, when Madeline undresses for bed, she "unclasps her bosom jewels one by one." Keats's manuscript reveals that when he revised the poem—when, that is, he brought it again to attention—he put it together differently, changing "bosom jewels" to "warmed jewels."[7] The result is that kind of marvelously rich and tactile image that we so admire in Keats. But there's more to it. Normally cold, the jewels have picked up Madeline's body heat: another set of exclusivities begins to break down. Essences intermingle—almost: hot and cold, stone and skin remain opposed. Madeline must lose *all* ordinary consciousness, a loss begun in the feast hall by her deafness to ordinary music, continued here by her putting aside the jewels, her undressing and falling asleep. To enter Special time fully, she must be both physically and spiritually naked, shed of all the trappings (and traps) of ordinary time.

When she sleeps, Porphyro emerges from the closet. What he prepares then is not unusual but Special: not just a feast like the one downstairs but an exotic feast. Though a consideration of the poem's sonic effects belongs more to part 2 of this study, we should note here how this stanza's sound is more Special than poetry's ordinarily unusual language. Highly wrought, rich and heavy with alliteration, assonance, short phrases, mostly end-stopped lines, and accented monosyllables, the passage enacts the moment:

> ... candied apple, quince, and plum, and gourd;
> With jellies soother than the creamy curd,
> And lucent syrops, tinct with cinammon;
> Manna and dates, in argosy tranferr'd
> From Fez; and spiced dainties, every one,
> From silken Samarcand to cedar'd Lebanon.
>
> (265–70)

But first, the door to the hall downstairs opens, and "the boisterous, midnight, festive clarion, / The kettle-drum, and far-heard clarionet, / Affray his ears, though but in dying tone" (258–60). Dying, not finer, tone: this music is a dead memory, an annoying, rather than liberating, reminder of where we've been. Formerly providing an entryway into something like Special experience, here it gets in the way—or, more exactly, demands to be transformed. It had its place, but another music is needed now.

The ordinary music is loud. Thankfully, it's also far away. Yet even if it were closer, we suspect Porphyro needn't worry. We've seen Madeline unaware of the noise in the midst of it. Porphyro hasn't, so he worries she'll be awakened. Having yet to enter Special time himself, he remains conscious of an exclusivity between sound and silence, between the music of the clarionet and the music of the mind. Madeline is beyond such awareness. Porphyro wishes for some "Morphean amulet," and is much relieved when "the hall door shuts again, and all the noise is gone" (257, 261). The varied pacing with which Madeline and Porphyro enter Special time is one of the great narrative feats of this poem. It also gives Keats a chance to show the real power of music. Not having quite achieved Special consciousness himself, Porphyro doesn't understand the depth and character of Madeline's sleep. But he will soon, and he will find a way to do it with music.

Ordinary music cannot awaken Madeline. Neither can ordinary language. With the banquet ready, Porphyro tells Madeline to wake up. She does not.

> Shaded was her dream
> By the dusk curtains:—'twas a midnight charm
> Impossible to melt as iced stream ...
>
> (281–83)

Gazing on her, his attention wanders from the banquet, the moonlight, the golden fringe on the carpet. All that is special to ordinary consciousness fades, and Porphyro "mus'd awhile, entoil'd in woofed phantasies" (288)—not unlike Madeline's being "hoodwink'd with faery fancy" earlier.

Yet fancy and fantasy, though necessary, are not sufficient. Special time requires not mere drowsiness or sleep but another kind of awareness—and another kind of music, as far removed as possible from that of the feast hall.

> Awakening up, he took her hollow lute,—
> Tumultuous,—and, in chords that tenderest be,
> He play'd an ancient ditty, long since mute,
> In Provence call'd, "La belle dame sans mercy":
> Close to her ear touching the melody;—
> Wherewith disturb'd, she utter'd a soft moan:
> He ceased—she panted quick—and suddenly
> Her blue affrayed eyes wide open shone:
> Upon his knees he sank, pale as smooth-sculptured stone.
>
> (st. 33)

The hollow lute is, like an empty sign, a shaped not-there-ness, a recognizable void, a determinate indeterminacy. Like the Special poetry discussed in the Chapman's Homer sonnet, it is a pure serene waiting to be filled by the player's hands *and* surging emotions. Once it begins to sound, the emptiness resonates like a live temple with the full range of the moment's interpretive possibilities. The lute, the hands, the emotional tumult—together these create the tenderest of chords: music is the mystical realm of many-at-once; harmony is the preservation and transformation of both soul and body, of both sculpture and life. The Pythagorean attitude toward music re-collects all the materials of rhetorical music; notes and chords and rhythms, even while continuing to signify to the senses music's own kind of sense, also lead the mind beyond sense and the senses. Music is understood as empty signs: signs because they are recognizable from past experience as able to convey meaning, empty because past meaning gets re-collected with each interpretive occasion. These signs point toward blank plenitude, toward the many-at-once-ness in which identities, while remaining what they are, empty and combine to make new identities.

Special music makes all good things possible for the lovers, much as an image of Special music allows the poet to set up the possibility of those good things. In this image itself, Keats presents us with something of an empty sign in need of interpretation, which is fitting since music and poetry meet when they do similar things in different ways. The music in the feast hall had been instrumental; now, apparently, we have a song: chords and melody, "an ancient ditty" with a title. Is sung music then the emblem of Special time? Perhaps in song and in song only, the opposition between verbal and musical language breaks down.

Perhaps in song, words and music together become something new, something belonging less to the cold northern climate of the castle than to the Provençal regions where iced streams melt easily, a place where the joys of life can be said *and* sung—not just in the past but continually.

It's debatable whether song is a seamless blending of opposites. Granted, sung words differ in effect from spoken words or instrumental music. But part of that effect is a counterpointing of modes of signification. Verbal and musical utterances do not make sense in the same ways and at the same pace within their respective utterances. The words and the music of a song are bound to disagree at certain points, and the song-writer has to know how to make such disagreements contribute to, rather than detract from, the song. More to the point, poetry and music may not need each other to act like each other, as Keats's own version of "La Belle Dame sans Merci," written soon after, suggests. That poem unfolds in a musical way; further, the music that the knight hears gains its power from being so impossible, so unreal. His (and our) experience is so musical that it needs no music, or rather, the ballad's words have an ideal setting. Hovering between verbal and nonverbal, this music dwells *in* the imagination and acts *like* the imagination. We are free to imagine it as we choose (which is, for us as well as the knight, an opportunity and a dilemma).

If poetry can act musically without music, then perhaps music can act verbally without words. Note Keats's description: Porphyro's song is "long since mute," which could mean that in Porphyro's and Madeline's day (or, less likely, in 1819), the song had not been heard for a long time. Or it could mean that for a long time the song has had no need of words: not mute because silent but mute because nonverbal. Its musical power is well established as a resource with which to enter Special time, to re-collect interpretations already in place.

But are there really no words? Though Porphyro *plays* the song, Madeline says when she wakes up that Porphyro's *voice* was just at her ear (308). Was he singing after all? Or is she talking about his whisper-ing to her before that (276ff.)? Then again, since she didn't wake up as he asked, did she really hear his whisper? Perhaps she had some verbal experience when he was "close to her ear touching [not singing] the mel-ody." Perhaps this music is so powerful, so perfectly suited to Special time, that, like the ideal musical setting of "Belle Dame," it has an ideal set of lyrics: words that hover just beyond the verbal. The combined presence of melody and absence of words may itself be the source of its power: signification without explicit reference. It can suggest as words do, without the limits on suggestiveness imposed by ordinary language, where the vast possibilities of combinatory meaning, though active, are given little priority. Porphyro's is a song of the imagination. (And, it seems, an imaginary song as well: no such "ditty" or short song exists; the fifteenth-century work from which Keats likely got his title was a poem, and a very long one at that.)[8]

At least this is one way of regarding a very difficult, almost willfully obscure, moment in the poem. As befits Special time, we are given many contradictory signals at once. As befits Keats's attention to music, we are also being taught to recognize that part of poetry's task is to give such signals. We are taught this by the way the poem unfolds—more specifically, by the way it unfolds its musical ideas: rhetorical has given way to Pythagorean. We must exercise our own Negative Capability here, and not reach irritably after fact and reason.

Or try not to. Such reaching is part of how the mind works; interpretation follows emptiness. Keats seems to admit this in his choice of song title. Since Madeline herself hardly seems a belle dame sans merci, perhaps the poet wishes us to understand that the lovers are in the enthrallment of the imagination, havened but also trapped within a situation as rich and as artificial as a medieval lover's complaint. Pure beauty, because essentially empty, has no mercy, no connection with ordinary emotional needs. What seems wonderful now, the poet may be hinting, will seem a threat later. The lovers are in a Special place: isolated within the castle, deep within imagination. Their condition cannot last. Dreamers awaken; songs end. Said or sung, the joys of life pass. And the revelers: what if, when they sleep off this night, they find their enemy here in the innermost place of their stronghold?

These considerations belong to ordinary time. They will return. But for now, the lovers have entered Special time, and they have done so by means of music—not the snarling trumpet but the hollow lute. Madeline enters into a state that is neither waking nor dreaming. She is both joyful and fearful at seeing Porphyro; she wishes again for "those complainings dear" (313). As when notes combine "in chords that tenderest be," exclusivity has broken down altogether. Finally,

> Beyond a mortal man impassion'd far
> At these voluptuous accents, [Porphyro] arose,
> Ethereal, flush'd, and like a throbbing star
> Seen mid the sapphire heaven's deep repose;
> Into her dream he melted, as the rose
> Blendeth its odour with the violet,—
> Solution sweet . . .
> (316–22)

The lovers melt together. (Their sexual consummation is more explicit in a passage Keats added and then withdrew at his publisher's request.)[9]

Melt: a change of state over time, a pure act of "as if," a going-forth and combining like waters in a stream, odors in the air, notes in music. Maleness and femaleness are brought again to attention and put together differently in a "solution sweet." The word choice is masterful: a solution is a combination and an answer. Combination belongs to the dizzy void, the many-at-once-ness, the overpoweringly blank plenitude of Special time; answers belong to ordinary time. In the same moment, the sexual act fulfills and extinguishes itself. The time in which the lovers melt together will end; being Special, it will end quickly:

> . . . meantime the frost-wind blows
> Like Love's alarum pattering the sharp sleet
> Against the window-panes . . .
> (322–24)

Even in the duration of "as if" or "like," threats await; time is passing. "St. Agnes' moon hath set" (324). Besides regret and danger, what can follow?

Another kind of re-collection begins. Coming out of imagination and back to ordinary time, Madeline and Porphyro confront the essential difficulty of that return: is the breakdown of exclusivity in the end anything but a reinstatement of exclusivity? After all, sex (at least the heterosexual activity of this poem) is impossible without an opposition between male and female. The lovers return to their former, anxious state, but with different anxieties. Madeline wakes up fully and enters ordinary consciousness again. Seeing that Porphyro is real, she becomes afraid that he'll really go away. And she perhaps suspects, as we may have suspected, that he took advantage of her when she wasn't quite awake (328ff.). Porphyro too becomes aware once more of the passage of ordinary time: "Arise—arise! the morning is at hand" (345). Ordinary material begins to reappear, though different. Madeline is a "silver shrine": silver is not just a precious material but one that bears the mark of having passed through Special time. Now it is a holy place, a refuge (337). But that refuge itself has become something different: no longer a lovers' retreat but a potential prison.

Porphyro must leave. But he will take Madeline away with him. He says the sleet blowing against the windows is "an elfin-storm from faery land" (343). The breakdown of exclusivity between "is" and "like" survives as metaphor: a stronger link than simile between opposition and identity. The combinatory aspect of Special time endures the transition back to ordinary time as a residue of enchantment, and, more to the point, as the insight of both poet and character that the storm is at once a hazard and a boon. It presents a danger; yet in that very danger lies opportunity, since it's unlikely anyone but fleeing lovers would venture out into it. If they leave now, they won't be followed. They can go else-where and love undisturbed. This is the essence of Keats's finer tone: a way of extending Special time, if not infinitely, then indefinitely—what Earl Wasserman calls "the spiritual repetition of the happiness of human life."[10]

Curious, though, that we don't actually follow the lovers. Also curious that we don't hear about any more music once they leave. Music not only had been a structuring idea in the poem, but had provided *the* essential moment of the poem when Madeline started into that waking / dreaming state of Special time. Yet in the end, Keats remains skeptical about music's ability to take that final step, to move from Special time back to ordinary yet different consciousness. He solves one problem—the ability of consciousness to experience opposites at once—only to set up others. The circumstances under which that consciousness can occur are so special that it cannot be achieved under any other conditions; further, those conditions are so special that they cannot sustain themselves. Love may not flourish anywhere but in an isolated chamber of a danger-ous castle. Music may be able to be rhetorical and mystical, but in the end it may have nothing to do with affect, with the most basic concerns of life-in-time. Poetry is fine, Keats said, but philosophy is finer. And if that's the case, then what's the point of love, of music, of poetry? Though flights of the imagination are wonderful in every sense, what if imagination, able to break down every other opposition, cannot break down the opposition between itself and the circumstances of ordinary life?

Once more Keats uses the music of words to help articulate his skep-tical attitude toward music and what music represents. Describing ordi-nary music, Keats says that "the silver snarling trumpets 'gan to chide" (31); he describes Special music as "an ancient ditty, long since mute" (291). With its harsh consonantal grating and hissing, the first nicely conveys the poet's dissatisfaction with the music of the feast hall. But if the second is meant to embody Porphyro's soft playing on the lute, it misses the mark with its bouncy *d* and *t* sounds and choppy short vow-els. One could argue for a union of opposites—harsh words mitigated by gentle music—or for some message here about words being unable to capture the feel of Special music. But the one is too easy, the other too clever. Keats may in fact be jarring our ears in order to insure that we'll question what does *not* jar our ears but should: the hollow lute's tones. With sound, the poem enacts its own skeptical attitude toward sound—and toward itself.

But the artwork can only question itself with artistic means. Experi-ence is shared by poet and character; but both remain within poetry. The lovers find, apparently, the finer tone; they find, apparently, a renewed ordinary time by going off into the danger / safety of the storm. But that's just the point. They go off. We don't see them again. Nor do we hear about any music as they go off. They're far away, and the whole thing happened long ago. Then the poem ends. We return from our Negative Capability and discover the need to interpret: Have the lovers, by returning to their respective but now changed identities (assuming that's what they did), discovered a way to make their souls? By reading, have we discovered a way to make ours? Like "La Belle Dame sans Merci," the poem becomes a musical experience. Its signification is finally empty—or, more precisely, it signifies, finally, our need to interpret. This is perhaps as it should be. As in music, meaning arises out of falling-away-in-time. Interpretation arises out of loss, distance, absence, emptiness. In Romantic theory, an origin, to be an origin, must be left behind in time and returned to in memory. To know is to know what is gone.

The simultaneity of meaning and loss may also explain why the end of the poem is so dark. It returns to a very different feast hall. All those who never get beyond ordinary consciousness, who never seek the finer tone that both arises from and redeems loss, suffer all the pains of ordinary time: the baron and his warrior-guests dream horrible dreams; Angela dies palsy-twitched and deformed; and the Beadsman, unsought for, sleeps among his ashes cold (st. 42). Much as his breath burned only in the poet's figures of speech, so these people, Keats reminds us, live and die only in the work of the poet. But that is where the lovers live, too. "And they are gone: ay, ages long ago" (370). As in *Endymion* and *The Fall of Hyperion,* Keats uses something like a dream within a dream— not just poetry but the poetic long ago and far away—to lead back to ordinary though different consciousness. But is the difference a finer tone or a recognition of the finer tone's impossibility? No answers here. Instead, we get the chance to do what Keats advised Shelley to do: load every rift with ore (L390), fill in each gap with the precious materials of the imagination, interpret the empty sign.

All this goes some way toward explaining the poem's ending, as well as the absence of any overt mention in the poem of affective music. But Keats is still struggling here. Song finally fails as an emblem of the highest art. What else is there? Can music (*pace* Shelley) be an emblem of art's connection with ideas? Can that connection remain valid outside the strict boundaries of art? "The Eve of St. Agnes," though it demonstrates how language conditions the perception of reality, is also at pains to distinguish what happens in language from what happens in reality, even to the point of underlining its own status as a linguistic event. Keats knew that the empirical distance between art and life can't be made to disappear simply by declaring that "reality" is built by language. Within such a construct there remain discrete moments—moments when we can accept poetry as real and other moments when we cannot. Eventually, after many more attempts over an extraordinary few months, Keats would find a place in his poetry for all kinds of music, even the affective. Doing so, he would find a way to connect his poetry with life beyond the artwork. The introduction noted how Wordsworth and Coleridge argued that the poet differs from others, the secondary imagination (which creates art) from the primary imagination (which is consciousness), only by degree. Keats is not persuaded. Not yet. Nothing is real until experienced, and Keats has yet to experience, fully and for himself, the reality of poetry's link with life-in-time. But he would, and before too much more time had gone by.

From fancy through imagination to the finer tone (maybe): in "La Belle Dame sans Merci" and "The Eve of St. Agnes," Keats attempts to trace this trajectory with music as assisted by narrative. As we've seen, music is assisted elsewhere by, say, the syllogistic structure of the sonnet. All along, though, Keats was working on ways to let the pattern of Romantic time itself shape his poetry. The results of this effort are visible on both a local and a global level. We'll examine each in turn, beginning with the local, since the global proceeds from it. We've noted briefly how stanzaic shapes, rhythmic events, and rhyme schemes contribute to meaning. In Keats's work, much more depends upon the perception of organized sound. Music remains central to his accomplishment—I'm tempted to add "as a person and as an artist," but I sense he would have resisted the distinction.

PART TWO

Inspecting the Lyre:
Music as Prosodic Model
in Keats's Poetry

6

Melos and Meaning

I'VE argued that poetry can be described as musical when its pattern of unfolding over time contributes to meaning in ways that are similar *in highly specific ways* to the patterns of unfolding that govern the meanings of musical compositions. We saw in part 1 how the deployment of musical imagery can create such a condition. The temporal unfolding that *is* the poem—a move from rhetorical through Pythagorean to affective musical imagery—enacts Romantic time much as the musical compositions of the day could with their rounded binary form (A-B-A'). The sound of poetry can also act in musical ways.

A thorny issue. When we describe a poem's sound as "musical," we often mean something like mellifluous: lots of open vowels, an avoidance of harsh consonants. Recall that we observed in the introduction, first, that criteria for pleasant sound can change with time and place, and second, that music itself generally sounds unpleasant insofar as dissonance provides music with its drive toward the resolution that ends the piece. Proceeding from observations like these, Northrop Frye has argued that Romantic poems in general and John Keats's in particular are "for the most part unmusical": their prosody emphasizes smoothness, slowness, end-stopped lines, stressed monosyllables, complex assonance, and metrical regularity; whereas truly musical poetry emphasizes roughness, rapidity, frequent enjambment, polysyllables, simple alliteration, and syncopation.[1] Not everyone agrees. E. C. Pettet has said that "among our poets [Keats] is certainly one of the most musical" because of the "resonance and beauty of word music" in his works.[2]

Yes and no to both critics. As Karl A. Zaenker argues, "ultimately, each art is its own province, and presents its own exigencies for experiencing it, which the other, by its own internal make-up, must miss, and rightly so, for if it failed to miss the other, it couldn't be itself."[3] Just so.

Poetry has its own ways of becoming musical. Physically embodying the rough sound of music (however "rough" is defined) is one way to allow combination to approach copriority with reference. Another, as we've seen, is the patterned deployment of musical imagery. Still another is the use of sound to organize time according to the patterns that music uses. Romantic poetry does this.

But is Romantic poetry unique in doing so? What Peter Conrad has called the "inspired unreason" of poetic language, where sound demands an attention at least partially independent of sense; what D. W. Harding has described as a willingness to expand our attention beyond semantical meaning:[4] surely these obtain in all poetry. It's arguable that a verbal utterance becomes a poem in the first place by putting rhyme, rhythm, assonance, and so forth into the foreground. As such, even the Augustan poetry that most of the major Romantic poets claimed to loathe is musical. The heroic couplet, by embodying a spirit of reason, containment, and wit, has an explicit combinatory dimension. I want to emphasize again, though, that poetic musicality involves a sharing of highly specific qualities with music. What makes Romantic poetry musical are the degree and purpose of its meaningful sound. The self-image of the Romantic poet is a singer. The Augustans shun a convergence with music; the Romantics actively seek it.

A contrast may be helpful. Alexander Pope, the arch-Augustan, said that "[e]xpression is the *Dress* of *Thought*." Sound reinforces verbal meaning, though such reinforcement should be subtle. Pope argued against poems that "ring round the same *unvary'd Chimes,* / With sure *Returns* of still *expected Rhymes.*"[5] Instead,

> The *Sound* must seem an *Eccho* to the *Sense.*
> *Soft* is the Strain when *Zephyr* gently blows,
> And the *smooth Stream* in *smoother Numbers* flows;
> But when loud Surges lash the sounding Shore,
> The *hoarse, rough Verse* shou'd like the *Torrent* roar.[6]

Onomatopoeia writ large. The open and prolonged sound of the word "smooth" in the third line above, given an even more leisurely pace when it becomes "smoother"; the half-alliteration between "smooth" and "stream"; the assonance between "smoother" and "number": these produce a gently sonorous, breathy effect. But in the next line, "surges lash" cannot be pronounced quickly *and* clearly. Also, in the final line, the sounds produced by the ending of "rough" and the beginning of "verse," as well as those produced by the ending of "verse" and the beginning of "should," do not exist in English. Thus a strong pause is enforced between those words; the language sounds as heavy as the weather it describes. The word boundary's spilling beyond the foot boundary only to crash up against an accented, self-enacting monosyllable ("loud sur- / -ges lash," "the Tor- / -rent roar") also makes the words sound as harsh and restless as wind and waves. Sound echoes idea.

Not an end in itself, sound can still be used to create particular effects. Because such effects possess a degree of independence from sense, they are often ironical or witty. Pope says the artist may

> From *vulgar Bounds* with *brave Disorder* part,
> And *snatch* a *Grace* beyond the Reach of Art,
> Which, without passing thro' the *Judgment*, gains
> The *Heart*, and all its End *at once* attains.[7]

The word "heart" sounds less like the first stressed word in the above passage's fourth line and more like the final stress in the third line. For a moment, a triplet rhyme and a corresponding Alexandrine line are suggested. But the rest of the line reveals this suggestion to be an aural illusion, and the couplet closes conventionally. A master at this sort of thing, Pope was not averse to showing off. With sound, the artist reaches beyond the bounds of art, just as the sound of "heart" reaches beyond the bounds of the couplet—precisely the kind of wit and daring Pope advocates here. Yet the whole effect remains rigidly controlled. Note the perfect iambs, each of which is a logical sentence unit, in "Ănd snátch / ă gráce / bĕyónd / thĕ réach / ŏf árt." Further, such effects depend on visual signals given by reading from the page—which is itself suggestive. This is poetry meant to be seen, not heard, or, more precisely, to have its sonic effects subject to its written appearance.

Sound contributes to but does not cause meaning. For Pope, "*Musick* resembles *Poetry,* in each / Are *nameless Graces* which no Methods teach."[8] But music does not resemble poetry in sound being a way of creating meaning in and of itself. To seek this in poetry is to be like fools

> Who haunt *Parnassus* but to please their Ear,
> Not mend their Minds; as some to *Church* repair,
> Not for the *Doctrine,* but the *Musick* there.[9]

The passage's sound itself seems to mock those fools. The triplet rhyme is a bit of sonic luxury that will distract some readers from seeing the greater elegance of the clever, extended simile and the chiastic shape (but . . . not . . . not . . . but), and perhaps even cause their ears to be offended by the final line's metrical substitutions and violated foot boundaries ("Nót fŏr / tĥe Dóc- / -trĭne bŭt / tĥe Mú- / -sĭck thĕre"). For the wise reader, these devices, balanced one against the other, will reinforce the pleasure of the passage's rhetorical savoir faire.

As James A. Winn points out, the Augustans generally "pilloried music for its ambiguity, its fluidity, its 'femininity'." Not long after Pope, Samuel Johnson called music "a method of employing the mind, without the labour of thinking at all."[10] Poetry is the superior art; it should not strive to act like music, an art made of nothing but sound. Yes, sound has its place. Johnson took Milton—and even Pope—to task for not being more assiduous about fitting ponderous language to ponderous ideas, lighter language to lighter ideas.[11] Sound should reinforce particular points, and particular points should be reinforced by sound.

Given that Romantic time moves both forward and recursively, it's not surprising that Romantic thought both departs from and carries on Augustan values. We've seen, for example, Shelley's and Lamb's antipathy to what they perceived as music's emptiness of ideas. Similarly, Romantic prosody looks both forward and back. In some respects, the sound of Romantic poetry is the dress of its thought; in others, it is not. Romantic prosody can reinforce a particular point. But what makes it musical is the degree and purpose of its meaning. We can call this dimension of poetry "melos": "the quality of sound and rhythm in a poem created by . . . the conscious or intuitive arrangement of various consonant and vowel groupings . . . and degrees of stressed syllables."[12] In Romantic poetry, melos achieves greater priority. Sound becomes a thoroughgoing intensification of the overall poetic experience. This it does by striving to forge a link between language and time in ways similar to what happens in music.

B. H. Fairchild exemplifies Romantic melos with William Blake's poem "Night" from the *Songs of Innocence*. The following is the fourth stanza:

> When wolves and tygers howl for prey
> They [the angels] pitying stand and weep;
> Seeking to drive their thirst away,
> And keep them from the sheep.
> But if they rush dreadful;
> The angels most heedful,
> Receive each mild spirit,
> New worlds to inherit.

The first four lines feel real and trustworthy. Their hymnal form (*abab* rhyme, alternating four- and three-beat lines) reminds one of tradition, its essentially iambic rhythm is close to spoken English, and it delays its rhymes. All these provide a satisfying complexity.[13] The lines sound the way that mature awareness feels. Their melos reinforces the reality of the world's dangers and the possibility, though by no means the certainty, of heavenly aid.

The second four lines alter the relation between sound and sense. Here, the anapestic rhythm and the rhymes that come after only two beats create a singsong effect. Fairchild says that "[w]hile we tend to accept the sense of diversity within totality of the more complex ballad stanza [actually the hymn stanza or common measure, a close relative], we tend to resist the false simplicity of the two- and three-stress couplets." An alternate interpretation might be that belief in heavenly aid can come only by sloughing off complex, adult, experiential awareness, trusting instead the knowledge that proceeds from innocence. In either case, though, this fact remains: a large part of the way we feel about the poem's meaning arises not from anything the poet says but from how his words sound. Melos "becomes sound articulate, carrying its own semantic potential."[14]

We should not forget, however, that sound in poetry is a distant relative of sound in music.[15] For instance, while poetic rhyme and musical consonance can both indicate moments of rest, poetry has no equivalent for the strict system of note and chord relations that determines what is and what is not consonant. And in music, a similar sound with a different meaning indicates defamiliarization, not closure (e.g., adding a seventh to the tonic chord gives it a new function as the dominant of the subdominant). More to the point, sound cannot have sole priority in verbal language as it does in music. No matter how explicit its combinatory dimension becomes, the referential dimension of verbal language will never cease to have priority—not without the words ceasing to be words.

But poetic sound can approach copriority with reference. John Hollander has written at length about the sort of expressive rhythms we see in Blake. According to Hollander, an organization of sound can establish a contract: when the poet chooses a particular metrical pattern or rhyme scheme, the reader understands that meaning will be made in particular ways. The sonnet indicates one way of ordering thought, the ballad another. As Fairchild puts it, sound "can have a distinct role in the total semantic power of poetic language."[16] I'll argue that this distinct role in regard to Romantic poetry is the ability to provide what the music of the day also provided: an enactment of Romantic time by means of sound employed re-collectively.

An example from Keats is in order. When in part 1 we saw "La Belle Dame sans Merci" end where it began but in a very different "now," we noted a link between what the poem says and how it unfolds. We can find another, equally important link between what it says and how it sounds. Like Blake's "Night," "Belle Dame" uses a traditional form—more or less. Usually the ballad stanza, rhyming *abcb*, alternates four- and three-beat lines. In Keats's poem, three four-beat lines are followed by a two-beat line:

> Oh what can ail thee, knight at arms,
> Alone and palely loitering?
> The sedge has wither'd from the lake,
> And no birds sing.
>
> (1–4)

All the poem's other stanzas regularly employ three four-beat lines followed by a two-beat line, as in the following:

> I see a lily on thy brow
> With anguish moist and fever dew,
> And on thy cheeks a fading rose
> Fast withereth too.
>
> (9–12)

That prevents an alternate scanning of the second and fourth lines of the first stanza in three beats (Ălóne / ănd pále- / -lў lóitĕrĭng; Ănd nó / ⌣ bírds / ⌣síng), which would make this a proper ballad. Such a scanning would also make the rhyming syllable of the second line the latter portion of an unstressed elision—not likely. This is a ballad stanza, but a highly unusual one. The pause normally found at the end of the second line is moved to the end of the fourth line, and that pause is lengthened considerably when it finally arrives. The second line seems overlong; the fourth line, with clashing iambic and spondaic feet (Ănd nó / bírds síng) ends abruptly and heavily, creating a vast silence, a palpable emptiness. This dramatizes the poem itself, where a voice of rational puzzlement is brought up short by awe and dread. Like the knight's dream, the sound of the stanza is both too much and too little. Not just an echo to the sense, or a reinforcement of a particular idea, the sound of the poem is a large, vital, and independently functioning aspect of the poem's overall effect. We attend to referential and combinatory experiences at the same time and to the same degree; the story and the melos count equally. Further, because the pattern of the sound is a modified ballad stanza, it is at once familiar and foreign, its asymmetry, like the idea of fairy enthrallment, both attractive and disturbing. Sound thus creates the many-at-once-ness we've seen Keats associating with Special time, which is the location of all the knight's joys and sorrows.

Keats handles the rhythm of that concluding two-beat line very loosely, adding syllables here and there, and alternately observing and breaking the foot boundary (Ănd nó / bírds síng; Ănd thĕ hár- / -vĕst's dóne; Ănd hĕr éyes / wĕre wíld; Ă fáir- / -ў's sóng). These rhythmic variations can be heard in several ways. They give the poem a folky feeling, a hand-hewn, seemingly unpolished charm. But they also interrupt the feel of the rest of the lines, which are iambic, almost indolently so, with very little metrical substitution. The effect is, of course, neither unpolished nor indolent but highly accomplished and utterly appropriate. The rough sound of the last line is in tension with the ease and fluidity of the rest of the stanza, much as the knight (and perhaps the speaker too) is wrestling with himself about the meaning and value of his memories. Again, the shortness of the final lines, as full of quietness as of words, adds to this effect. Consciousness seems to fail; so, therefore, does language. A long silence follows.

The poet, like the knight, seems enthralled by the imagination. This enthrallment causes him to be, when not silent, relentlessly terse. Yet where the poem uses silence, it is not itself a silence. It is a particular utterance, whose sounds (and silences) enact it in self-challenging, thus self-re-collecting ways. That is the degree to which melos is important here. Its purpose also involves a complex act of re-collection.

First, the poem's sound re-collects literary history. Keats himself labels it "A Ballad." He wants us to connect this work with poems that, though they often focus on the supernatural, can counteract the disturbance associated with that focus by being part of a deep, stable, and abiding tradition. The loosely handled rhythm of the stanza's final line may embody the voice of the folk: not a vulgar but a wise superstition that accepts the existence of intangibles yet distrusts them. But, as far as I can determine, no poem in exactly this shape exists in the English ballad tradition.[17] The French ballad of the same name, written by Alain Chartier in the early fifteenth century, uses an eight-line stanza rhyming *ababcdcd* in anapestic trimeter. The version of that ballad Keats likely knew, a translation wrongly ascribed to Chaucer, also uses an eight-line stanza with the same rhyme scheme but in iambic pentameter.[18] Keats, that is, borrowed only the title. The stanzaic shape is very much his own. Poetic tradition is brought again to attention, yet put together differently when Keats invokes and changes the ballad stanza. The sense of disturbance that the knight, speaker, and reader experience together here is made that much more powerful by a brand-new kind of ballad stanza, which at once adds to and disturbs the fabric of tradition. Any comfort that the past can provide comes into question. The poem's re-collective melos enacts the poem's deep ambivalence about memory.

Second, the poem re-collects Keats's own work. The luxury of sound and image characteristic of his early verse are here: "I met a lady in the meads, / Full beautiful, a fairy's child"; "I made a garland for her head, / And bracelets too, and fragrant zone"; "She found me roots of relish sweet, / And honey wild, and manna dew." Note the sonority produced by the diphthongs and long vowels on metrical strong points. But rather than marring the poem with overindulgence, these luxuries contribute to its effect. They are pitted against the knight's regrets and, as important, against the brevity and severity of the stanza form, made even more severe by its truncated last line.

As in music, the sound of words becomes an experience where reference shares priority with emotions whose power resides in our ability to feel them undeniably and our inability to name them precisely. Thomas MacFarland has noticed a "rapturous or singing tone" in much Romantic poetry, which causes a feeling of rushing-toward, a sense of the not-there-ness of objective obstacles. This allows entry into what Mac-Farland calls "the void that is the home of true feeling."[9] We might qualify MacFarland's point. Keats found the creation of such a "rapturous tone" too easy. He wanted his poetry to have more backbone. Accordingly, he uses sound to re-collect his work—a move that also enacts the knight's experience. Like the knight's trip to fairyland, imaginative indulgence, as embodied in the indulgent language Keats associated with his early work, is brought again to attention and put together differently. The sound of the poem, a tension between luxury and severity, moves us toward emptying the words of prior significance. New interpretations become necessary.

Finally, the poem re-collects itself. Each stanza both preserves and destroys each preceding stanza: same general sonic pattern, new words. More important, the final stanza closes the poem with a near-verbatim repeat—return with a difference—of the poem's opening. Such is typical of folk ballads. But not thus typical is the ambivalence and skepticism created thereby. All's changed now that we've heard the story and, with an after-Special consciousness, find ourselves again on the cold hill's side. What does this return with a difference tell us about the value of the knight's experience? About the poet's? About ours? How do we move to the far side of enthrallment if going back and going forward always complicate each other?

The poem leaves us wondering whether there's such a thing as the present or the past; the sound of the poem takes us both back-to and away-from. Its melos provides a way of feeling with words the power and the mysteries of the fairy's song. We *hear* the difficulty of moving from imagination to insight. Perception and memory become modes of

each other. Like music, and like the melos of the stanza here, consciousness is repetition with a difference. But the difference repeatedly lapses
into silence. How, after all, can you speak, or even properly think about,
what you've heard, be it the song of a fairy or of a bird? The simultaneity, as in music, of here-and-now-ness with falling-away-ness resists attempts at referential fixity. Hearing defies words. That's why it's so
troublesome, and so important, to the Romantic artist of words, who
seeks ways other than (or in addition to) silence and emptiness to express
the meaning of repetition with a difference.

The manifold act of re-collecting by means of sound provides Romantic poetry with a very specific set of approaches to musicality. Keats's melos, like the music of the day, re-collects the past, as embodied in the
history and given materials of the art, in the artist's prior output, and in
the artwork's own prior events. As we'll see, his use of sound is both
highly unique and well grounded in theories and practices of the day.

7

The Romantic Uses of Sound

THE years between about 1750 and 1830 are often called music's classical age, the Romantic era in music coming later in the nineteenth century. This presents difficulties related mostly to terminology. Like academic disciplines, "ages" often have more to do with scholarly convenience than with lives as lived. The rigid distinction between classical and Romantic (or any related and similarly rigid distinction like Apollonian / Dionysian, expressive / structural, free / formal, subjective / objective, individual / social) is both facile and inaccurate. Most of what happens in music later in the nineteenth century also happens in, or is at least prepared by, so-called classical pieces, with differences residing more in style than in actual materials or fundamental compositional values. Those classical pieces—music written by, or in the style of, Haydn, Mozart, and Beethoven—account for most of the compositions the Romantic poets would have known. When they said "music," they meant this body of work. This is where we should turn first for any insights music can give us into Romantic thought.

Charles Rosen has identified two urges in this music. One is toward "absolute" forms. Tonal relations organize music. Its structural principles derive from its own materials: the major and minor scales, and what we noted in part 1 as Rameau's "hierarchical arrangement of the triads based on the natural harmonies or overtones of a note." Music, that is, achieves coherence by virtue of the physical characteristics of sound and sound alone. The second urge is toward making the motif—a very brief melodic figure—the basic element of composition.[1] The two urges are closely related. To go forward coherently in time, a composition must be able to move with alacrity from one tonal area to another. A long and fully worked out idea like a melody inhibits, in fact, largely obviates this movement. Tied to itself, the music is unable to enter a new area until the entire melody is sounded. And it is reluctant to do so: if the musical thought is complete as it is, why go elsewhere? The motif, often just a couple of notes, is inherently incomplete and restless. It demands context and change.

Some examples will clarify these points. The Overture to Mozart's *The Magic Flute* (1791) is a hybrid of musical forms. Ostensibly it is a "French overture." Lully originated this form in France in the 1650s, and Handel often used it as an introduction in the operas and oratorios he wrote in the 1720s and 1730s. The form begins with a slow and stately opening in dotted rhythm ("dot" refers to the notational marking that increases a note's rhythmic value by half; hence, "dotted rhythm" is typically long-short-long-short). Then follows a faster fugal section (various voices take up and develop a motif contrapuntally).[2]

This form was by Mozart's time respectable but antiquated. Mozart demonstrated that it continued to have possibilities. Once the fast fugal section begins, his overture becomes a sonata (a first theme is introduced in the home key, followed by a second theme in the dominant key, which sets up the need for an exploration and resolution of this tonal disagreement). To hear and understand this overture, then, is to re-collect music history. Tradition is brought again to attention and put together very differently in order to show that music, in looking back, looks forward too. The old French overture and fugue gain new life, and the newer sonata gains depth.

The piece's introductory passages consist of nothing but arpeggiated chords. Again, Mozart brings old forms up to date: now, unlike in the French overture's heyday, music needs only the barest of materials to build itself. The first theme of the fast fugal section is likewise sparse: little more than a series of repeated notes followed by another series a perfect fifth higher. The second theme, though somewhat more melodic, is still little more than a call-and-response scale figure in the flute and oboe.

For a sonata to achieve closure, it must sound in the home key material formerly heard in a foreign key; the second theme must return in the tonality of the first theme. When Mozart brings back that second theme, the instrumentation and texture (call-and-response in the high winds) remain the same as on first hearing, and the figure is sounded in the home key. But the figure is recontoured. It need not be recovered unchanged. Tonality largely provides all necessary closure. When we hear, in one key, something like the first theme and something like the second theme, we are satisfied.

Haydn proves a similar point about the adequacy of tonality as a structural device. In the first movement of his Symphony no. 104 (1795),

Haydn sounds the first theme in the home key. Then, when the moment arrives to establish a second key, he chooses to sound that first theme again in the key of the dominant. This is all that is needed for the music's structural necessity. This alone creates the need for tonal argumentation and resolution. That the same theme is sounded twice doesn't matter. That the theme itself is little more than an insignificant motif doesn't matter. Motif articulates structure; it is not structure in itself. It acquires significance by being developed over time in different keys until, in the end, it can be heard twice in the same key.

To understand the full meaning of this passage, one must, of course, understand the dynamics of the tonal system. But one must also appreciate the composer's past work, which helped define those dynamics to begin with. Haydn was an inveterate experimenter. Remember, this is his one hundred and fourth symphony. In the course of his long career, he moved the symphony from a slight and unprepossessing form toward the massive proportions and self-conscious importance it would assume in the nineteenth century.

This moment, then, re-collects Haydn's prior output. The creative insight that allows Haydn to sound one theme on two tonal levels springs directly out of his more than one hundred previous attempts at delineating the symphony's capabilities. The listener who fails to bear this in mind fails to understand fully Haydn's triumph here.

Building upon Mozart's and Haydn's accomplishments, Beethoven proved himself an even greater master of motivic development and instrumental form. It is, therefore, one of the ironies of music history that he has achieved such formidable status for a composition that makes extensive use of a melody—and a sung one at that. His symphony no. 9 seems a radical departure, both from his earlier works and from the age's basic compositional principles. Yet if the work looks ahead, it also looks back. For years, Beethoven had tried without success to set to music Schiller's poem "Ode to Joy." He finds a solution in the final movement of his final symphony. Indeed, we can conjecture that Beethoven wanted to achieve here a summing up; though sketches for further work exist, he seemed to know this would be his last symphony.[3] The major Romantic poets, Keats included, probably never heard this symphony (it was finished in 1823). But its last movement fulfills, in re-collective ways, the music they did hear.

The fourth and final movement opens with a dissonant chord and a burst of wild energy. Then it sounds the themes from the preceding three movements. Such had never happened in a multimovement work before. Beethoven wants us to understand the work as a *whole*. But if he tries for greater unity, he also tests that unity. He sounds the themes once more only to reject each. In doing so, he reminds us that each prior movement had taken its motifs as far as they could go. Something else is needed now. Slowly, the "Ode to Joy" theme assembles itself, rising finally out of the low strings into the clarity of the violins. Various instruments take it up and embellish it. Then the melody, fully formed, is given resoundingly to the entire orchestra.

Even this is not enough. The melody dissolves back into fragments, the rhythm becomes increasingly restless, and the ensemble falls apart. The orchestra comes together again only to sound that crushingly dissonant chord once more, plunging back into wild energy.

Now emerges the human voice. The effect is extraordinary and, as one realizes so often with this composer, inevitable. By this point, the music seems to have nothing more to give from within itself. To do further work—which Beethoven invariably elects—the music must now use all that it has excluded from itself. "O Freunde, nicht diese Töne!" Words sung by the baritone, added to Schiller's poem by Beethoven himself: O Friends, not these (instrumental) tones. Music must return to what it has departed from. That is, it must return to the human voice and, in so doing, move forward. Return involves difference. An entirely new range of possibilities opens. Music is now liberated from the voice (as the previous movements more than proved). It is thus now able to join with the voice as an equal partner.

Once this happens, the "Ode to Joy" theme is itself broken: tossed between various instrumental and vocal colors and groups of colors, pushed through various harmonic contexts, given unexpected, sometimes shocking rhythmic characteristics. What could have been a simple theme-and-variations becomes instead a set of transformations. Now, melody and motivic development are put together in dozens of new ways over the course of the phenomenal duration that follows.

Such radical development could cause the music to slip its own bounds. It could become so lost in difference that any element of repetition or continuity becomes impossible to sense. Beethoven courts this state deliberately. A large part of the interest in the symphony throughout lies in hearing how close Beethoven is willing to steer toward sheer noise without actually entering chaos. Flirting with structural disaster arises necessarily out of the symphony's own initial materials: the entire work had begun with the interval called the open fifth, with the violins sounding the notes D and A. Neither major nor minor, this is a consonant but cold sound. The entire symphony is largely an effort to fill in this interval with either a minor or a major third. Until one or the other establishes itself definitively, the piece will remain in tonal limbo.

Beethoven re-collects music history. All previous assumptions about musical adequacy are questioned. For music to achieve emotional depth and complexity, the open fifth must be filled in, as composers several hundred years earlier had learned to do, with either a major or a minor third. But under what conditions can such a filling-in survive? How long can the music go without filling it in? The idea of tonal adequacy comes under fire. In fact, the idea of musicality itself is questioned. Such questioning can be found especially in those passages that more nearly resemble noise than music yet serve a purpose in the overall composition, reminding us graphically that music is in essence an emerging out of raw, ordinary noise.

The open fifth and the sheer noise that so often follows release a tremendous amount of energy, because at stake is nothing less than the coherence of the major-minor system on which the piece is built—and toward which the piece directs a steady barrage of challenges. Throughout, the minor seems to be the one that will survive—not reassuring, since minor is prone to instability. Finally, at the end of the last movement, the orchestra and choir use their fully combined and fully developed powers to drive the music toward a finale in major that is as glorious as it is brief.

The movement re-collects Beethoven's own work, and in quite a literal way. He had been sketching the "Ode to Joy" theme for years. Each attempt is marked by the style in which he was composing at the time. The final version brings all these together. It emerges out of the music much as it emerged out of his notebooks—slowly, painfully, searchingly, and at last, definitively. The music built on this melody brings again to attention and puts together differently all that Beethoven had worked with previously: his twin urges toward severe economy of basic materials and expansion of those materials on a massive scale; the motif and the concomitant idea of constant development, which allow instrumental music to achieve coherence; and the human voice. If Beethoven lacked anything as a composer, it was a facility for writing idiomatic vocal music. Here, he finds a way to succeed by treating the voice as a vital part of the orchestra. The vocal parts themselves are extremely difficult to sing, but they work magnificently as members of the overall ensemble.

The music re-collects itself. In the opening of the movement, the preceding movements' themes, formerly adequate, are dismissed, dismantled, then reassembled as the "Ode to Joy." This re-collective urge continues unabated throughout the rest of the movement, where the theme that had finally proved adequate is itself subjected to the utmost permutations. The very idea of coherence, of the musical composition's ability to be called a unified composition, is thoroughly tested. As recently as the previous movements in this symphony, Beethoven had answered such challenges with largely inherited gestures of closure; for example, the first movement, being in sonata form, can end when its

home key subsumes material formerly heard in a foreign key. Those answers are no longer adequate. Solutions don't work twice. The
ongoingness of time adds new complications. Mozart had suggested this
by recontouring the *Magic Flute* Overture's second theme. In Beethoven's hands, Mozart's suggestion becomes both an architectural principle and a challenge to any architectural principle. The symphony
brings itself again to attention and puts itself together differently in order
to discover its own ultimate stress load.

Establishment, departure, return with a difference: the past is saved
from both deadness and loss, the present from anomie. The music becomes an enactment of the joy of Schiller's poem; it finds ever-new ways
of using what has gone before. Meaning is what you lose—which explains both the power and the evanescence of the joy to be found here at
the very end. The agony of loss becomes part of joy, loss being the necessary precondition for the joyful act of finding again all that has been
lost, thus of finding all that is new.

Romantic prosody uses sound in similar ways to similar ends. Wordsworth argues that

> not only the language of a large portion of every good poem, even of the
> most elevated character, must necessarily, except with reference to the me-
> tre, in no respect differ from that of good prose, but likewise that some of
> the most interesting parts of the best poems will be found to be strictly the
> language of prose when prose is well written.[4]

Poetry, Wordsworth believes, should not be an occasion to inflict upon
language "the gaudiness and inane phraseology of many modern writers . . . [or] POETIC DICTION, arbitrary, and subject to infinite
caprices."[5] Rather, it should be written in "language really used by
men," specifically by those who lead a

> [h]umble and rustic life . . . such a language, arising out of repeated expe-
> rience and regular feelings [in relation to what is most basic in man and
> nature], is a more permanent, and a far more philosophical language, than
> that which is frequently substituted for it by Poets . . . [6]

Even so, Wordsworth grants that the poet "is only selecting from the
real language of men, or, which amounts to the same thing, composing,
accurately in the spirit of such selection." The poet must use "true taste
and feeling" to preserve what is beautiful and "as immortal as the heart
of man." Because the "particular purpose" of poetry is "that of giving

pleasure," and to as wide a range of persons as possible ("the vast empire of human society"), the poet must "separate the composition from the vulgarity and meanness of ordinary life."[7]

How can the poet do so? According to Wordsworth, poetry should follow "the fluxes and refluxes of the mind when agitated by the great and simple affections of our nature."[8] Our affections possess a rhythmic quality, a flux and reflux in response to the comings and goings of those things that move us most. In fact, it is the very process of coming and going that affects us most: the essence of Romantic experience is the sense of time as a simultaneity of nowness and passing-away. At the most basic level of our being, the Romantic argues, we are always in the process of losing what we have; and we are likewise always in the process of recovering what we've lost. Poetry is the language of this process. Taking its origin from the act of re-collecting, it repeats (with a difference) what has already been. It will thus involve what Abrams calls "figures of speech and rhythm by means of which words naturally embody and convey the feelings of the poet."[9] Language is by its nature rhythmic, full of varying stresses, accents, and intonations, which echo the rhythms of experience.

Echo, but in a very general way: as Abrams also points out, "Justification of rhythm had proved a particularly troublesome point" for Wordsworth.[10] Why should a poet move from language's generally rhythmical feel, which enacts experience's generally rhythmic feel, to the specific devices of poetic diction? Because, Wordsworth argues,

> by the act of writing in verse an Author makes a formal engagement that he will gratify certain known habits of association ... the music of harmonious metrical language, the sense of difficulty overcome, and the blind association of pleasure which has been previously received from works of rhyme or metre of the same or similar construction, an indistinct perception perpetually renewed of language closely resembling that of real life, and yet, in the circumstance of metre, differing from it so widely—all these imperceptibly make up a complex feeling of delight, which is of the most important use in tempering the painful feeling always found intermingled with powerful descriptions of the deeper passions.[11]

Rhyme and meter—the reassuring, trustworthy, and time-honored "co-presence of something regular"[12]—allow us to feel emotions either painful or so intense that we cannot distinguish them easily from pain.

The poet is "a man speaking to men." He feels what we all feel, only more deeply. The sound of poetry not only makes the intensity of basic passions more bearable, it also allows poetry "to divest language, in a certain degree, of its reality."[13] The poem is recognizable as ordinary language, but it also feels decidedly unordinary. Rhyme and meter make deep feeling both bearable and communicable.

In Wordsworth's view, then, the sound of poetry both cools you down so you can feel without pain and heats up language so you can talk about what you feel and be understood. "[T]he perception of similitude in dissimilitude . . . is the great spring of the activity of our minds, and their chief feeder."[14] Rhyme and meter, which enable such perceptions, establish pleasurable and calming relations within the poem: different meaning, similar sound; every-changing words, ever-constant beat. Rhyme and meter also enact the relations between this poem and other language; poetry is at once similar to and different from ordinary verbal utterances. And they enact the relations between this poem and other poems. The presence of meter and rhyme allows me to recognize this utterance as poetry. I thus allow myself to feel a powerful emotion that is like, but is not the same as, what I've felt when I've read or written poetry before. Poetic sound re-collects language—both ordinary language and poetic tradition, which is the "ordinary" language of poetry.

Such re-collection is evident in Wordsworth's poetic practice. *Lyrical Ballads,* Wordsworth states, was intended to relate or describe "incidents and situations from common life" with the language really used by men, yet in an artful form, and with "a certain colouring of imagination" thrown over them in order to provide access to "the primary laws of our nature."[15] Accordingly, Wordsworth adopts a fairly plain style and the traditional form of the ballad. Yet in preserving these he also transforms them: his is not the language really used by men but a composition made in the spirit of a selection of that language. His handling of the ballad stanza is as individual as Keats's.

For Wordsworth, then, melos re-collects both ordinary language and literary history in an attempt to make each more accessible to the other. The blank iambic pentameter of *The Prelude* uses "the language really used by men" as well as the prosodic form of *Paradise Lost* to establish a new kind of epic. Its concern is the growth of the poet's mind: the ways in which the individual imagination shapes and is shaped by the patterns of time. "Tintern Abbey," also a personal response to temporality, uses that same meter to create a new kind of landscape poem, whose concerns encompass the viewing "I" as much as the view:

> In darkness and amid the many shapes
> Of joyless day-light; when the fretful stir
> Unprofitable, and the fever of the world,
> Have hung upon the beatings of my heart,

> How oft, in spirit, have I turned to thee
> O sylvan Wye! Thou wanderer through the woods,
> How often has my spirit turned to thee![16]

It's difficult to hear the meter in this passage as superadded, so perfectly does the move from enjambed, staccato, and metrically variable phrases to the long, end-stopped, regularly iambic phrase of the final line enact the poem's charting of the path from restlessness to peace.

Meter may have calmed down the poet, but it also adds passion and pleasure to ordinary language. More exactly, it allows the passion and pleasure in ordinary language to show itself more forcefully. The means by which any art is organized tend to arise out of its materials. The English language has inherent stress, most frequently iambic stress (a sharp distinction between accented and unaccented syllables, the accent going forward in longer words, themselves often preceded by unstressed articles, auxiliary verbs, and so forth). On this score, Wordsworth said only that

> metre obeys certain laws, to which the Poet and Reader both willingly sub-
> mit because [the laws] are certain, and because no interference is made by
> them with the passion, but such as the concurring testimony of ages has
> shown to heighten and improve the pleasure which co-exists with it.[17]

Melos is "blind association," little more. According to Wordsworth, what makes a poem worthwhile, finally, is its truth,[18] which poetic sound, as a re-collection of language and literary history, articulates and makes palatable.

Coleridge also argued that sound is an addition to poetry. But, he says, "if metre be super-added, all other parts must be made consonant with it."[19] Unlike prose, each part of a poem must be equally worthy of attention. Every word counts. Sound is not added *after* but *during* the process that gives rise to the poem. Meter and rhyme, as recurring sounds and accents, allow all the parts of a composition to balance, to contribute equally to an overall effect.

> A poem is that species of composition, which is opposed to works of sci-
> ence, by proposing for its *immediate* object pleasure, not truth; and from
> all other species (having *this* object in common with it) it is discriminated
> by proposing to itself such delight from the *whole*, as is compatible with a
> distinct gratification from each component part.[20]

Imaginative literature steers away from truth, at least as an immediate object. A poem does this particularly well because its parts are as delight-ful, thus as worthy of attention, as the whole poem. A large part of this delight, this steering away from truth, arises out of the sound of the poem. The sound of words when regarded *as* sound abstracts them, as Kevin Barry says, from social and historical impediments. Through words for which the making of referential sense is no longer the sole governing urge, certain thoughts can now make themselves evident. If the word-as-sound does this anyway, then what Edward W. Sapir calls "rhythmically self-conscious speech"[21] will do this even more forcefully. For Coleridge, unlike Wordsworth, sound does not temper passion as much as excite attention; meter and rhyme have the power to remove us from ordinary emotion and ordinary meaning.[22]

Poetry, however, is in the end not meter or rhyme or anything else technical. Along with Wordsworth, Coleridge argues that

> What is Poetry? is so nearly the same question with, what is a poet? that the answer to the one is involved in the solution of the other. . . . The poet, described in *ideal* perfection, brings the whole soul of man into activity . . . [23]

In the poet the sense of wholeness, of unity, is most acute. Because, in Coleridge's view, the poet's thoughts and feelings are grounded in this sense of wholeness, his language will be that language where all parts balance with and contribute to the whole—not, say, a work of fiction, where pleasure rather than truth may also be the immediate object, but a poem, where the individual components of rhyme and meter are as important as the overall statement. But although a poem needs to be a certain organization in sound to be a poem, poetry—the poet's thoughts and feelings—is ultimately removed from that organization. My poetry must take on a physical body of sound to be a poem, since only by "exciting a more continuous and equal attention than the language of prose aims at" can my poetry be made known. Yet I can compose in "a studied selection and artificial arrangement, as will partake of *one*, though not a *peculiar* property of poetry."[24] I can use *this* arrangement of sound to produce *this* pleasure that leads ultimately to truth, or I can use *that* arrangement of sound to produce *that* pleasure that leads ultimately to truth. Whichever I choose, I will be guided by pleasure, not truth: truth, my feelings and thoughts in themselves, is the goal of poetry; pleasure, a way to excite the mind into a contemplation of truth, is the goal of the poem as a path to that truth.

Two possibilities open. First, I can revise my poem to produce a different pleasure without changing its essential truth. Second, if I want to make truth my immediate object, I may have to abandon poetry altogether. Both possibilities were realized often in Coleridge's career. He left numerous fragments like "Christabel," which was revised so much and so often that he finally decided it couldn't be finished at all. He tried and abandoned numerous styles, like the early "conversation poems," only to give these up in favor of other kinds of sound arrangements. He composed two very different versions of "The Rime of the Ancient Mariner" (another original approach to the ballad) and, still unsatisfied, added a marginal gloss in prose, albeit in an archaic style. Eventually he more or less gave up poetry altogether in favor of prose, philosophy, criticism, and conversation.

Coleridge says that an "artificial arrangement" like rhyme or meter can facilitate recollection, by which he means simple remembrance.[25] A poem is memorable because words-as-sound boost ordinary verbal attention; the part is dramatized and made memorable in order to remain available when the poem is evaluated as a whole. But Coleridge's idea of poetic sound also facilitates re-collection in our sense, which helps to explain why he should do more revising and abandoning than composing—or, more precisely, why composing, revising, and abandoning tend to shade into one another in Coleridge's thinking. For the Romantic, poetry should enact the poet's experience (What is poetry? = Who is the poet?). With ordered sound, it can do so. Melos carries the reader forward with "the pleasurable activity of mind excited by the attractions of the journey itself," which, interestingly, Coleridge compares with "the path of sound through the air; at every step [the reader] pauses and half recedes, and from the retrogressive movement collects the force which again carries him onward." By means of rhyme and meter, the poem enacts the re-collective pattern of time, the inextricability of time's moving forward and circling back. Yet, while a poem "blends and harmonizes the natural and the artificial, [it] still subordinates . . . the manner to the matter."[26] In a poem, *how* remains subordinate to *what*. Rhyme and meter, being added, can be added in any number of ways without changing the essence of the poetry.

Thus part of the poem's essence, of the lived truth that a poem both records and enacts, is the reality or the possibility of revised and abandoned poems. Sound re-collects the poet's prior output. Melos balances part and whole over time, therefore providing a delightful approach to truth. But the presence of melos is a reminder that this truth either has been or could have been approached before, and either will be or can be approached again. To understand this poem, this enactment of time, we must understand the poet's past poems. Though crucial to the poem, sound remains secondary. The pleasure that sound creates is the poem's object; the truth that sound excites contemplation of is the poem's reason for being. And that truth can be recorded and enacted in many ways, since it does not reside in any particular arrangement of sounds. Thus any particular arrangement of sounds—any individual poem—can be revised infinitely, and perhaps should be abandoned altogether as the poet seeks a more stable and truthful expression of his poetry.

This dilemma is characteristic of Coleridge, who was wont to make distinctions for the sake of reconciling them, and then found he could not do so, perhaps because they never should have been split asunder to begin with. So Shelley might have argued about pleasure and truth, sound and idea. Harold Bloom says that "Shelley's genius desired a transformation of all experience, actual and literary, into the condition of lyric." Shelley was ever attempting what A. W. Schlegel describes as a "musical expression of emotion in language," what William Hazlitt calls that state in which "[t]he music of the mind"—thoughts and feelings as they unfold and interact—"is answered and expressed by the music of language"—the sounds of words as *they* unfold and interact.[27]

According to Shelley,

> Sounds as well as thoughts have relation both between each other and towards that which they represent, and a perception of the order of those relations has always been found connected with a perception of the order of those relations of thoughts. Hence the language of poets has ever affected a certain uniform and harmonious recurrence of sound, without which it were not poetry, and which is scarcely less indispensable to the communication of its action, than the words themselves, without reference to that peculiar order.[28]

For Shelley, the sonic body of poetry *is* poetry; the idea *is* the seamless and unified melos it assumes.

Essential to poetry is the perception that Being has a vitally metaphorical character. Poetry marks

> the before unapprehended relations of things and perpetuates their apprehension, until the words which represent them, become, through time, signs for portions or classes of thoughts . . . [29]

Both ideas and objects are intimately related for Shelley. Characteristics found in *this* thing or thought are found also in *that* thing or thought. This phenomenon can be enacted in poetry by metaphor, which allows us to see the connections and recurrences between things and ideas that we might not see otherwise. It can be enacted also by means of rhyme and meter, the regular recurrence of sounds. As we saw in part 1, this is why Shelley said music is valuable: having rhythm and recurrence, it is an important model for poetry. But music lacks ideas; thus, it cannot enact the rhythm of thoughts and feelings. Poetry can. (Shelley left no comment about whether poetry was also superior because, though it can and should be heard aloud, its music can be experienced by the individual imagination reading silently and alone, whereas music generally has to be heard, and usually in a public performance at that. Though he did remark on how thrilling it was "to *read* the compositions of the most celebrated writers of the present day.")[30]

Reference in poetry is important. Poetry speaks of actual things and feelings and ideas. But because it demonstrates not just their actuality in and of themselves but also the actuality of the relations among them, poetry needs combinatory meaning as well. Poetry means a poem: a specific organization of sound, because poetic sound embodies the rhythms and rhymes of Being. The poetic thought or perception assumes one shape and one shape only. *This* perception of some vital relation takes *this* arrangement of sound and none other; only this arrangement of sound can apprehend and preserve that particular relation.

As self-contradictory as brilliant, Shelley veers between discussing poetry as poems and discussing poetry as any worthwhile endeavor of human consciousness:

> [I]t is by no means essential that a poet should accommodate his language to this traditional form [meter], so that the harmony, which is its spirit, be observed . . . The functions of the poetical faculty are twofold; by one it creates new materials for knowledge, and power and pleasure; by the other it engenders in the mind a desire to reproduce and arrange them according to a certain rhythm and order which may be called the beautiful and the good.[31]

Any perception and preservation of vital relation could be called poetry. This is because poetry is that which

> makes immortal all that is best and most beautiful in the world; it arrests the vanishing apparitions which haunt the interlunations of life, and veiling them, or in language or in form, sends them forth among mankind . . . [32]

Which allows that rhyme and meter may be superadded after all: perhaps other veilings are possible.

By and large, though, Shelley argues that

> it were as wise to cast a violet into a crucible that you might discover the formal principle of its colour and odour, as seek to transfuse from one language into another the creations of a poet. The plant must spring again from its seed, or it will bear no flower . . . [33]

Poetry is poems: that form of language which is utterly untranslatable, either into another language or into another poem. If it is a veiling, it is nevertheless a localization, a covering up that is also a particular act of making available.

Both Wordsworth's and Shelley's theories allow for a re-collection of tradition. For Wordsworth, old sound can be added to new ideas. For Shelley, sound and idea begin together. New ideas require new sounds. "[E]very great poet must inevitably innovate upon the example of his predecessors in the exact structure of his peculiar versification."[34] Among his predecessors, the poet must count himself, and here we see the distinction between Coleridge's and Shelley's ideas of revision. For Coleridge, a poem can be rewritten because, though the pleasure might change, the truth will not; thus the poem re-collects the poet's prior output. For Shelley, all details of the poem, as well as the poem itself, push themselves into the past as soon as they exist.

Thus the poem re-collects itself. It brings again to attention a vital relation within Being and puts that relation together differently. The poem is not Being, rather an apprehension and preservation of some aspect of Being already past. It enacts both that aspect and its already-past-ness. The poem preserves from decay this visitation of the eternal—this and none other. The rhymes and rhythms become prior to all present and future rhymes and rhythms. More important, the poem will never be any other poem, nor will any other poem ever be this one. The poem exists because it is always in the process of becoming a memory. Devices like rhyme and meter enact repetition and difference. Melos enacts meaning. In fact, it is an important part of the meaning it enacts. Neither meaning nor melos, then, can be repeated—or rather, they can be repeated but always differently. Poetic shapes are always available, but only as re-collections of themselves.

Shelley's poetic practice bears out this sense of self-as-predecessor, of poetry as undoing itself in the act of making itself. Heterogeneity is the characterizing force of his career. We find in Shelley a greater diversity of sound structures than in any other of the major Romantic poets. Most of those structures were either his own highly wrought, utterly unique shapes, or his own distinctive use of given forms. In either case, the sound of the poem *is* the poem. More accurately, the sound enacts the ideas so thoroughly that it is impossible to imagine reference apart from combination.

"Prometheus Unbound" re-collects and rejects an array of poetic shapes no less assiduously than it re-collects and rejects an array of moral systems. "Ode to the West Wind" enacts the independent and careening force of its subject with headlong, breathless periods, yet also enacts the relatedness of the forces of nature with tightly controlled terza rima stanzas and concluding couplets. Such tension within the sound of the poem deepens considerably the poet's cry to the wind, "Be thou me." Does the poet want to be as free as the wind in order to fulfill its ends, or does he want to harness the wind to his own ends? Similarly, the stanza of "To A Skylark" moves from short, heavy trochaic lines to a long, flowing iambic line. This rhythmic shift embodies the poet's move between reserve and release, between wariness of and desire for the skylark's harmonious madness. "The Keen Stars Were Twinkling" embodies, with a strong yet delicate shape, the fragile oneness of moonlight, music, and feeling that it yearns for. In the moment we appreciate how suited sound and idea are to each other in these works, we understand their inapplicability elsewhere.

We can draw some conclusions about how the Romantic uses of sound allow for intersections between poetry and music. Our interest is not in how poetry is music but in whether it can be musical: how does the poem's sound, a crucial component of verbal language's combinatory aspect, contribute to the poem's meaning?

The experience of sound itself is crucial to the Romantic poets when addressing this issue. Coleridge's wedding guest is held spellbound by hearing the Ancient Mariner's story, whose boat had been driven forward by the sounds made by spirits.

> And now 'twas like all instruments,
> Now like a lonely flute;
> And now it is an angel's song,
> That makes the heavens be mute.[35]

"Frost at Midnight" uses the occasion of hearing—even the night's silence—to initiate and guide its exploration of time.

> ... the old church-tower,
> Whose bells, the poor man's only music, rang
> From morn to evening, all the hot Fair-day,
> So sweetly, that they stirred and haunted me
> With a wild pleasure, falling on mine ear
> Most like articulate sound of things to come![36]

Consciousness is consciousness of time; it begins with hearing. Wordsworth's "Tintern Abbey" opens thus:

> Five years have passed ... and again I hear
> These waters ... Once again
> Do I behold these steep and lofty cliffs ...

I hear before I see. I see because I hear.

> I cannot paint
> What then I was. The sounding cataract
> Haunted me like a passion.[37]

With poetry's rhythmical and figurative language, I can convey what a picture cannot: what I heard, thus what I felt—and feel. For the Romantic, music not painting is a paradigm for the arts; similarly, hearing rather than seeing initiates awareness. A striking example among many in *The Prelude* is the poet's description of his ascent of Mount Snowden: hearing the sound of many waters gives rise to the reflections that follow about the essence of consciousness. By listening, Wordsworth begins to realize that the mind both remains what it always was and becomes something new: an emblem for the workings of the universe itself. That sound comes up through a chasm in the clouds—through a gap.[38] Much as the gap in the open fifth of Beethoven's Ninth Symphony creates the need for the symphony itself, so interpretation comes out of emptiness. The gap is interpreted by hearing.

Hearing leads to interpretation because even random noise, an emptiness of order, has a tendency to acquire a pattern when heard. Coleridge, on listening to breaking ice in the German highlands, muses that "there are sounds more sublime than any sight *can* be . . . more utterly absorbing the mind's self-consciousness, in its total attention to the object working upon it"; Shelley wonders in "Mont Blanc" whether silence is vacancy after all when consciousness is present.[39] Wordsworth, following the lines quoted above from the beginning of "Tintern Abbey," goes on to supply the sounds he hears with context and qualities ("rolling from their mountain-springs / With a sweet inland murmur"). In various versions of *The Prelude*, he changed "The mind of man is fashioned and built up / Even as a strain of music," to "The mind of man is framed even like the breath / And harmony of music," and revised that much later as, "Dust as we are, the immortal spirit grows / Like harmony in music."[40] With its appeal to the atemporal and corresponding devaluation of mortal experience as its own ground and justification, this last trivializes somewhat the poet's magnificent sense of humanity's worth (and loneliness). Nevertheless, common to all three versions is the notion that the mind, like music, is fashioned, built up, framed. Consciousness is harmony.

"Harmony" should not be confused with "consonance." Whether the word is used figuratively or literally, it refers to something that causes but is not synonymous with consonance.[41] Properly speaking, "harmony" is the name used in the Romantics' age for those dynamics, systematized by Rameau, with which music organizes itself as music. The set procedures of harmony allow music to move from consonance to dissonance and back to consonance, thus transforming sound into meaning—a transformation enacted palpably in Beethoven's Ninth Symphony. Harmony pushes music forward. It allows music to destroy and preserve its past.

By extension, harmony can be a name for experience that has become context. Shelley implores the skylark:

> Teach me half the gladness
> That thy brain must know,
> Such harmonious madness
> From my lips would flow,
> The world should listen then—as I am listening now.[42]

He says to the West Wind:

> Destroyer and preserver; hear, oh hear . . .
> Make me thy lyre, even as the forest is:
> What if my leaves are falling like its own!
> The tumult of thy mighty harmonies
>
> Will take from both a deep autumnal tone . . . [43]

Hearing tends to be organized by certain patterns. When consciousness is present, sound is associated with harmony, and harmony is associated with motion. Note the dissonant and jarring sound of the phrases "harmonious madness" and "tumult of thy mighty harmonies." Harmony is systematic restlessness. It makes dissonance meaningful. Intellectual beauty, says Shelley in his hymn to that quality, is "Like hues and harmonies of evening . . . Like memory of music fled":[44] a zone of temporal transformation, a re-collection of what passes. For Shelley, such transformation implies a moving-forth and moving-back, something to be welcomed and something to be wary of. Teach me *half* the gladness. Be thou me, destroyer and preserver. I want to become other than what I am, but I also want to remain what I am. Like Asia in "Prometheus Unbound," the poet goes forth from self and returns changed to self.[45]

Such describes Romantic time; such allows sound to link music and Romantic poetry. We've noted that for the Viennese classicists, hearing is memory. Music is a manifold act of re-collection. To make sense of this music, the listener must bring again to attention and put together differently music's past, the composer's prior output, and the preceding material within the piece itself. As we saw with Mozart, we must place the piece in the context of its received elements, that is, the particular musical traditions that govern the ways in which ordinary sound can be meaningful; as we saw with Haydn, we must understand what the composer has done previously in order to understand fully this particular accomplishment; and, as we saw with Beethoven, we must relate each passing moment in the composition itself to each moment that has come before, because notes and chords and rhythms *mean* by participating in a patterned unfolding. Indeed, in the case of Beethoven, meanings are subject to such extensive challenges that the solution to any tonal problem consumes itself in the moment that it offers itself. Sound re-collects the past, as embodied in the art's history and given materials, in the artist's prior work, and in prior events in the artwork.

Likewise in Romantic prosody. Wordsworth's theories suggest that we must be aware of how a given poem uses both ordinary language and poetic tradition (poetry's ordinary language) to make, with materials already used, a statement never made before. Coleridge's theories suggest that we must understand what the poet has already written, the shape of the poet's own experience, as enacted by his poetic output, being crucial to the poet's meaning. And Shelley's theories suggest that we must be aware of how the poem both builds and unbuilds itself with the same gestures. These kinds of awareness are all created and guided in poetry by melos, by the organization of rhymes, rhythms, lines, and stanzas, which re-collect, as in music, what is prior in the art, in the artist's work, and in the artwork at hand.

Romantic theory, then, makes poetic sound both crucial to poetry's function and similar in specific ways to musical sound. This helps explain why so many Romantic poets called even their longest works "songs" and "hymns" and the like. Romantic prosody allows verbal language, using its own means, to act very much like the music of the day. Even though that music was instrumental, even though Romantic poetry was seldom really sung, the two arts saw themselves as enactments in sound of the process by which consciousness, in a manifold act of re-collection, makes meaning of and for itself. (We observed in part 1 that the image of song is used almost by default; Keats would seek better images throughout the great odes, finding it finally in "To Autumn," as we'll see in part 3.)

In poetry and music both, to hear is to perceive duration. For the Romantic, the world is a history, not a moment; the landscape poem begins not with something seen but with something heard. If harmony is, then it is passing. Sounds begin, progress, decay, and die. The presence of sound is the possibility of the pastness of sound. But in passing, sound supplies an opportunity for re-collection. Hearing is the realm of harmony, of simultaneous destruction and preservation. To hear is to perceive and participate in time's pattern. That pattern is the origin, that participation the purpose, of consciousness itself—the haunt and main region of the Romantic song.

In our model of Romantic melos, ordinary language seems to correspond with Keats's ordinary time, whereas poetic tradition suggests Keats's unusual but ordinary time. Both exist as points of departure. In manipulating, organizing, combining and recombining them, the artist breaks down their exclusivity, eventually returning to the realm of the ordinary with something new. Ordinary consciousness at best gains insight; ordinary language gains depth and resonance. Now sound and sense, combination and reference contribute equally to meaning. The moment of hearing begins with the perception of words as words only: not purely referential, since this never exists, but with a very low combinatory value. By making sound a more important component of verbal meaning, we enter a special realm where words acquire, for the moment, both fullness and emptiness, a more explicit combinatory dimension and a less apparent, less determinable referentiality. Then we return with a new sense of the word. When melos comes to attention, verbal language has already been re-collected; poetic language allows time's shape to be felt. From ordinary to Special to ordinary with a difference: the pattern of melos is the pattern of Keatsian time.

So associative logic suggests. But we need more evidence about Keats and sound. Having examined the milieu he worked in, we need to examine his place in and response to that milieu. I wish to bracket here as much as possible the larger issue of intention. My concern is not to debate, as the question has been endlessly debated, whether such can govern poetic meaning, therefore critical interpretation. It is rather to discuss what particular ideas might be active in that meaning. What may have informed Keats's thinking to begin with? Did he know the works of the major composers of the day, and, if so, did he hear in them what we hear in terms of sound and re-collection?

A resounding maybe. As we saw in the preface, Charles Cowden Clarke, Keats's friend and sometime mentor, introduced the young man to much music. Many in Keats's circle, as Linda Barlow has shown, were well acquainted with music. Keats often attended gatherings at the home of the famous organist Vincent Novello, and Joseph Severn, the young painter who watched over Keats on his deathbed, played the piano often for his friend, not only in Rome but also during the two years or so preceding their voyage to that city. But Keats had known and loved Mozart and Haydn well beforehand (as early as October 1816, Keats made a pun on the resemblance between the composer's name and that of his new friend, the painter Benjamin Haydon).[46]

To know and love Haydn and Mozart, one must understand musical structure, at least enough to be able to respond appropriately to the ways in which notes and chords and rhythms in the tonal idiom establish basic patterns such as tension and release. Keats had no musical training. But given that he was an unusually intuitive person, it's not unlikely that he could have *felt* the workings of the music, much as he claimed to be able to feel the delight in motion a billiard ball might feel. Apparently, Keats had a good ear as well, and knew much music by heart: he and his brothers and friends would often perform "concerts" in which each would imitate an instrument of the orchestra; these concerts would go on for hours at a time. Keats was usually the bassoon.[47] This perhaps suggests that he sang in a deep voice. More important, it also suggests that he could pick out the bass line, which requires more skill than singing the main melody. We know, then, not only what music was in the air, we also know that Keats was listening, and listening well. At some level he must have heard and understood the music's re-collective character. Such would be true for any competent listener, and doubly so for one as keen and perceptive as Keats.

Regarding prosodic theory, Keats left no formal treatise. Again, we have to speculate. Christopher Ricks has said that the preface to *Endymion*, in which Keats evaluates his performance in that poem, is "most convincing as a sigh, and not as a statement that should be altogether believed."[48] In a way, this is true of all Keats's critical statements, since they are more random comments than literary dogma. Nevertheless, they deserve some consideration. In a letter to John Taylor, Keats says that poetry should "surprise by a fine excess . . . it should strike the Reader as a wording of his own highest thoughts, and appear almost a Remembrance" (L69–70). This is not dissimilar from what Wordsworth, Coleridge, and Shelley put forward. These poets—all of whom were known to Keats, both personally and by their work—argued that poetry provides something new because it provides something familiar. It uses sound to return with a difference both to ordinary language and to literary history, to the poet's prior output, and to prior events within the poem itself.

Such accords with Keats's urges. Carl Woodring points out that Keats often veers between "trust in original genius" and trust in "genres from the traditional store." That is, his creative energy largely proceeds from a tension between continuity and innovation. This tension is often manifested by, and receives a resolution in, Keats's treatment of prosody. Douglas Bush finds in Keats's work "an almost physically felt intensity of image and sound"; similarly, Jackson Bate finds it "almost impossible to draw a line between sensuous and spiritual experience in Keats's poems." And David I. Masson says that Keats's poems are full of spell-like, almost incantatory patterns like "repetition or inversion of a melodic line in music," and which, being "probably related to something fundamental in human nervous construction," allow for a short circuit of ordinary consciousness, a stirring of the whole organism to response.[49] The whole organism: it's arguable that the primal perception is of the mother's heartbeat—a rhythmic sound, an aural perception of both ongoingness and repetition. No wonder, then, that sound seems to dominate young consciousness: children respond readily to poetry and music, and can often sing in perfectly intelligible words before they can talk.

Having steered close to assertions about influence a few pages back, I veer now toward the archetypal arguments I am also trying to avoid. Whatever is "fundamental in human nervous construction" nevertheless takes specific manifestations. We should focus now on the more tangible level of the poet's works. Ricks argues that Keats's misspellings and aural confusions often provide a clue into his imaginative processes. For example, Keats's spelling of "jeapardy" seems to indicate his sense of the dangers of jealousy. These confoundings, says Ricks, may be for Keats something like a chord in music, a way for two meanings to coexist in one moment.[50] Not many into one but many at once: this is the mark of Keats's Special experience, wherein the imagination embraces life's complexities and contradictions. The sound or appearance of a compound word, the way it unfolds over time, becomes a way into this Special state. Combination, always present but tacit, becomes explicit.

Of greater interest than puns and misspellings is Keats's "principle of melody in verse." The evidence for this "principle" comes from a letter written by Keats's friend Benjamin Bailey, which states that Keats mentioned to him in conversation that poetry should produce a "pleasurable richness" derived from the nonrandom repetition and alternation of both vowels and consonants "like differing notes in music," sometimes in the individual line, sometimes throughout an entire passage.[51] Notice the intricate patternings of vowels in the following lines:

And still she slept an azure-lidded sleep

Nor let the beetle nor the death moth be

And bid old Saturn take his throne again

Already with thee! Tender is the night

Bate provides more than enough examples of such patternings to demonstrate that they are important in Keats's work.[52] But we need to evaluate particular instances. For example, the link between "and" and "an" in the first line above, or that between "with" and "is" in the last line: these prove little, involving unstressed function words. But the pairings in the third line seem crucial to its meaning. Assonance reminds us of something the words do not explicitly refer to: the "throne" belonged of "old" to Saturn, who must now "take" his throne "again" (for Keats they would have the same long *a*). Combination—sound unfolding over time—achieves copriority. Similarly, the two clauses of the fourth line begin with the same accented vowel sound ("already" and "tender"); this makes the components of what might otherwise seem a rather paratactic line sound inevitably paired.

Obviously, Keats believed a tightly worked out melos to be integral to the poetic process, and he practiced this belief more assiduously than perhaps any other poet of the era. The actual sounds of words, in themselves and in combination with other words, are crucial to the meaning of the poem—under certain conditions. We should not make more of this so-called principle than it merits. Sound per se occupies less of Keats's attention than of Poe's or Swinburne's.[53] For those poets, melos was an end in itself; for Keats, it is a poetic means: crucial, but also one of many.

As Bate points out, Keats used his principle most consciously when, sitting at the bedside of his dying brother Tom, he wrote *Hyperion*. With much time on his hands, he worked out the poem slowly and deliberately.[54] Doubtless, too, the attention to technique would have provided welcome distraction from these trying emotional circumstances—a good example, perhaps, of Wordsworth's point about melos as the copresence of something regular to keep passion from overflowing its bounds.

Keats came to reject the deliberateness of the language in *Hyperion;* similarly, he never again spent so much time poring over melos itself. But the process of sound manipulation did become part of his ability to produce and guide poetic meaning. Much as Special time ought to lead both away from and back to ordinary time, so language-as-sound ought to lead away from and back to ordinary language. Prosody doesn't turn language into music; it allows verbal language to re-collect itself in musical ways. This is the case in Keats's poems, which we should now consider in depth.

8

The Verse Paragraph

I F Poetry comes not as naturally as the Leaves to a tree," Keats wrote
his publisher when citing his "axioms" as a poet, "it had better not
come at all" (L70). But the process by which poetry comes "naturally"
can be long and involved. Keats has often been thought of as a poet of
immediacy; yet the past, whether a burden or a blessing, informs all his
poetry. The poet re-collects. This applies to his experience—and to his
work. While Keats's collected works don't display the overt heterogeneity of Shelley's, they do attest to much experimenting with given
forms. Some he mastered; most he did not. But he learned from his failures, since they helped him to focus his goals and abilities as an artist.
This is especially true of those poems written in verse paragraphs.

"Sleep and Poetry" (1816) shows that from early in his career, and
well before any recorded mention of his ideas on prosody, Keats was concerned with the re-collective possibilities of melos. The poem opens with
a series of questions:

> What is more gentle than a wind in summer?
> What is more soothing than the pretty hummer
> That stays one moment in an open flower,
> And buzzes cheerily from bower to bower?
>
> (1–4)

Susan Wolfson has argued that Keats acts most characteristically when
he asks questions. Seeking a wide range of knowledge and experience,
Keats also sought to keep his poetry and his thinking open.[1] Rather than
drawing conclusions, he asks. Rather than accepting the given or imitating the past, he seeks repetition with a difference. Note the delicate
rhythmic variation (repetition with a difference) in the last line of the

above passage: the language itself moves from bȯwèr (elided) to bówĕr (trochaic). This urge towards openness is enacted on a broader level by the question format itself, and by the breaking of the couplet between lines 2 and 3. Sense spills across the rhyme's boundary. Like the poet, the form of the poetry asks, What is more?

But the break is cautious. It occurs between a main and a subordinate clause, and the entire thought is contained by the end of the fourth line. This is appropriate. The questions that the poet has asked are little more than rhetorical. He quickly answers them, and the few more that follow, by talking about sleep—"Soft closer of our eyes! / Low murmurer of tender lullabies!" (11–12)—and about the pleasures of indolence and dreaming. For a moment, the poet had "stood tip-toe" (to borrow from another poem written around the same time). Then he became content to let the energy of the couplet override his urge to go beyond. He sinks back down to luxurious, dreamy images and sound patterns: "Light hoverer around our happy pillows! / Wreather of poppy buds, and weeping willows!" (13–14). The vowels and consonants here are predominantly soft, the line endings weak. Yet a tough sense of craft is active. That sense, in fact, determines the choice of those vowels and consonants to begin with, just as it unites, by means of rhyme and alliteration, the varied ideas of restfulness imaged by pillows, poppies, and willows.

The poet seeks to bring this active sense more into the foreground. He goes on to ask what is higher, fresher, more strange, more beautiful than sleep and the luxuries of dreams. A more prolonged series of questions follows. These questions seem less rhetorical, seem to be searching more assiduously for fresh definition and language. In the forty lines that follow, the couplet breaks three more times. Urgency develops. More and more, the verse strains against itself, chafing at the narrow focus of the closed couplet. Finally, the poet's questions lead him to speak of that which is higher than mere fancy and indolence. At the same moment, the couplet breaks again and repeatedly:

> O Poesy! for thee I hold my pen
> That am not yet a glorious denizen
> Of thy wide heaven—Should I rather kneel
> Upon some mountain-top until I feel
> A glowing splendour round about me hung,
> And echo back the voice of thine own tongue?
>
> (47–52)

The first break in this passage occurs in the middle of a phrase, and the sentence is allowed to run beyond the break of yet a second couplet. The sense of rupture, of breaking of bonds, is far more acute than that created at the beginning of the poem. Having sensed the kind of energy generated even by a cautious break in the form, the poet lets momentum and tension build until just the right moment. As poetry is more powerful by far than dreaming, so the prosodic arrangement here is more powerful than anything else thus far in the poem. The poet has set up the vital and contrasting forces of indolence and activity, fancy and imagination, sleep and poetry. Now he shows that these are not opposites as such. Poetry needs visions; a "sense of real things" is useless without the glories of the imagination. And sleep needs poetry; indolence without "tender lullabies" offers little attraction. The creative tension between these is enacted by Keats's alternately closed and broken couplet.

This tension is the specific source of energy that *is* this moment. Sound allows the artwork, in the manner of Shelley and Beethoven, to re-collect itself. The arrival of poesy and the concomitant breaking of the couplet re-collect how the poem's opening gesture was cut short, showing thereby how that gesture can be put together differently and better. Keats also re-collects poetic tradition, in the manner of Wordsworth and Mozart. Farther on in "Sleep and Poetry" he says of Augustan poets:

> with a puling infant's force
> They sway'd about upon a rocking horse,
> And thought it Pegasus.
> (185–87)

Keats repeats the format of Pope yet puts it together very differently. Not only does he break the couplet regularly, he also makes sound more than the mere wit he perceived in Augustan poetry. A pseudohistory of English literature follows. Keats wants to show the glories of the past in order to inspire glories of the future (and to denigrate the Augustan betrayal of those glories). With its anti-Augustan treatment of melos, this poem is a foretaste of those future glories.

A foretaste—at least in the poet's mind, at least when he wrote it. It could be argued that Keats himself is doing a bit of swaying on a rocking horse here. The balance of "Sleep and Poetry" continues breaking the couplet, frequently heightening the sense of rupture by making the break coincide with a paragraph break. Emphasizing expansiveness, Keats allows the poem to lose the creative tensions he'd manipulated so well in the first fifty lines or so. Energy seems to run down. By creating tension, by actively engaging tradition for the sake of forming new tradition, by using sound as a way of re-collecting poetry, Keats's idea of the couplet seems in a way more interesting than Pope's, which, according to some tastes, goes too far in the direction of sheer restrictiveness. But it remains an interesting idea only.

In fact, Keats's best work is seldom found in the couplet. He never found the right balance for it, though he kept trying. *Endymion* (1817) does not often rise even to the low level of creative tension in "Sleep and Poetry." Here, the couplet is broken, not as a contrast to moments of integrity, but constantly. We not only get the breathlessness that mars so much of Keats's early work, we get it, without respite, for four thousand lines. As we saw in part 1, the poem offers some insights into Keats's development, and contains some passages of real beauty. It bursts so with its own enthusiasm, however, that even Keats's most ardent admirers seem to feel compelled to apologize for it. Keats himself, in the poem's preface, called it "a feverish attempt, rather than a deed accomplished," full of an adolescent "mawkishness" that would cause "all the thousand bitters which [sensitive readers] must necessarily taste." By the time Keats got to book 4, he'd grown tired of the sonic arrangement he'd chosen. There, we begin to see something new: not a closing of the couplet but little lyrics and songs interrupting the couplet texture. These had appeared, widely scattered, in earlier books; in book 4, Keats seems to be admitting that the lyric is really where he belongs. As we'll see, his attitude toward such an admission was highly mixed.

Keats's early verse epistles generally observe the closed couplet, but none is a terribly accomplished work. *Lamia* (1819) is a great poem, and it too observes the couplet assiduously. Whether Keats's decision to do this was prompted by artistic or commercial concerns is hard to say. He'd written most of the great odes by now and was looking for new challenges. He also needed money, and felt such a "sensational" story, narrated in the still-popular Augustan form, would sell well (L268, 308).

In calling up a technique employed in his own earlier work, and in breaking with the ways that those poems themselves broke with poetic tradition, *Lamia* becomes a re-collection of a re-collection. One wonders if Keats had any notions of how he might incorporate what he learned here: in the poem's Drydenesque style, the paragraph rather than the couplet is the basic unit of thought, which mandates an argument that must be firm because it is deployed over many lines. The poem nevertheless shows a certain exhaustion, a certain capitulation to old ways of thinking. Early in adulthood, Keats asserted that we can have Isaac Newton's *Optics* or the beauty of the rainbow but not both.[2] He was at a dinner party and had been drinking heavily when he said this, so he may have spoken at least partially in jest. To be sure, his greatest poems question such exclusivity. Not *Lamia*. The speaker there asks,

> Do not all charms fly
> At the mere touch of cold philosophy?
> There was an awful rainbow once in heaven:
> We know her woof, her texture; she is given

In the dull catalogue of common things.
Philosophy will clip an Angel's wings,
Conquer all mysteries by rule and line,
Empty the haunted air, and gnomed mine—
Unweave a rainbow, as it erewhile made
The tender-person'd Lamia melt into a shade.

                                    (2.229–38)

Here, though the couplet avoids the stop-and-go effect or barrage of witticisms that this form tends to encourage, its integrity is generally observed. Here also Keats works with a highly polarized view of the world, of the relation between reality and imagination. One kills the other. Such is a possibility in Keats's finest works; yet in those poems Keats also sought other relations, few of which can be found here.

Whether closed or broken, the couplet may have been for Keats too closely associated with compositional values alien even to this traveler among unknown identities. Repetition with no real room for difference: such was a difficulty Beethoven faced with theme-and-variations, a form, like the couplet, affiliated with the eighteenth century. Beethoven's true voice is mostly absent from his compositions in that form. Late works like the final movement of the Ninth, composed after Beethoven had had ample opportunity to establish his own voice in his own forms, do achieve a breakthrough (the formidable Diabelli Variations also come to mind). Keats didn't live long enough to have a "late" period as such. No real breakthrough came for him in the particular inherited form of the couplet.

Keats experimented with other inherited forms such as blank verse. Bate's description of the melos of *Hyperion* is worth citing here. The poem has "greater strength and severity of line" than many of Keats's earlier efforts. Adjectives are cut in favor of verbs, or are turned into lists following the noun; shorter, more "native" (Anglo-Saxon rather than Latinate) words are employed; the past participle is used as an adjective to convey a feeling of captured strength; the verb often begins the line, with nouns and verbs, as well as nouns and adjectives, being frequently inverted; the first foot is often trochaic, creating a sense of weight and dignity; and a caesura often comes early in the line, thus tending to quicken the pace of the rest of the line.[3] In other words, Keats had been studying Milton, and was using that poet's style in a very deliberate fashion.

In Miltonic tradition, the poet addresses himself to elevated subjects, and seeks a fittingly grand style far removed from ordinary, conversational tone. As we've seen, this poem is where Keats most carefully attended to his "principle of melody in verse." Notice in the remarkably resonant passage that follows the consistent placing of long vowels on stressed beats, the complex interplay of *s* sounds, and the tight web of alliteration and assonance:

> Deep in the shady sadness of a vale
> Far sunken from the healthy breath of morn,
> Far from the fiery noon, and eve's one star,
> Sat grey-hair'd Saturn, quiet as a stone,
> Still as the silence round about his lair;
> Forest on forest hung about his head
> Like cloud on cloud. No stir of life was there,
> Not so much life as on a summer's day
> Robs not one light seed from the feather'd grass,
> But where the dead leaf fell, there did it rest.
> A stream went voiceless by, still deadened more
> By reason of his fallen divinity
> Spreading a shade . . .
>
> (1–13)

Like Shelley, Keats seems to believe that sound must somehow *be* the poem—that is, our attention is directed not to sound in itself but to sound as an enactment of the poem. Keats achieves this with *Hyperion* insofar as the sound is at the same remove from daily speech as the myth is from daily life.

Yet in the case of this poem, Keats, like Coleridge, found melos to be a precipitator of revision. He abandoned the poem after two and a half books. Reasons aren't hard to find. We can dismiss the savagely personal reviews of *Endymion* that appeared while he was writing it. He'd distanced himself thoroughly from his early epic by then, and he had more artistic resilience than that.[4] Keats says that he gave up *Hyperion* because he was spending too much time on intricacies. The style may have been native to Milton; it was not so to Keats. The sound of the poem is too careful, too calculated, too self-conscious. He wanted, he said, to give himself up to other sensations (L292). For Keats, part of being a writer was living, not poring over a poetic style belonging neither to oneself nor to one's age. *Hyperion* repeats Milton, but without the finer tone of Keats's voice. He wanted fancy, and he wanted flights of imagination, but he wanted "a pair of patient sublunary legs" too (L268)—a way to bring imagination back to the ordinary. His thoughts were turning from mythical subjects toward "the mind of man"; his sound was thus aiming for a less epic, more humanly proportioned melos.

Keats abandoned the epic melos, but not many months later he tried, characteristically, to find a place for it within an overall poetic statement.

Being far removed from the ordinary, myth can't be *all* of poetry; but can it be *some*? In *The Fall of Hyperion*, Keats tries again to work out the relation between the imagination and life-in-time. One way he does this is by seeking a fruitful exchange between high poetic diction and ordinary speech.

> Fanatics have their dreams, wherewith they weave
> A paradise for a sect; the savage too
> From forth the loftiest fashion of his sleep
> Guesses at heaven: pity these have not
> Trac'd upon vellum or wild Indian leaf
> The shadows of melodious utterance.
> But bare of laurel they live, dream, and die;
> For Poesy alone can tell her dreams,
> With the fine spell of words alone can save
> Imagination from the sable charm
> And dumb enchantment.
>
> (1–11)

The spell of words here is markedly less ponderous than in the opening of *Hyperion* quoted previously. A different sonic arrangement excites a more delightful contemplation of whatever truth there might be in dreams and myths. The poet shows us how a more ordinary melos for poetry—not "melodious utterance" but its shadows—can save dreams from irrelevance and extinction.

The bulk of *The Fall of Hyperion* is such a dream, in which the poet encounters Moneta. She gives him a vision of fallen Saturn and the contest between the Titans and the Olympians. Moneta is the goddess of memory. This is fitting. Keats is re-collecting his own work: the passages revolving around the gods are reworked lines from *Hyperion*. Keats is trying to save his earlier work, like myth, from irrelevance. He brings these again to attention yet returns to them with a difference. Now the myth is a dream within a dream. This vision can lead far into the imaginative realm, yet can also, Keats hoped, lead back to reality. Apropos of this focus on reality, there are also echoes in Moneta's name of money, suggesting that she provides a valuable experience, but also suggesting that material concerns cannot be separated from spiritual ones, as Keats, had he not believed so on principle anyway, would have come to believe now that he was almost desperately poor.

Unlike Haydn's plundering of his own past work for new ideas, however, Keats's effort here seems, finally, a cut-and-paste job. The conversational blank verse in the new passages conflicts with the Miltonic tone and godly subject matter of the old passages. Further, in both its diction and its use of the all-seeing I, it sounds more like Wordsworth than the voice Keats is struggling to develop. He can't find that voice simply by shifting from a long and lovely verse paragraph composed in the spirit of Miltonic titanisms to an equally long, equally lovely paragraph composed in the spirit of a selection of the language really spoken by men.

Acknowledging a second failure with this material, Keats gave up on *The Fall of Hyperion*. Yet he never abandoned the notion that poets prove their worth in the epic. Unsuccessful in this form, he came to see all his work as a failure. Later generations have been kinder. Keats did not, like Wordsworth, establish a new kind of epic. But he did develop his own unique kind of extended composition, as we'll discuss in part 3. Pulled by his genius toward the modern short lyric and lyric sequence, he learned from his failures where his strength did *not* reside.

Some of Keats's shorter poems in verse paragraphs such as "Fancy" (1818) show his strengths developing. This was one of Keats's first efforts at exploring crucial thoughts in a short poem with less brevity and greater flexibility than the sonnet.[5] Such an effort, as we'll see, would become increasingly important in Keats's career.

> Ever let the Fancy roam,
> Pleasure never is at home:
> At a touch sweet Pleasure melteth,
> Like to bubbles when rain pelteth;
> Then let winged Fancy wander
> Through the thought still spread beyond her:
> Open wide the mind's cage-door,
> She'll dart forth, and cloudward soar.
>
> (1–8)

These lines manifest Keats's "melody in verse" nicely: notice the assonance that forges a strong link between "pleasure" and "never," "wide" and "mind," "forth" and "soar," as well as the alliteration that joins "winged" and "wander."

Notice also the trochaic meter. Blake, by using that rhythm in "The Lamb," gives his language a nursery rhyme sound (like, say, "Twinkle, Twinkle, Little Star"). The falling rhythm of trochaic meter makes the verse feel whimsical yet heavy-handed, the product of a mind innocent of finesse. There is, however, a certain ominousness about it as well. English—the spoken English of adults, that is—tends to be iambic. Though the accent generally moves forward in multisyllabic words, these words are generally preceded by particles. Such particles—modal auxiliaries, prepositions, possessive pronouns, and so forth—are missing from more youthful speech because they belong to a mature view. When I stop saying the trochaic "Dada" and begin saying the iambic "my Dad," I show that, among other things, I am beginning to feel that much as my father is not everyone's father, so my point of view is not everyone's point of view. To use trochaic meter, then, may be to get a taste of recovered innocence. But this meter can also create a sense of disturbance because it violates the language's natural stress pattern. The flip side of nursery rhymes: they often articulate not childhood joy but childhood dread, or serve as ghastly warnings about what happens to small people bad and good. Surely few poems have terrified more generations of children than the morbid—and trochaic—"Now I Lay Me Down to Sleep."

The meter of Blake's "Lamb" thus both invites us back into preexperience and prevents facile interpretations about the lamb's character (why did Christ have to become a lamb anyway, and what happened to that lamb?). Keats's use of trochaic meter in "Fancy" acts similarly, enriching the poem. Flights of imagination are countered by ponderous rhythm. This, combined with the use of rhymes delayed by only four beats, allows the poem's melos to enact what is for Keats a fundamental paradox: weighty cares create the desire for fanciful roaming—and also make such roaming, if not impossible, then brief.

In the fragment "The Eve of St. Mark," the four-beat lines arranged in couplets, along with the predominantly trochaic words that give the verse a falling stress,[6] make for a roughhewn feeling appropriate to the recounting of folk legend:

> Upon a Sabbath day it fell;
> Twice holy was the Sabbath bell,
> That call'd the folk to evening prayer.
> The city streets were clean and fair
> From wholesome drench of April rains,
> And on the western window panes
> The chilly sunset faintly told
> Of unmatur'd green vallies cold . . .
>
> (1–8)

Why Keats never finished the poem is impossible to say, though we can hazard a guess. At the time (early 1819), he was searching for a new style to get his work going again after illness and inactivity.[7] This was one attempt. It even went so far as to incorporate an imitation of Chaucerian-era verse (99–114). But re-collection wars with restrictiveness. Line length and rhyme are neither capacious nor flexible. Struggling with these strictures, the couplet breaks in most un-Chaucerian and unfolklike ways.

Keats had manipulated folk tradition to his own ends in "La Belle Dame sans Merci." Perhaps that poem owes much of its success to being written in stanzas. For Keats, the closed couplet seemed too restrictive, the broken couplet too free. Blank verse seemed too restrictive in that it necessarily invoked the spirits of Milton and Wordsworth, yet too unrestrictive in that composing in paragraphs allowed Keats to wander without resolution among disparate styles. We've noted that toward the end of *Endymion*, Keats switched from paragraph and couplet to stanza. Such a move points the way.

9

The Stanza

THE blank verse paragraph can be musical. Its utterances, not subject to articulation in terms of line endings or stanzaic boundaries, can run on freely and thus can quicken the pace of poetry, with "the sense variously drawn out from one Verse into another." So Milton himself asserted in his note on the verse of *Paradise Lost.*[1] As Keats discovered, this wasn't his kind of music: not enough to rub up against, perhaps, not enough of a focus for what he felt could be his too-indulgent imagination.

The stanza, which does provide a focus, can be musical too, though not necessarily for the obvious reason that it can be set to music. Such may be the case with some stanzaic poems. But these must have a regular rhythm and end-stopped lines. (Metrical substitution and enjambed rhymes, if they provide the songwriter anything, usually provide humor.) Such poems are usually not great, unless lack of complexity is part of how the poem works.

The musicality of great stanzaic poetry resides in its ability to enact re-collection. Each stanza is a return with a difference of all preceding stanzas. The poem's melos is ever the same, ever changing. This suits Keats. He is a questioner, a seeker of new possibilities for old material, and the stanzaic poem performs the same search. It moves forward by circling back on itself, and circles back by moving forward.

Bate characterizes "The Eve of St. Agnes" as leisurely, majestic, rich and varied in rhyme and meter, "extremely dynamic in its intensity" yet "strengthened and restrained by classical rigor" and a severe structure.[2] As such, the poem fulfills all the criteria we've observed, both in music and in poetry, for Romantic melos. First, it re-collects itself, between stanzas and within the stanza, by setting its materials into creative tension with one another. The length of its Spenserian stanza (nine iambic pentameter lines, with an extra beat in the ninth) encourages long periods and forward momentum. At the same time, the high incidence of repetition in the rhyme scheme *(ababbcbcc)* keeps the stanza turning back on itself. Further, the very form of the Spenserian stanza, because it is associated with the epic-length *Faerie Queene,* presupposes that the poem will re-collect itself on a large scale; the reader understands, even before beginning to read, that the same sonic shape will appear, changed, many times. Present and prior sound point to each other.

If Keats, by the form he chooses, brings to attention his beloved Spenser's work, he also puts Spenser together differently. The poem thereby re-collects poetic tradition—another criterion of Romantic melos. Keats's love story, like those in *The Faerie Queene,* is set among knights and ladies, and is both sensual and spiritual. But Keats's brand of sensuality is unredeemed by Spenser's brand of spirituality. No Christianity or courtliness for these lovers, no relying on the preachings of what Keats called an "ideot parson" and "the Bench of Bishops" (L215) or on "the divine right Gentlemen" (L164) and "the tyranny of the nobles" (L312). This is an allegory of the imagination. Clifford Adelman has said that the music of the feast hall affrays Porphyro's ears in Madeline's chamber because Keats wants him—and us—to be mindful of all previous chambers.[3] Consciousness re-collects. It attends equally to present and past. Time is both ongoing and gone. Similarly, stanzaic patterns from literary history are always available as vehicles for discussing and enacting time. Part of this availability is an awareness of them *as* historical, the stuff of old romance. If they are to live again, they must be given something new.

The melos of the poem also re-collects Keats's own work. The assured details of the poem point to Keats's prior experience. A few months before, he'd struggled with *Hyperion.* "The Eve of St. Agnes" was written much more quickly, but we can see the effects here of having pored over his principle of melody in verse. Consider the nested shapes formed by the vowels in the poem's first line:

St. Agnes' Eve—Ah, bitter chill it was!

Sound moves forward to circle back on itself, and circles back to move forward.

The pause after the second foot forces the following three feet to hurry, thus making them vital and urgent. This is fitting. The first, two-foot phrase is a statement of fact, the second a response, whose emotion is heightened by its stylistic disjunction with ordinary speech (not "it was a bitter chill" but "bitter chill it was"). The pace of the first phrase is slowed, thus made more weighty, more full of thingness without affect, by the heavily accented long vowels of ǣ in "Agnes" and ī in "Eve" (given that Keats was a Londoner, "saint" should probably be pronounced "sn" and is thus unstressed). The second, three-foot phrase has a short vowel on each accented syllable. The quickening of pace produced thereby adds to its emotion. Linear and circular, slow and fast, fact and feeling, long and short: with sound, opposition is re-collected as creative tension.

Throughout the poem, rhythmic variations within stanzas are kept to a minimum for maximum effect. When they do occur, they occur early in the line, and almost never in the final line. Stanza 37 is typical:

> 'Tis dark: quick pattereth the flaw-blown sleet:
> "This is no dream, my bride, my Madeline!"
> 'Tis dark: the iced gusts still rave and beat:
> "No dream, alas, alas! and woe is mine!
> Porphyro will leave me here to fade and pine.—
> Cruel! what traitor could thee hither bring?
> I curse not, for my heart is lost in thine,
> Though thou forsakest a deceived thing;—
> A dove forlorn and lost with sick unpruned wing."

From variation to regularity: note the initial trochees of the second, fifth, and sixth lines above, the spondaic and pyrrhic feet ('Tĭs dárk / quíck pát- / -tĕrĕth) midway in the first line, and the anapestic effect (fŏr mў héart) midway in the seventh. The endings of those lines are regular. The final line is entirely iambic, with only one, barely audible crossing of the foot boundary (ŭnprún- / -ĕd wíng). Strong closure arises in each line; an even stronger finality emerges at the stanza's end.

Another of Keats's axioms about poetry:

> Its touches of Beauty should never be half way therby making the reader breathless instead of content: the rise, the progress, the setting of imagery should like the Sun come natural too him—shine over him and set soberly although in magnificence leaving him in the Luxury of twilight. (L70)

As we saw in part 1, musical imagery in "The Eve of St. Agnes" rises, progresses, and sets. It guides the reader through the forms of Keatsian experience—ordinary, Special, changed ordinary—and in the end leaves the reader free to interpret. The same could be said of its melos. Sound should rise, progress, and set, a motion Keats achieves in this poem with rhythmic variation. The poem seems to breathe, to open and close, to inhale sharply and exhale easily, over and over. Every step it takes is a meshing of past and present, regularity and variation, repetition and difference. Every line, every stanza is both end and beginning.

Such a move, though it allows the poem to develop "naturally," also inhibits finality. The stanza can close; the stanzaic poem, ever aware of the possibility of one more breath, can only stop. We might recall here the jarring we often receive in the final movement of Beethoven's Ninth. For example, the "Janizary March" in that movement reworks the "Ode to Joy" theme into a joke at the expense of the fad then raging in Vienna for Turkish military music. But if we laugh, we should do so uneasily. The spare bassoons, percussion, and high winds here contrast disturbingly with the glory of the sustained tutti preceding this passage. That tutti could have provided a resounding close to the symphony; instead, this plucky march follows. Even more disturbing is that the word *Gott* (God), sung at full volume by the full chorus, had caused the music to fall apart into the long silence, out of which this most irreverent music arises. Any grasp on the infinite, the composer seems to be telling us, any sense of final answers must yield to time's ongoingness. The artwork, like consciousness itself, exists precisely because it is always in the process both of becoming the past and of bringing the past back changed.

In part 1 we saw Keats make a similar move when he describes Porphyro's song. The sound of the phrase "an ancient ditty long since mute," being so appropriately inappropriate, jars us. We also observed that there's reason to believe Keats wanted to create a certain ironic distance with this poem, a certain distrust about the attractiveness of such a story. With melos he does so. Any sense the reader might have of this as an ideal moment of fulfillment is undercut by the sound of the passage. Both Beethoven and Keats, then, offer us not answers but a vast range of interpretive possibilities. Sound enacts idea: there can always be one more stanza, in much the same way that in Beethoven's Ninth there can always be one more transformation. Like that composition, "The Eve of St. Agnes" has an organic uniqueness. Its melos is perfectly suited to its meaning because they both rise, progress, and set. But part of organicism is the possibility of new growth: no final answers. "The Eve of St. Agnes" remains open *and* achieves coherence. This is one source of its greatness.

We should pause here to consider that for every success such as "The Eve of St. Agnes," there are numerous lesser works such as "The Cap and Bells; or, The Jealousies" (1819). The majestic pace and frequently repeated rhymes of the Spenserian stanza are wretchedly unsuited to the satirical breeziness Keats is trying for here:

"Dear Princess, do not whisper me so loud,"
Quoth Corallina, nurse and confidant,
"Do not you see there, lurking in a cloud,
Close at your back, that sly old Crafticant?
He hears a whisper plainer than a rant:
Dry up your tears, and do not look so blue;
He's Elfinan's great state-spy militant,
His running, lying, flying foot-man too,—
Dear mistress, let him have no handle against you!
                                                        (st. 6)

Byron shows in *Don Juan*—which, interestingly, Keats despised[4]—that ottava rima works much better for satire, with an interwoven sestet and a concluding couplet that epigrammatically unweaves the whole thing. Keats used ottava rima for the tiresome "Isabella" (1818). Not only is the story relentlessly maudlin, but its ottava rima stanzas seem perversely unsuited to the story's gravity. Not that ottava rima is always inappropriate for a grave utterance. A hundred years later, Yeats would create with this form a muted despair, a sense of magnificence built up in the first six lines, then torn down in a couplet that gains power through subtlety (for example, "Nineteen Hundred and Nineteen"). But this is "Isabella":

Why were they proud? Because their marble founts
Gush'd with more pride than do a wretch's tears?—
Why were they proud? Because fair orange-mounts
Were of more soft ascent than lazar stairs?—
Why were they proud? Because red-lin'd accounts
Were richer than the songs of Grecian years?—
Why were they proud? again we ask aloud,
Why in the name of Glory were they proud?
                                                        (st. 16)

It is perhaps not fair to quote this stanza, approaching self-parody as it does. But the rest of the poem is not much better. In fact, among his longer works Keats himself disliked this poem most. As Bate points out, the "quick walk" of the ottava rima "partly succeeds in modifying the sentimentality."[5] Yet for those unwilling or unable to share the pathos that even Keats was trying to eliminate from his verse, the poem remains hysterical (in every sense). When sound and story clash, they should do so for some effect; a disagreement between combination and reference shouldn't demonstrate that the poet had, on this occasion, a tin ear.

Elsewhere, Keats performed better. Like Wordsworth and Mozart, he was ever seeking a creative tension between tradition and originality. At worst, he grafted on an inappropriate tone or story, as in "Isabella." At best he produced works new yet strangely familiar. Some of his stanzaic poems could actually be song lyrics. "Unfelt, unheard, unseen" (1817) may have been composed with that in mind:

> Unfelt, unheard, unseen,
> I've left my little queen,
> Her languid arms in silver slumber dying:
> Ah! through their nestling touch,
> Who, who could tell how much
> There is for madness—cruel or complying?

Note the skill with which the poet shifts from the iambic yet jerky feel of the anxious first line to the smooth, languid, dying-away feel caused by the falling stress in the third line's major words. Such rhythmic skill is apparent in other lyrics, such as "Hither, hither, love" (1817 or 1818):

> Hither, hither, love,
>   'Tis a stately mead;
> Hither, hither love,
>   Let us feed and feed

And "You say you love; but with a voice" (1817 or 1818):

> You say you love; but with a smile
> Cold as sunrise in September,
> As you were Saint Cupid's nun,
> And kept his weeks of Ember—
> O love me truly!
>   (st. 2)

"Stay, Ruby-Breasted Warbler, Stay" (1814) and "Apollo to the Graces" (1818) were actually written as lyrics to melodies Keats knew. If "Extracts from an Opera" (1818) were intended to be set, the music has been lost.[6] But their songfulness, that is, their ability to use a perfectly regular ballad stanza to create nonetheless interesting words, remains:

> The stranger lighted from his steed,
> And ere he spake a word,
> He seiz'd my lady's lily hand,
> And kiss'd it all unheard.

There are also the songs in *Endymion* which we mentioned earlier, including this metrically extraordinary performance:

> O Sorrow,
> Why dost borrow
> The natural hue of health, from vermeil lips?—
> To give maiden blushes
> To the white rose bushes?
> Or is't thy dewy hand the daisy tips?
>
> (4.146–51)

Though some of this material borders on preciousness, all of it shows the artist actively seeking a melos. Keats tended to do more searching when the stakes were low, being cautious in his "important" works. Yet as we noted in part 1, "light" entertainment has its place in Keatsian experience, as in "The Gothic looks solemn" (1817) in which Keats pokes good-hearted fun at academic life:

> There are plenty of trees,
> And plenty of ease,
> And plenty of fat deer for parsons;
> And when it is venison,
> Short is the benison,—
> Then each on a leg or thigh fastens.
>
> (st. 3)

The rhyme of "parsons" and "fastens" is less of a howler if we remember Keats's Cockney accent, though this itself is part of its humor. Too often struggling to be a proper and important poet, Keats here pokes fun at himself as well as at Oxford with a rhyme that works only in a "low" dialect.

A heavy trochaic rhythm, combined with an elaborate rhyme scheme, creates the mock seriousness, transport, and incantatory feel of the "Spirit here that reignest" (1818):

> Spirit here that reignest!
> Spirit here that painest!
> Spirit here that burneth!
> Spirit here that mourneth!
> Spirit! I bow
> My forehead low,
> Enshaded with thy pinions!
> Spirit! I look,
> All passion struck,
> Into thy pale dominions!

One suspects that this poem was a sort of Haydn-like exorcism: the demeanor and subject of *Endymion*, already feverish, pumped up beyond all possible seriousness, and thus dispatched.

In a far more muted tone, one of Keats's most moving lyrics is the Shelleyan "In drear nighted December" (1817). Its exquisite shape and dignified brevity barely rise up from silence even as the poet seems barely able to rise up from resignation:

> Ah! would 'twere so with many
>   A gentle girl and boy—
> But were there ever any
>   Writh'd not of passed joy?
> The feel of not to feel it,
> When there is none to heal it,
> Nor numbed sense to steel it,
>   Was never said in rhyme.
>
> (st. 3)

All of these experiments are minor works. One set of experiments was decidedly not minor: the great odes. In developing the melos for those poems, Keats brought to bear what he'd learned from all his varied attempts—again, and differently. Here, finally, he finds his voice and his vehicle.

IO

The Ode Stanza

IDENTITY can confine one's perspective. Keats believed that the poet needs to go forth from his own habitual self in order to discover the fullness of life. He often described the poet as a "camelion" rather than a great individual (L157). That he alone among the major Romantic poets did so has caused us to believe that this is the key to his thought. It is not. What Keats called "the wordsworthian or egotistical sublime"—the seeing of all experience in terms of the self—isn't the only way to poetic success (L157). But neither is Negative Capability. Or rather, Negative Capability and soul making must balance each other.[1] The imagination must dream, but must also awake and find its dream to be truth (L37).

The need for balance is evident in Keats's approach to melos. The poet needs to assume a negative character in order to learn, as it were from the inside, what past poets have done, thus to master the craft of verse writing. Melos is re-collection. But the poet also needs to find a voice. Great poetry balances repetition and difference, much as it balances rigor and exuberance, propriety and indulgence. The best poetry, Keats believed, occurs between these hypothetical limits. His imagination needed something to push against. He needed the creative tension he found when placing his voice within the given forms of prior poetry, most productively in the stanza. But he needed to find *his* stanza.

Bate has said that "[n]o poet of the last two centuries has so well exemplified, in his own habit of composition, that organic inseparability of style and subject to which we pay lip service as an ideal, though we often seem at a loss when we confront it concretely."[2] Maybe. Though "organic inseparability" owes more to New Critical formalism than to Romantic prosodic theory; organism doesn't necessarily exclude separability, since living things can lose parts of themselves as they grow and change over time. Even Shelley couldn't decide exactly how melos and meaning become and remain related. But Bate is right insofar as Keats spent his entire career trying to put into practice a belief that no poetic utterance succeeds unless enacted by its own poetic shape.

I say "poetic" deliberately. Shelley said that fiction involves "detached facts" related to each other solely by circumstance:

> The story of particular facts is as a mirror which obscures and distorts that which should be beautiful: Poetry is a mirror which makes beautiful that which is distorted.[3]

Shelley seems to have little room in his theory for the narrative poems he himself would write, or for the notion that poetry, whether lyric, epic, dramatic, or narrative, is, no less than fiction, conditioned both by the temporal circumstances in which it is written and by its own pattern of unfolding in time.

But Shelley's point is well taken. As Kramer argues, the central insight of Romanticism was the discovery of the individual consciousness as a phenomenon worthy of attention in its own right.[4] Romanticism was thus an undeniably poetic movement, in that poetry is organized primarily by the gestures of consciousness. More particularly, it was a lyrical movement. Ever re-collective, Romantic poets were sometimes too conscious of history, therefore anxious of their place, if any, in it. But, though the ghosts of mighty predecessors moved slowly through their minds and were a trouble to their dreams, the major Romantic poets did their best work in the lyric. And for a reason: the lyric's function is not to tell a story—as epic, dramatic, and narrative poetry must do to some degree—but to enact the intense emotions that make up the deepest experiences of consciousness. Being intense, the lyric tends to be brief. True to their Shakespearean and Miltonic pretensions, though, all the major Romantic poets, Keats included, would test the limits of this brevity by exploring longer lyric utterances, sometimes with the assistance of narrative. We noted in the last section how Keats's use of the Spenserian stanza re-collects literary tradition; we could point out here that another way it does so is in its length. "The Eve of St. Agnes" is far shorter than *The Faerie Queene*. At least some features of epic are thereby enabled to enter into a briefer poem. Brevity itself becomes part of that link the Romantics sought between poetry and life. A short poem is easier to re-collect: to read, put aside, and read again with insight acquired over time.

Andrew Welsh has argued that lyric poetry has several "roots." In each, sound and sense are intimately related. Song tends toward regularity and is often a social occasion; chant tends toward irregularity and complex patternings, and often has religious or mystical applications; speech freely alternates regular and irregular, and, in English, is the provenance of both iambic rhythm and the occasional departure from that rhythm.[5]

The lyric poet, then, can be a singer, a sorcerer, or a "man speaking to men." Lyric poems can exist in opposition to ordinary speech, or they can employ Special speech, or they can lead back to a changed ordinary speech. Keats, at one time or another, was all three kinds of lyricist. Sometimes he composed in regular stanzas, sometimes in complex sonic patterns, sometimes in a conversational yet not inartistic style. He wanted to re-collect all the kinds of lyric available to him, even as he wanted to re-collect all the kinds of time available to consciousness. He found a way to do both at once.

Though the lyric can follow the course of a single thought or feeling, and thus can be extremely brief, it can also trace a longer, more involved emotional history. This possibility may have been some comfort to Keats as he came up against his failures in epic. Perhaps the lyric could offer an opportunity for the extended composition with which poets prove their worthiness. Accordingly, Keats experimented with longer short poems like "Fancy," which he called a "rondeau" because it brought back its opening lines late in the poem. It enacted return with a difference (though, with its couplet rhymes and four-beat lines, not in a complex and deeply satisfying way).

He also experimented with the ode. This most extended and exalted of lyrics was traditionally associated with music. The word "ode" itself comes from the Greek *aidein*, "to sing or chant."[6] For Keats, as for many other poets, the ode is as close as poetry comes to music, and coming close to music is what the Romantics wanted to do with their poetry. Keats's odes, the greater as well as the lesser, are seldom without copious references to music: song, Apollo, lyres. Moreover, their melos enables Keats to discover and exploit his most characteristic voice. Much as the ode provided a structure for the choral celebrations of the ancient Greeks, so it provides Keats with an opportunity for the kind of soaring yet patterned flight he most valued.

In the ode Keats can be equally "mad" and "temperate." So he describes himself in the "Milton's hair" ode, which we examined in part 1. We also noted there that the poem's irregular form creates the breathlessness that Keats was trying to eliminate from his verse. "God of the golden bow" (1816 or 1817) also uses the free or irregular ode form. Perhaps Keats wished to show himself capable of designing his own poetic shape, thus to be worthy again of the god of poetry and music, whom he feels he violated by jokingly donning a laurel crown one evening at Leigh Hunt's house.[7] The more mature Keats might have laughed this off in the kind of wry letter he wrote even when dying. This poem is panting, youthfully sincere, and hopelessly conventional in diction and imagery. Unlike Wordsworth or Mozart, Keats here offers little that's new to tradition:

> God of the golden bow,
>   And of the golden lyre,
>   And of the golden hair,
>   And of the golden fire,
>   Charioteer
>   Round the patient year—
>   Where, where slept thine ire,
> When like a blank ideot I put on thy wreath—
>   Thy laurel, thy glory,
>   The light of thy story?
> Or was I a worm too low-creeping for death,
>   O Delphic Apollo?
>   (st. 1)

Keats had similarly limited success with regular odes. Neither the Horatian "To Hope" or "Ode to Apollo" (both 1815) seems to hold his attention. The latter appears to be a Pindaric ode written by a poet so preoccupied with "correct" diction that he fails to see he's not gotten the form quite right:

> Then, through thy temple wide, melodious swells
>   The sweet majestic tone of Maro's lyre;
> The soul delighted on each accent dwells,—
>   Enraptured dwells,—not daring to respire,
> The while he tells of grief, around a funeral pyre.
>
> 'Tis awful silence then again:
>   Expectant stand the spheres;   ·
>   Breathless the laurel'd peers;
> Nor move, till ends the lofty strain,
> Nor move till Milton's tuneful thunders cease,
> And leave once more the ravish'd heavens in peace.
>   (st. 3, 4)

Keats must have sensed, as he would sense also in the verse paragraph, that his voice was not coming through in given ode forms. He abandoned them early on.

Keats knew he needed more discipline. The Spenserian stanza offered a tight organization, a spacious line, and a strict yet flexible rhyme scheme. But Keats desired his own discipline. In "The Eve of St. Agnes," he'd gone as far as he could go then with Spenser's melos. Bate has pointed out that whenever Keats felt himself to be at a creative impasse, he turned to some new style; recall the radical shift from "St. Agnes" to "St. Mark," written immediately afterward. But this poem was also a dead end. In any case, both were narratives: not lyrics—the latter being the kind of poem to which, Keats was learning, he was more suited. He wasn't altogether pleased to discover this. He seemed to believe that the lyric was not an altogether serious mode. Paul Fry notes that for Keats it was always "a vacation from the labor of writing long poems."[8] Still, his little lyrics, insubstantial in themselves, helped him refine and expand his technique. He learned that he felt more at home in the stanza than in the paragraph, and in a five- rather than a four-beat line.

To make his short poems carry more weight, Keats often turned to the sonnet. This form offered at once great freedom of statement and the discipline of a given form: a looser shape, but a shape nonetheless, and one with a prestigious tradition. Keats often put pressing thoughts into sonnets while trying to figure out how to write more ambitious poems.[9] From early on, he could compose sonnets with great skill and great ease: "On First Looking into Chapman's Homer" was written in a matter of hours, "On the Grasshopper and the Cricket" in a fifteen-minute sonnet writing contest with Hunt. While many of these early sonnets are shallow, others like "On Seeing the Elgin Marbles" (1817) show the development of Keats's distinctive voice:[10]

> My spirit is too weak—mortality
>   Weighs heavily on me like unwilling sleep,
>   And each imagined pinnacle and steep
> Of godlike hardship tells me I must die
> Like a sick eagle looking at the sky.
>   Yet 'tis a gentle luxury to weep
>   That I have not the cloudy winds to keep
> Fresh for the opening of the morning's eye.
> Such dim-conceived glories of the brain
>   Bring round the heart an undescribable feud;
> So do these wonders a most dizzy pain,
>   That mingles Grecian grandeur with the rude
> Wasting of old time—with a billowy main—
>   A sun—a shadow of a magnitude.

In his "important" early works, we hear Keats attending to poetic propriety, even conventionality; in the sonnet, we hear Keats himself more clearly—the poet of light and shade, spring and autumn, immediacy and re-collection:

After dark vapours have oppressed our plains
   For a long dreary season, comes a day
   Born of the gentle south, and clears away
From the sick heavens all unseemly stains.
The anxious month, relieving from its pains,
   Takes as a long lost right the feel of May,
   The eyelids with the passing coolness play,
Like rose-leaves with the drip of summer rains.
And calmest thoughts come round us—as, of leaves
   Budding—fruit ripening in stillness—autumn suns
Smiling at eve upon the quiet sheaves—
      Sweet Sappho's cheek—a sleeping infant's breath—
   The gradual sand that through an hour glass runs—
      A woodland rivulet—a poet's death.

As was typical of the day, his early sonnets, including this one, "After Dark Vapours" (1817), were usually Petrarchan. Keats would come to associate that form, like the broken couplet, with all that was wrong with his early poetry. What he called its "pouncing rhymes" indulged the ear too often and too predictably,[11] tending, as in the sestet of the above poem, toward a random catalogue of too-sweet imagery.

In 1818, he turned to the Shakespearean form, from which he learned much: balance and repetition within the line, parallelism, alliteration, antithesis.[12] But this form also had difficulties. Keats felt it was "too elegiac." Its three iambic pentameter quatrains called to mind inevitably the use of that four-line form by eighteenth-century graveyard-verse writers. More important, the three quatrains sounded too distinct from each other, while the concluding couplet sounded too distinct from the rest of the poem, often lapsing into epigram.[13]

Unable to find what he wanted, Keats invented. "O thou whose face" (1818) is a completely unrhymed sonnet. "If by dull rhymes" (1819) has a highly involved and unique rhyme scheme:[14]

If by dull rhymes our English must be chain'd,
   And, like Andromeda, the sonnet sweet
     Fetter'd, in spite of pained loveliness;
Let us find out, if we must be constrain'd,
   Sandals more interwoven and complete
To fit the naked foot of Poesy;
     Let us inspect the lyre, and weigh the stress
Of every chord, and see what may be gain'd
   By ear industrious and attention meet;
     Misers of sound and syllable, no less
Than Midas of his coinage, let us be

Jealous of dead leaves in the bay wreath crown;
So, if we may not let the muse be free,
She will be bound with garlands of her own.

This sonnet has the gently binding, more interwoven sound Keats wanted. For one thing, the ordinary boundaries of the sonnet at the end of the fourth and eighth lines are overrun. Notice the soft partial rhyme of "crown" and "bound"; the distant rhymes of "chain'd" and "gain'd," as well as "sonnet sweet" and "attention meet," joined in the one case by being the same part of speech, in the other by the same inversion of noun and adjective. Notice also the low-stress linking verb "be" in line 11 matching the low-stress final syllable of "Poesy" in line 6, which makes the penultimate line's accent on "free," both as a sound and as an idea, that much more striking. Also striking is the effect of the final two lines; because they do not rhyme with each other, they are epigrammatic and memorable without seeming pat.

The difficulty here is that there is too little restrictiveness. In a sonnet where anything can happen, nothing can surprise. The poem, though skillful, does not show much of the artist maturing by facing given technical problems—what Wordsworth called "the sense of difficulty overcome." The question is, Did Keats as an artist really need to overcome the particular difficulties of the sonnet? A truly successful sonnet imposes a world view. Its structure—a quatrain, followed by another quatrain, followed by a sestet—typically mandates a specific argument, a set way of seeing: if X, and if Y (usually a counter to or an elaboration on X), then Z. In a very general way, this is the pattern of Romantic time (X and not-X both return with a difference in the poem's resolution). But Romantic time also requires much more intensive, and extensive, exploration of the relation of present and past, presence and absence, X and not-X. Hence Keats also faced a related problem: the sonnet's brevity. Whether Petrarchan or Shakespearean or free, the sonnet remained "a fresh if minor challenge."[15] Though it provided discipline, it also seemed to end before any ideas could be tested fully. Writing a few good sonnets, yet seeing his true calling in the long poem, he remained unsatisfied. This combination of small-scale competence and large-scale ambition urged him on.

Perhaps the experience of writing "If by dull rhymes" in the spring of 1819 catalyzed something: the sonnet could be manipulated. What Bate calls "the associational drag" of the sonnet was finally loosened.[16] If the sonnet could be manipulated in terms of its rhyme scheme, why not also in terms of its length? Here was a way to use something like the sonnet and something like the long poem, yet in Keats's own particular shape.

Here was a way to turn the burden of the past into an opportunity. England's poetic glories could be brought again to attention and put together differently with a single gesture at once utterly familiar and utterly new.

Keats's solution—one of those brilliant and simple strokes that characterize the great artist—was twofold. First, he broke up the sonnet into smaller units, and second, he deployed those units over a larger yet patterned stretch of lyric time. The result is the form in which Keats wrote his great odes. Typically, a Shakespearean quatrain is followed by a Petrarchan sestet to form the individual stanza.[17] Keats takes the best of both sonnet types and dispenses with the pouncing rhymes, the elegiac strings of quatrains, and the concluding epigrammatic couplets. Thus, the stanza itself is both roomy and tight, offering more lines than the Spenserian stanza, a more compressed logic than the sonnet, and a greater flexibility of rhyme than either. Departures from this scheme could themselves be productive of meaning, unlike in other set forms where departure generally means violation or incompetence. Most important, this stanza could be used in the single poem as many times as needed to begin, develop, and conclude an extended yet shaped flight of the imagination.

Structural integrity and emotional freedom combine. Keats finds his voice, even while fulfilling the criteria of Romantic melos. The way that the artwork sounds over time establishes, departs from, and returns with a difference to what is prior for the art (as per Wordsworth and Mozart), for the artist (as per Coleridge and Haydn), and for the artwork itself (as per Shelley and Beethoven). The melos of the individual ode stanzas re-collects the sonnet tradition, as well as Keats's own efforts in the sonnet. The melos of the poem as a whole, by means of the stanzaic shape that moves forward and back, re-collects itself. It also re-collects Keats's earlier attempts in the ode, as well as the history of the English ode and, indeed, of the English lyric itself. Special and ordinary language renew each other. The singer, the sorcerer, and (to borrow Wordsworth's idea if not his narrow phrasing) the person speaking to persons: all these come together. Like music, the odes' melos turns time's pattern into a source of meaning and value. So does the odes' overall form, as we'll see in the following pages.

PART THREE

The Songs of Spring: Music as Organizational Principle in Keats's Poetry

The Extended Tonal Organization

Thomas MacFarland has described Wordsworth's *Prelude* as "Beethovenian, not only in its grandeur but in the tentativeness with which it searches for themes and prospects after it is actually underway."[1] Keats's greatest poems are motivated by similar, and similarly musical, energies.

For Keats the greatest poetry was epic: Milton's *Paradise Lost*, Spenser's *Faerie Queene*, Wordsworth's *Excursion*, which Keats cited as one of the "things to rejoice at in this Age" (L48). Great poetry was also dramatic: Keats expressed a hope that Shakespeare presided over his own work (L12). He associated his grandest plans with these two kinds of verse. "I think I shall be among the English poets after my death," he writes his brother George as he dismisses harsh reviews of *Endymion* and prepares to write *Hyperion* (L161). And to his friend Benjamin Bailey he writes, "One of my Ambitions is to make as great a revolution in modern dramatic writing as Kean has done in acting" (L276).

The evidence—*Endymion, Hyperion, Otho the Great, King Stephen*—suggests that Keats's talents did not lie much in the way of epic or drama. These are all either fragments or works of lesser quality. Paul Robinson, when discussing Keats's failure to master larger and more complex forms, argues that, as is the case with Schubert, intensity, not comprehensiveness, makes his great art what it is. But, continues Robinson, Keats is for that reason a lesser artist than Chaucer or Shakespeare or Milton, whose work is "longer and richer, if not more beautiful."[2]

Faint praise. We might respond, yes, but Keats died at twenty-five. This misses the point too. Keats was not Shakespeare or Milton, and, though it's impossible to say for sure, he probably never would have written like either. As long as we judge him by standards we use to judge those artists, we'll miss the source of his power and the magnificence of his accomplishment. Perhaps what Keats called "the grand march of intellect" had by his day rendered suspect any poetry that did not "think into the human heart" (L96). Lyric poetry, organized primarily by feeling and thought, can do this in ways that epic and drama, organized primarily by more concrete events, cannot. Keats wanted to write epic or drama, but his gift, like his era, was lyrical.

The lyric has become the prevailing mode in modern poetry. This tells us both that Keats was on the right track and that his work helped determine the right track for modern poets. Though Keats himself may not have appreciated his own accomplishment in the lyric, later writers have. As I argued in part 2, Keats's ode stanza re-collects the roots of lyric: song, chant, spoken language. The great odes themselves do even more. Keats did write a great large-scale work, for that is what I take the odes to be. Their coherence as a group proceeds from Keats's discovery of how to bring dramatic tension and epic scope into the already expanded purview of the lyric.

The ode is traditionally the most important and exalted of lyric forms. It provides an opportunity for lyric poets to demonstrate the full extent of their powers and speculations. As Paul Fry points out, the ode "raises questions more steadily than any other poetic mode about the aesthetic shibboleth of the unified whole." But, according to Fry, the ode by its nature also experiences a tendency toward what he calls "prolepsis."[3] Raising questions so energetically, it simply must cut itself off at some point in order to end. The ode's grandeur and eager questioning surely appealed to Keats's ambitious and searching mind; if he could do anything important in the lyric, he could do it here, and perhaps he could find some way to avoid prolepsis as well. In the great odes, he doesn't so much abandon each poem as enable it to give way to another ode. The boundaries of the individual poem break open.

What exactly allows for this move from one poem to the next? Though many critics have argued that some principle unifies the odes, few have made a concerted effort to find it, much less to explain it. Helen Vendler believes that "the most important context for each of the odes is the totality of the other odes." She asserts that the odes are related in special ways, specifically that each of Keats's efforts in that form somehow extends or comments on earlier efforts.[4] Vendler goes on to give readings of the odes individually. While each is excellent, none throws much light on her assertion about the odes' unity.

According to Vendler, the temporal organization of the odes—the ability of later odes to comment on earlier ones—is crucial to how they work. In our terms, poetry is in essence re-collection. But we can be more specific. Understanding begins as intuition. Whenever the issue of temporal organization arises, intuition suggests that a good place to begin looking for an analytical method is music, the art where time is most palpable and most palpably organized. This intuition seems correct here, and for two reasons. First, the ode began in ancient Greece as a musical entity and has remained closely associated with music ever since. Second, music was always important to Keats, frequently providing a vocabulary and a model for his most crucial concerns.

Not surprising, then, that in the great odes Keats most fully succeeds as an artist, nor that music is central to that achievement. Bernard Blackstone has said that "a use of a musical analogy will prevent the odes from being considered, as all too often, in isolation from each other and from the rest of John Keats's poetry, thus making the odes appear incoherent (or, worse, darlings of New Criticism)."[5] In other words, these poems refuse to yield to premature resolution, and there's more to this refusal than illogic or irony.

But what musical analogy should we use (and must we use an analogy)? Linda Barlow believes the odes constitute a group because each displays the same musical organization: in following Stillinger's "basically Keatsian shape" of real–ideal–changed real, each is like the sonata in music with its A-B-A' pattern.[6] But this provides only a very general analogy with music. The formula A-B-A' can describe any number of rounded binary forms in music, whereas the sonata involves highly specific events. And Barlow's model says little about how one ode moves to another in a sequence—if, in fact, such is the case.

Perhaps we're on the right track and need only to broaden our scope. David Michael Hertz has argued that large-scale structure in music enacts small-scale events; the overall piece seems so right because its logic is the logic of its component parts.[7] For example, the chord progression C-G7-C is enacted and echoed on a large scale by lengthy regions of time involving tonal stability, instability, and recovered stability. The means of organization arise out of the materials being organized.

Such may be true of poetry as well, and this is what I meant when I said at the end of part 1 that in Keats's use of music, the global proceeds from the local. We've seen that for the Romantics the act of hearing, like the act of knowing, involves an established meaning, a departure from that meaning, and a return to that now-enriched meaning. The moment is itself a duration of Romantic time. Perhaps, then, Barlow's sense of the individual odes being like the sonata may be accurate and relevant. Each ode follows a rounded binary pattern—the pattern that, on a local level, informs the use of melos, and, on a global level, informs the odes as a sequence. Whereas "The Eve of St. Agnes" and "La Belle Dame sans-Merci" are organized by the deployment of musical imagery, the odes as a sequence, though they may use such imagery, are organized by *a sonatalike musicality.*

Why the sonata? For one thing, it is the most logical place to look for the paradigm of what music is supposed to be in the late eighteenth and early nineteenth centuries. Able to organize a vast and variegated amount of musical material with strictly musical means, the sonata tended to be for the age's composers what the ode was for the age's lyric poets: a means of working out their most important ideas. Further, the sonata is dramatic: a conflict between restlessness and repose, between formal integrity and innovation, between regions of time marked by varying degrees of tonal stability. It's also epic: a large, complex, serious piece of music that wrestles with large, complex, serious matters like the adequacy of music's own materials to provide coherence and resolution. And it organizes its epic scope and dramatic tensions with an essentially lyrical shape. That is, the sonata signifies dramatic conflict on an epic scale by enacting temporal and emotional experiences, such as loss and recovery, which are the stuff of lyric.

We're attempting to clarify poetry by examining music, and here, it must be admitted, we're clarifying music with poetic terms. I'm not sure there's any way around this. Poetic analysis must sometimes borrow from the rich vocabulary with which musical analysis describes combinatory meaning. But to understand exactly how music means, musical analysis must sometimes borrow from the rich vocabulary with which literary criticism describes referential meaning and emotional experience. Poetry is like music because music is like poetry: a methodological loaded deck.

The more fruitful way to regard the situation, however, is this: We use poetic terms to understand music, then, having achieved an understanding of music, we effect a return with a difference. Those terms, enriched by their passage through another art, can now tell us more about poetry. In that light, the sonata can clarify how Keats's urges toward epic and drama found fulfillment in the lyric.

We ought to be more precise about what happens in the sonata. It is *an extended tonal organization.* That is, using tonal relations, it moves coherently through several regions of time. In the first, tonal stability is established and then questioned; in the second, tonal stability is lost; in the third, tonal stability is recovered and reaffirmed. The first movement of Beethoven's Symphony no. 5 offers a good example of the form.

The movement begins with the famous dot-dot-dot-dash motif: a note rapidly repeated three times careens into a sustained note. This motif is then repeated at a lower tonal level. Notice that the composer suggests three things right away: the piece will be an interplay of opposing forces, such as headlong energy and sudden braking; it will be an interplay of repetition and difference; and, because the source of both repetition and difference is the ability of a severely brief motif to be placed on various tonal levels, the piece will also be an interplay between minimal materials and maximal development. Beethoven will demonstrate what grand music can be built by relying solely on the organizing power of tonal relations.

The movement quickly develops a rich and restless texture. The home key is established in correct fashion by the sounding of the dominant chord (G) followed by the tonic chord (C minor). Typically, Beethoven accentuates this establishment of the tonic by a sudden, brief forte: when the home chord appears, the music gets very loud and then pauses. Beethoven wanted to make music as self-sufficient as possible. Tonality was one way to do this, texture another. As Wallace Berry says of this movement, "Extreme foreground manifestations hav[e] vital and consistent signification."[8] This is something relatively new in music history: dynamics and orchestration become part of the structure, indispensable to how the music makes sense.

The music begins again on another tonal level. The dense, active texture builds up once more, leading to a modulation, or change of key, to the relative major (the key that uses the same notes as C minor but whose center of tonal gravity is E-flat). This again is the correct move. So is the sounding here of an eight-note theme that is much more melodic, much less rhythmically driving, than the initial four-note motif. Again, texture articulates structure. Now the piece is a dual entity. It experiences allegiances toward different keys. Though each key is stable in itself, their copresence in the single piece destabilizes the music. Thus the composition is provided with a reason for moving forward in time. Structural dissonance creates a need for resolution.

The new tonal area is itself destabilized. Key feeling slides back into minor. Then the major key returns. All the instruments sound the four-note motif, and the dynamic level swells to a double forte. With its loud, fully orchestrated, repeated progressions from dominant to tonic, this passage feels like a cadence or ending. But we're ending in the wrong key. We began in C minor. Now we're in E-flat. The opening motif has returned; but where is its tonality? Beethoven creates unease amid this definitive major-key cadence. We may sense an ending; but we sense an even stronger need to carry on, to work out precisely and satisfyingly the relationship between C minor and E-flat major.

Now ends that part of the sonata called the exposition. (The music is marked with repeat signs here, but this is one instance of a repeat with virtually no significance. Before electronic recordings and mass media, an audience needed to hear the themes and tonal progressions more than once to become familiar with them. Since the repeat adds nothing architecturally, an observation of it today is pedantic, and most modern conductors ignore it.) The development section follows. Here, the four-note motif is tossed about from key to key. Sometimes it's combined with the second, eight-note theme; sometimes the second theme is heard alone in various permutations. Characteristically, Beethoven develops at length material formerly heard in passing. The trivial becomes the grand. For example, a motif sounded by the horns that had introduced the second theme in the exposition is brought back in the development, then is broken up and echoed extensively between strings and winds in slower time values (quarter and half rather than eighth notes). All tonal feeling loosens. Numerous keys are formed and deformed. Motivic material is fractured and recombined until there's nothing left but one note repeated quietly. Everything has been deprived of whatever power it had in the exposition. Now the music will discover what, if anything, can rebuild itself.

After some false starts that increase the tension, the four-note theme finally returns. Intact, it clings tenaciously to C minor in the loudest and longest-held notes of the movement. Now begins the recapitulation. The initial measures of the exposition are repeated note for note. C minor has proved able to recover its own materials (the four-note motif). But it has one more task. Can it bring into its tonal gravity the materials of E-flat (the eight-note melody)? Again building the tension, again demonstrating how much music can be extrapolated from minimal materials given the power of tonal relations, Beethoven prolongs the issue. Recall the pause early in the exposition. Now that silence is filled by a meandering oboe. A hole in the texture is filled, but what fills it sounds improvisatory, arbitrary, out of place. The music is less solidified than challenged—in the recapitulation, where questions ought to be tending toward answers.

The oboe leaves off, the interruption is glossed over. The music moves on to the second theme. But we're not allowed to forget that we've passed through this disturbance. The movement re-collects itself no less than it re-collects, with all its "correct" and "incorrect" touches, the traditions of the sonata form itself, including Beethoven's own earlier and more conventional sonata movements. In the exposition, the second theme had been introduced by the horns; in the recapitulation, it is introduced by the bassoon. This makes for a softer, deeper, darker tone. The oboe's woodwind sound has led, via the bassoon's woodwind sound, to yet another disruptive moment.

Beethoven isn't changing things as much as acknowledging that things have changed. The recapitulation returns to the materials of the exposition. But return involves difference. The changes in the music—texture is structure—articulate our changed perception of that music. To find tonal stability, the music must first lose it. Recovery exists because of loss; loss will then be part of how recovery feels. The individual phrase must progress from tonic through dominant to tonic for the tonic to have any power; similarly, the home key of the sonata must progress from the stability of the exposition through the lack of stability in the development to the recovered stability of the recapitulation. But having lost the ability to resolve once, can the music regain that ability?

It does. This is the moment that makes the sonata what it is, the specific return with a difference that sets the sonata apart from all other rounded binary forms: *the second theme must be heard in the tonality of the first.* Only then will the home key really feel like home. Accordingly, the second theme is played in C major. Something of a compromise to please all parties: the second theme gets to keep its major feel, but the tonal center is now C, not E-flat. The music is structurally complete, though, as we'll see, Beethoven manages to find more work for it to do, eventually charting a course back to minor, whose reappearance is both satisfying and disturbing. Resolution by its nature is questionable. In an art made of time, answers and compromises work for only so long.[9]

To explore what the sonata offers poetic analysis, we must address this issue: Before it is epic or dramatic or lyrical or anything else, the sonata is an extended tonal organization—a procedure for organizing large-scale regions of time with tonal relations; can the same be said of poetry?

A sonata is not a sonnet. The words resemble each other by etymological accident.[10] More to the point, musical meaning is primarily combinatory—the unfolding of a patterned duration that is in itself a coherent experience. Verbal language is primarily referential. Combinatory meaning is always present but usually tacit. If, in a verbal utterance, combination can share priority with reference, then that utterance can act musically. It can make temporality an unusually active component of its syntax, organizing the experience of time with the efficiency and complexity of a musical composition.

What exactly do we mean by musical compositions? To avoid the difficulties (and vagueness) of transhistorical analyses, deep structures, and the like, we should first explore whether the music of the age can help us. In the compositions that the Romantics knew, organization means tonality: musical sense can be established solely by tonal relations. To assert that Romantic poetry can be organized musically, then, is to assert that Romantic poetry can be organized tonally. Is this justifiable?

Obviously, poetry lacks notes and chords, thus key relations. But, as John Neubauer puts it, "[t]he demand that all the original connotations of a term be relevant in the new context is clearly impossible to satisfy. We should ask rather whether the term has a specific function and, perhaps, a new dimension of meaning in the new context." Calvin Brown speaks of poetic "keys" as "different phases of one basic idea," that is, contrasts between tenses, between moods, between strong and weak alliterative schemes, and so forth. But, Brown concludes, these are "only very general analogies." They entail no relations inherent in the material itself such as relations among keys or among a scale's notes and chords.[11]

Northrop Frye says that the "emphatic use of thematic words" is like tonality.[12] This is also a very general analogy. In music, tonality establishes structure; theme only makes that structure more easily perceivable. Further, a theme in music is the musical surface, whereas a theme in poetry is (supposedly) an abstract statement summarizing the poem but not appearing within the verbal surface. Arguably, theme doesn't even exist in poetry. David Perkins has called "unwarranted" the assumption that any abstract statement can summarize a poem. As Michael Black puts it, the meaning of the poem is the experience of the poem.[13]

Meaning as experience: Black describes this as "the music of words," the rhythm and resonance of mental sounds and mental activity, a complexity of symphonic powers and extent. Music turns experience into meaning, and it uses tonality to do so. Perhaps, as Black senses, poetry does this too. But we must try to define poetic tonality in poetic terms. Steven Scher warns that we should avoid metaphorical paraphrase of the effects of one art in terms of another.[14] We're looking for residents, not tourists.

M. L. Rosenthal writes of "the basic or radiating unit of poetic structure" as being "a specific quality, and intensity, of emotionally and sensuously charged awareness."[15] He calls this the poem's tonal center. Such is not a theme, Rosenthal says, except in the musical sense. A qualified yes: theme in music is not structural, which is what Rosenthal argues that tonality in poetry is. But like a theme in music, the tonal center of a poem can't be found anywhere but in the language, texture, and pace of the poem itself.

Keats himself was attracted to this musical term. We saw in part 1 that he believed the finer tone is in essence an again-ness, something added to experience by memory. As an example of this phenomenon, Keats chose the re-collection of a musical performance (L37). He does say "tone" rather than "tonality," and tone in music means the individual note, which has little if any organizing power in itself. But Keats's finer tone is clearly something that acts like tonality in music; both organize a range of interpretive possibilities by ordering the experience of time. Like poetry itself, the finer tone, though not music, acts musically.

Others have used such terms in similar ways. Hertz speaks of reading in a "tonal" way: a systematic ordering of question and action that reduces (and, we might add, thereby enables) potential meanings. D. W. Harding speaks of "a readiness for the time being to allow one range of allied emotions to be more easily activated than another; the corresponding fact in literature is the 'key' or 'register' in which we feel a work to be written, preparing us for one sort of emotion rather than another (and opening the way to special effects of contrast . . .)."[16]

These formulations of verbal tonality all involve two notions: first, a center or focus of affinities around which certain thoughts and emotions cluster; second, a clustering that takes place only in and over a patterned duration (recall Hertz's "systematic ordering" and Harding's "readiness for the time being"). The recurrent use of musical terms in these descriptions—tonality, key, register, rhythm, harmony—suggests, if nothing else, that there is something in poetry that consistently makes its readers think about music, and in ways involving not general analogies but specific literary qualities.

We can hazard a definition. Tonality in poetry is not any particular utterance but rather *a range of possible utterances* governing and governed by a particular complex of affiliated ideas, feelings, and language. I do not mean a union of form and content—they're never disunited to begin with and every utterance has *some* temporal shape—but rather a means for allowing referential and combinatory gestures to embody and enact each other in such a way that they make equal and equally palpable contributions to meaning.

Tonality is a poetic means particularly appropriate to Romanticism. Tonality is re-collection insofar as *these* ideas, feelings, and language achieve meaning when brought together as a combination unique to this poem that differs from the meanings they achieve alone or in other combinations. And tonality is re-collection because the relations within and among such complexes occur only in and over time. Tonal meaning is temporal unfolding. For tonality to work as an organizing principle, it must demonstrate the power of tonal stability. This stability must be tested: established, then lost, then recovered. That test is most effectively accomplished by a contest between at least two tonal centers. Tonality means tonal relations: no change in key, no need for resolution, therefore no large-scale shape of time. A tonality comes into being as a complex. It is an affiliation; it includes. Thus it also excludes. Its adequacy can therefore be questioned, which is what a second tonal center does. The relation between the two is worked through until one tonality proves itself. It does so not by eliminating or repressing the other, thus demonstrating an awareness of itself as unstable, exclusive, and inadequate after all, but by "comprehending" the other. It finds a place within itself for the materials of the other.

As we've observed, poetry lacks the relations found in music: no tonic and dominant, no minor and relative major in verbal language. But in the idea of exclusivity, Romantic poetry has a relation as inherent to itself as key relations are to music. For Keats, Romantic time means a move from ordinary through Special to a different kind of ordinary time. The characteristic feature of ordinary time is a sense of exclusivity between its usual and unusual forms, between the way time feels when experience is understood as "reality" and the way time feels when experience is understood as "fancy." One calls forth the other even as it calls the other into question. A sense of the world as constituted upon opposition follows. From that sense all imaginative experience departs, and to that sense all such experience returns, changed somehow.

I wish, then, to refine what I asserted earlier about the odes: as a sequence they are organized by a sonatalike musicality residing within the materials of poetry itself. Though differing in fundamental ways, music and poetry can share what Lawrence Kramer calls "structural rhythms"—ways of organizing change and provoking interpretation.[17] I will call such sharing "cognate structural rhythm." By structural rhythm, I mean the pattern and pace of the artwork's unfolding, the ways in which the experience of time, as organized by the artwork, govern the artwork's meaning. By cognate, I mean those phenomena that, though they act in ways unique to each art's language, take their origin from the same or similar gestures of consciousness. Using tonal relations, longer poetry can dispense with narrative scaffolding. The experience of consciousness of and over time is the fundamental concern of Romanticism. Poetry organized tonally according to a structural rhythm cognate with the sonata is the expression of that concern.

We can predict that such poetry will move through several regions of time. The first will be "expository," involving the presentation of tonal stability and of a challenge or challenges to that stability. This destabilization will drive the poetry forward toward a hoped-for recovery of stability. The poetry will enter into a second, "developmental" region. Like Special consciousness, this region will cause previous material to lose its integrity. All tonal feeling will weaken. The sense of exclusivity between the tonalities will break down. Their relation will be re-collected for the purpose of being imaginatively explored, complexified, deepened. This prepares the poetry to enter a third, "recapitulatory" region. The original tonalities will be returned to with a difference, re-collected for the purpose of finding a resolution unavailable before the development. New relations and kinds of relations will become possible. At best, such a state will be insight. But the poetry, in acknowledging return and change, may wonder about the value of that change and the process that led to it.

Since the poetry must provide some cue that we are in *this* region and not in some other, each region will show a characteristic treatment of tonal feeling: stability yet diversity in the expository region, extreme instability in the developmental region, a different kind of stability in the recapitulatory region. Boundaries within and between regions will likewise have certain characteristics. Four types of boundary are possible: strong between regions, weak between regions, strong within regions, and weak within regions. Because tonality establishes structure, a strong boundary will involve a change of tonal feeling. Within a region, this means a shift from one set of ideas, feelings, and language to another; between regions, a loss or recovery of tonal stability. A weak boundary will involve some change other than a tonal one—a slight shift in, say, diction or imagery. Such boundaries will probably be found within regions, since those between regions should be more strongly marked.

In a sequence things have to be ordered. My ordering of the odes takes into account their compositional history, though our knowledge of when they were written is sketchy. Jack Stillinger's impeccable scholarship allows us to be sure only that "Ode to Psyche" was written before 30 April 1819; that "Ode to a Nightingale," "Ode on a Grecian Urn," "Ode on Melancholy," and "Ode on Indolence" were written sometime in 1819, perhaps in May, perhaps later; and that "To Autumn" was written during the afternoon or evening of 19 September 1819 in Winchester.[18] Conceivably, a poem I've placed earlier in the sequence was written later than some I've placed further on. All artistic careers involve advances and retreats. The arbiter is the experience of reading the poetry itself. As the following chapters will show, the order in which I place the odes is itself a patterned duration, a tonally organized unfolding. The ode stanza's melos re-collects what is prior for the art, the artist, and the artwork; the form of the odes considered as a whole re-collects what has priority for words: the balance between modes of signification is shifted in such a way that the combinatory dimension of verbal language, normally tacit, becomes explicit. Like music, the odes feel like Romantic time.

The Expository Region

For our model to work, we need first to find the odes' tonalities. Since tonality is the organization of time, we might expect that tonally organized poetry will devote attention to time itself. Such is the case, as a number of critics have observed.

David Perkins sees in the odes equally strong urges toward forgetfulness of and participation in process; Keats's imagination here impels him toward freedom from earthly limitations and toward sympathetic, emphatic responses. Christopher Salvesen calls the odes "a specific contest in terms of time," noticing in them a tension between the inaccessible past and historical continuity. John Barnard says the odes are a prolonged meditation on time: what's in and out of time, what's normal and not-normal time, and time as residing in or threatening the imagination.[1]

This dwelling on time can be seen in the odes' language itself. Jackson Bate has shown that the odes share features characteristic of Keats's mature style: few run-on lines, short native words, long vowels and bilabial consonants. Most interesting for our purposes are two things: first, metrical substitution is generally heavy (a trochee or spondee, seldom a pyrrhic) and generally confined to line beginnings, thus slowing the first several beats and quickening the rest; second, past participles are used frequently, providing a "highly dynamic power, caught momentarily in repose . . . a rich and heavy . . . music" that nevertheless has "strict sobriety and classical restraint."[2] Keats's style itself coordinates temporal experiences ordinarily exclusive, such as fast and slow, restless and restful, moving and still.

Apropos these experiences, Jacob Wigod says that Keats wanted "two irreconcilable things." He desired life in all its fullness and richness and variety. Stemming directly from this desire is a "profoundly melancholy awareness" that variety consumes itself. Because time gives and takes away, Keats also wanted "to arrest these ripe moments and hold them permanently."[3] Here we see the two tonalities, as well as the necessary relation between the two, that set the tonal organization moving through the process of working-out. One complex of ideas, feelings, and language is centered on an awareness of and a trust in time; opposed to that awareness and trust, yet emerging directly from them, is another complex of ideas, feelings, and language that desires freedom from time. This description doubtless appears reductive—as we've noted, no abstract statement summarizes poetry—but the odes themselves will bear out what I've sketched here.

The next task is to find what Donald Sutherland calls "an episode of potentiality":[4] those odes where these tonalities are established but not explored, or are explored minimally. The "Ode to Psyche" and the "Ode on Indolence" present such an expository region. Stillinger says that "Psyche" was probably written before all the other great odes, and that it "is not so clearly organized as the other odes and has frequently seemed the most difficult to integrate with the rest in a unified scheme."[5] These considerations are to the point. "Psyche" is a beginning. Less achieved than the other odes when considered by itself, it introduces concerns explored elsewhere. As the beginning of an expository region, it is itself as untrodden as that mental region where the poet wishes to be.

"Psyche" begins with a brief invocation. It seeks direct address, even direct control ("O Goddess! hear"), of an eternal entity. Yet it acknowledges process, in fact, embraces time's ongoingness. The poet's utterance is "wrung / By sweet enforcement and remembrance dear" (1–2). That utterance itself is composed of "tuneless numbers." It is tuneless poetry because it acts like the numbers of music but without the tunes that must be sounded by music itself, and it is waiting to be fine tuned, being now little more than an enforcement, albeit a pleasurable one, of a technique that succeeds by numbering syllables and counting stresses. The poet is aiming for high art. For now that art lies in the future. Like Beethoven's dot-dot-dot-dash motif, Keats's opening move tells us a great deal about what will happen in this poem and in the odes at large. The poet seeks immediate contact with that which is out of time. But he can do so only in time. He must, in fact, build that entity with a memory that exists only when it is built by the poem's words.

The poet details that memory:

> Surely I dreamt to-day, or did I see
> The winged Psyche with awaken'd eyes?
> I wander'd in a forest thoughtlessly,

> And, on the sudden, fainting with surprise,
> Saw two fair creatures . . .
>   (5–9)

The poet hurries the discussion, trying to move forward in time. What the poet experienced could have been a dream or a memory (and what exactly distinguishes the two?). But whether fanciful or real, the experience is *past*. An issue that will later become central—do I wake or sleep?—is here glossed over. The entire poem contains only two questions; they are both in the opening stanza, and the second is as rhetorical as the first. The poet wants to be declarative now. He wants to move from memory to prospective consciousness. Whatever happened, how can I use it now? I want to cease wandering thoughtlessly, and instead use my experience to steer a course into and through imagination.

This desire is both enacted and fulfilled by the relation between the second and third stanzas. The poem uses its own materials to move from old to new. In stanza 2 the poet bemoans the lack of an appropriate cult to worship Psyche; in stanza 3 the poet says, with much the same language, that he will dedicate himself to the establishment of such a cult.

> O brightest! though too late for antique vows,
>   Too, too late for the fond believing lyre,
> When holy were the haunted forest boughs,
>   Holy the air, the water, and the fire;
> Yet even in these days so far retir'd
>   From happy pieties, thy lucent fans,
>   Fluttering among the faint Olympians,
> I see, and sing, by my own eyes inspired.
>   (36–43)

Conventional religion is dead, the world desacralized. The poet will "build a fane." But he will locate this place of worship "[i]n some untrodden region of my mind" (50–51). This location is fitting: Psyche is the goddess of the soul, of the inner person. The poet is inspired by his own vision. Using his own mind, he will fulfill that most ardent desire of Romantic consciousness: the transformation of loss into meaning.

The future tense in the poem's final stanza is worth noting. The poet *will* do these things. The future *will* fulfill his desires. Time is the medium in which the poet achieves his goals. The traditional images of religion—the teeming censer, the pale-mouthed prophet—are brought again to mind, though put together differently, by being put, literally, *in* mind:

> And there by zephyrs, streams, and birds, and bees,
>   The moss-lain Dryads shall be lull'd to sleep;

And in the midst of this wide quietness
A rosy sanctuary will I dress
With the wreath'd trellis of a working brain,
   With buds, and bells, and stars without a name,
With all the gardener Fancy e'er could feign,
   Who breeding flowers, will never breed the same . . .
                        (56–63)

Out of this process comes poetry. Thoughts are branched, arranged like lines in a stanza; they murmur in the wind, speaking by means of the poet's inspiration, that is, his highest ideas, and his breath or lived experience, and his words or breathed utterances.

Only time can bring the poet to this state, since that state is not-now. "Psyche" recognizes itself to be moving toward the future by using the past as its vehicle. The poet admits he needs time: his desires began in memory, and their fulfillment is yet to come. My poem can act imaginatively; re-collecting its own materials, it discovers a many-at-once entity like "pleasant pain" (52), though it also admits that this is imagination of a low order. Now is not then, but it will be. I trust time, trust the way it ordinarily progresses. Therefore I trust the ordinary consciousness with which I perceive this time. From the imperative beginning to the prospective ending, the poet sounds sure, open, ready to embrace change for the sake of the future. That's what makes the tonality of this poem expository. That's also a reason why the lyric shape here is so loose, so variable, so very much itself a celebration of mutability. Notice the polarization between usual and unusual consciousness: I am aware of time as a simultaneity of nowness and passing-away-ness. I accept the passing-away-ness not because of imagination, the faculty that provides many-at-once, but because of fancy, the faculty that provides a picture of what is *not* here, *not* now. Things grow and die, the poet admits; but in admitting this, he can point to what's on the way.

The confidence expressed in the final stanza—"Yes, I will be thy priest"—is embodied by the last quatrain. In the other three stanzas the final four lines had stood alone by virtue of the rhyme scheme, but not until now do they stand alone and resolute as an independent grammatical unit. The alternated three-beat lines hurry the pace as the poet envisions himself moving forward in time toward a better future. The poet waits for warm love to arrive by an open casement—itself a closing-up and an opening-out, an end and a beginning. Keats has created a strong sense of both finality and expectation. Both past and future are certain.

But a darkness has been introduced. If "the gardener Fancy" must "feign," then is Fancy to be trusted? Is "feign" a pun on both "fane" and "fain," the poet expressing a suspicion that the religion of art is as questionable as it is desirable? The poem stops short of admitting that what it really wants is not the future but timelessness. How can it do so when it trusts so in time? The poet wants to use memory, but he also wants memory to be a means toward fixity. Witness the image the poet had used of the lovers Psyche and Eros. Statuesque in a statuesque landscape, they come close but do not actually touch:

> . . . couched side by side
> In deepest grass, beneath the whisp'ring roof
> Of leaves and trembled blossoms, where there ran
> A booklet, scarce espied:
> 'Mid hush'd, cool-rooted flowers, fragrant-eyed,
> Blue, silver-white, and budded Tyrian . . .
>
> (9–14)

The frequency of past participles here—verb as quality, action suspended—manifests the divided character of the poet's desire. He wants memory to be fixed: these images are certain because I feel as if they really happened. Yet he also wants memory to be fluid: because they also seem dreamed or fancied, I wonder what else I can do with them; how can they be something more than *scarce* espied? To usher in the future I want, I must change the present; but if I change the present, I run the risk of disturbing that vision I am remembering now—the vision that all my hopes are founded on. As the form of the poem is highly variable, never settling on any stable stanzaic shape, so the poet is thirsting for infinite variety and perpetual blossoming. But flowers that are never the same are nevertheless flowers that change and grow and die. Because the poet trusts time to fulfill his desires by changing the present into the future, he must also acknowledge that time takes away as much as it gives. How else would "these days" have become "so far retir'd from happy pieties"? Reality passes. Therefore permanence, even the permanent joy of infinite variety, is fanciful. Yet it is no less desirable for that. It may, in fact, even be more desirable (fane = feign = fain).

Recall that Beethoven builds his expository region on the tension between minor and major. This should not be understood to be a tension between "sad" and "happy." The minor scale tends to be restless because it involves chromaticism in its various forms; for example, in the key of C minor, the note B-natural is substituted for B-flat at cadential points to allow a half step, thus a stronger feeling of finality, between the seventh and tonic degrees of the scale. The major scale, having only one form, tends to be stable. "Sad" and "happy" are only the most obvious emotions related to these experiences. On a more complex level, the minor scale offers the listener a more palpably felt embracing of change, process, and dynamism than does the major. The second tonality (the relative major) uses the same notes as the tonic minor with a different center of tonal gravity, and enables a shift from the restless motif to a less urgent, more static melody.

We cross a similar boundary (strong within a region) between "Ode to Psyche" and "Ode on Indolence." Same problem, different tonality: not forward drive but stillness as a way of coping with time. "Psyche" implies that trust in time may be a concealed urge toward timelessness. "Indolence" follows directly from this implication, and attempts to proceed in the opposite direction. Here is a mind made blissfully unaware of temporality by its own low energy. Indolent even in his temporal setting, the poet describes three figures he saw "one morn" while in a dreamy mood of receptivity. Note the stillness, the frozen flow, of his memory—and of the frequent past participles with which he describes it:

> With bowed necks, and joined hands, side-faced;
> And one behind the other stepp'd serene,
>   In placid sandles, and in white robes graced:
> They pass'd, like figures on a marble urn,
>   When shifted round to see the other side;
>   (2–6)

The poet did not recognize the figures. They came again, and still he did not know them because "[t]he blissful cloud of summer-indolence / Benumb'd my eyes; my pulse grew less and less" (16–17). Time's manifestation in the body—the rhythm of the pulse—loses strength. The poet's condition here ("Pain had no sting, and pleasure's wreath no flower") is like the Beadsman's lifeless religiosity in "The Eve of St. Agnes." In both cases, the breakdown of individual qualities owes less to imagination than to lassitude. This semiawareness is unusual but ordinary consciousness: let me forget my cares for a while.

The figures passed by the poet a third time. When they turned their faces to him, he recognized them; he brought his two previous encounters with them again to attention but put these encounters together differently. The throstle's music of stanza 5 had given access only to a very dim and dreamy state of mind; similarly, the poet was still very much in the realm of ordinary consciousness when he recognized the figures:

> My sleep had been embroider'd with dim dreams;
> My soul had been a lawn besprinkled o'er
>   With flowers, and stirring shades, and baffling beams . . .
>   (42–44)

The figures he saw were Ambition, Love, and his "demon Poesy." At first he ached for wings to fly so that he could follow them; then he recognized this as folly. None of these was able to offer him anything that he would prefer over "evenings steep'd in honied indolence" (37). What the poet really wants is

> an age so shelter'd from annoy,
> That I may never know how change the moons,
> Or hear the voice of busy common-sense!
>
>   (38–40)

Here is the crux of the poem, the fullest statement of its tonality. The poet recognized the figures. He has had an encounter with them predating the indolence that they interrupted and that he now wants to regain. That encounter occurred in "Psyche," where the poet, inspired by a vision of Love embodied, made ambitious plans to write poetry. His indolence arose directly from these plans: given that perhaps what I really want is not the future but timelessness, why must I wait? I can achieve that state now by shutting down my mental energies, by attempting to locate my deepest, therefore most troubling, desires outside myself. If the figures are not-me, then I needn't worry overmuch about fulfilling or betraying them.

Memory disturbs indolence. Yet memory also provides the sense of indolence the poet wants to recover. Notice the present participles in Keats's description of what accompanies indolence: stirring shades, baffling beams. Indolence is itself composed of process. Fittingly, almost the entire poem is a memory—a sense of now as arising out of not-now. It moves from past to present tense only at the end, though not exactly in an effort to shift to the future. The poet wants the figures to vanish, and, if time stops, then they will not reappear. All will be as it was.

Perhaps an awareness of this state's contradictions—memory as a desire to be rid of memory—accounts for the stinging tone of stanza 6:

> For I would not be dieted with praise,
>   A pet-lamb in a sentimental farce!
> Fade softly from my eyes, and be once more
>   In masque-like figures on the dreamy urn;
>   Farewell! I yet have visions for the night,
> And for the day faint visions there is store;
>   Vanish, ye phantoms, from my idle spright,
> Into the clouds, and never more return!

As in Beethoven, we're ending the exposition more or less where we began, but something's wrong. The poem closes with the sort of direct address with which "Psyche" opened, yet we've begun to question it. Now and not-now, self and not-self are not as exclusive of each other as the poet might have us believe. Any utterance founded on this exclusivity and attempting to take control over it comes into question. There can be little doubt that further exploration must follow. Nor can there be doubt that the poet is up to the task. For one thing, all the questions we've raised as readers are raised first, albeit in passing, by the poet himself. For another, in "Indolence," finally, is the ode stanza established as we observed it in chapter 10. The poem may be *about* indolence, but the poem itself, at least in terms of its melos, is a highly accomplished act of bringing again to attention and putting together differently. Re-collecting what is prior for the art, the artist, and the artwork, it attempts to exorcise the love, ambition, and demon poesy *with* the demon poesy he so loves and for which he has such high ambitions. The figures themselves depend for their being on the poet's words.

The poem retreats from these contradictions. This retreat is itself part of its tonality. The poet is in the realm of ordinary if unusual consciousness, which is constituted on a desire not to face usual experience. But even a sheltered age is an age, during which, the poet implies, the moons would still be changing, though unbeknownst to him. Perkins says that for Keats, permanence is "lasting participation in some moment of fulfillment."[6] Here, the poet implies that this notion may not necessarily stand.

Subsequent odes will pursue such implications, challenging the ideas, feelings, and uses of language found here. Now that two tonalities have been established, the poetry has the dramatic tension necessary to drive forward through a quasi-epic scale of time. We trusted time. Then we questioned that trust. Then we questioned that questioning. Not that any of these was "wrong": under certain conditions, each is correct. Similarly, opposition and exclusivity, which acknowledge (and sometimes rejoice in) a gulf between now and not-now, are desirable under conditions that these poems detail. But, as Keats himself argued, the thinking principle awakens in time. We want to explore the other chambers of life's mansion, to see into the life of things. Now that we've read "Indolence," we can't go back to "Psyche." As Clifford Adelman puts it, there is "no resting place in reality or in dreams; the former is not living, the latter is enthrallment."[7] Where can we go?

13

The Developmental Region

PERKINS has called "Ode on a Grecian Urn" and "Ode to a Nightingale" the most complex and satisfying of the odes. Unlike the others, which tend to take only one side of an issue, these fight out a drama within themselves.[1] Their complexity makes them fitting for a developmental region. What was presented in the expository region will come under close scrutiny in an attempt to find what can and what cannot lead to tonal stability. The tonalities, as well as the relationship between them, will enter imagination. There, to paraphrase Coleridge, they will be dissolved, diffused, and dissipated in order to be re-created.[2] All will be doubt, uncertainty, mystery, and—for a time—there will be no irritable reaching after fact and reason.

"Grecian Urn" takes up where the expository region left off. It examines the made thing that "Ode to Psyche" wanted to build and "Ode on Indolence" wanted alternately to fly after and to fly from. Here we have a more detailed look at what happens when "the urn once more is shifted round." A strong boundary between regions is crossed: the entire feeling of tonal stability is gone.

The poet begins by addressing the urn:

> Thou still unravish'd bride of quietness,
> Thou foster-child of silence and slow time,
> Sylvan historian, who canst thus express
> A flowery tale more sweetly than our rhyme:

Though this is similar to the direct addresses in "Psyche" and "Indolence," the address, being no longer an imperative but an apostrophe, has lost its original force. But it has picked up another force. In the expository poems, it seemed an attempt to cross a perceived gulf between opposites—self and other, time and timelessness. Yet it functioned for the most part as a vehicle for getting on with other utterances: O goddess, listen to the following poetry; begone, visions, so I can be sheltered from annoy. Now the poet wishes to explore not only the ability of such an address to break down exclusivity but also the grounds of exclusivity itself. Such is the characteristic feature of Keats's Special time. The word "still" itself contains the many-at-once quality of Special time: the bride is both frozen in time and is not yet (but perhaps will be in time to come) ravished.

Jeffrey Baker says that Keats in this poem freezes the moment in order to move back and forth between poet and object. Again, a many-at-onceness, a dissolving of opposition between self and world. Perhaps. But the moment isn't exactly frozen, nor does that dissolution take place outside time. As Earl Wasserman puts it, the urn belongs to slow time, not to no time.[3] It approaches, but does not achieve, a state of fixity. It is not a child but a foster child, adopted by the poet as a means for examining timelessness in the temporal context of a poem. Both expository tonalities are present though different: silence shelters the urn from the busy voice of common sense, and slow time brings the future without creating change and decay, which are the usual ravages of time.

The poem's language helps to create this slow time full of silences. Special language for Special time: note the heaviness of the accented monosyllables, the short periods creating pauses in which to contemplate questions that come far more frequently than they'd done in the expository odes, the headlong rush created by enjambment, the cutting off of that rush with the braking action of end-stopped lines and choppy phrases:

> What leaf-fring'd legend haunts about thy shape
>> Of deities or mortals or of both,
>>> In Tempe or the dales of Arcady?
>> What men or gods are these? What maidens loth?
>> What mad pursuit? What struggles to escape?
>>> What pipes and timbrels? What wild ecstasy?
>>>> (5–10)

"Heard melodies are sweet," the poet goes on to say,

>>> but those unheard
>> Are sweeter; therefore, ye soft pipes, play on;
>> Not to the sensual ear, but, more endear'd,
>> Pipe to the spirit ditties of no tone . . .
>>> (11–14)

In a way, this is a rejection of actual music. Music is time. It is beauty that must end. Ideal music seems attractive. The grounds for seeing it so, as well as the grounds for its opposition to "real" music, will soon be questioned. For the moment, the poet can believe that without time, music cannot be consumed by itself. Such stasis also holds for (and holds) the lovers depicted on the urn.

> Bold lover, never, never canst thou kiss,
> Though winning near the goal—yet, do not grieve;
> She cannot fade, though thou hast not thy bliss,
> For ever wilt thou love, and she be fair!
> (17–20)

Like Eros and Psyche, the lovers will never touch and therefore never be consumed by their own desires.

Wasserman points out that the high incidence of negatives in this poem ("thou canst not leave / Thy song . . . nor ever can those trees be bare . . . never, never canst thou kiss") creates an indefinitely prolonged present; by the avoidance of positing, Keats achieves "an absolute extension of the time that passes."[4] Little in the poem is affirmed, much as nothing on the urn is real and therefore subject to decay: "Ah, happy, happy boughs! that cannot shed / Your leaves, nor ever bid the spring adieu" (21–22). The passion on the urn is far above the ordinary, time-filled passion that "leaves a heart high-sorrowful and cloy'd, / A burning forehead, and a parching tongue" (29–30). The urn, as a made thing, belongs to the realm of that-which-is-finished.

The use of the present tense throughout the poem is appropriate to this Special time of indefinite prolongation. But Special time is characterized by the breakdown of exclusivity in the imagination. It embraces contradiction. No surprise, then, that the poem itself does so. It seeks to be purely present, yet it points to the past: the stanza is the same as in "Indolence." In a similarly contradictory vein, the poem is and is not a ditty of no tone. It has no tone because, in relying for a part of its meaning on melos, it acts somewhat like music but without musical notes and tones; and it does have tone because the ode itself is a poem—the sonic product of a burning forehead and a parching tongue, of the thought of an active brain and the speech of impassioned language. The poem's sound itself seeks a slowing of time that is possible only when time moves forward. It seeks to pipe to the spirit; yet it must rely on the body—on the eyes if not the ears—to apprehend its patterned sounds.

A consciousness of its own contradictory many-at-once-ness grows throughout the poem. Characteristic of a developmental region, the tonal feeling shifts radically as the urn is yet again shifted. It's possible that a contemplation of timelessness can come only out of such radical shifts and contradictions, making it impossible to dwell fully on any one image, thus never allowing restlessness to set in. Time and timelessness, passing-away-ness and nowness are intimately related. Unheard melodies as tunes that unwrite themselves: tearing themselves apart so that they will not last too long, they present nothing but an eternally postponed start. The urn is both finished once and for all *and* never really begun.

Such a condition of apparent changelessness can be, for the same reason, attractive or repelling, as the poet discovers when he focuses on "those coming to the sacrifice." Because this image is fixed, the "lowing heifer" will always be caught in its terror, the town will always be emptied of its folk, "and not a soul to tell / Why thou art desolate, can e'er return" (39–40). The citadel will always remain desolate—empty and forsaken. No possibility for *telling*—for any use of language, including poetry—exists here.

If lovers that never touch can never part, neither can they ever really become lovers. What "Psyche" and "Indolence," and the earlier lines of this ode itself, had presented with confidence becomes a problem. The urn is "overwrought, / With forest branches and the trodden weed" (42–43). Here the "branched thoughts" of "Psyche" are both forever done branching and forever unable to begin branching. The poet realizes that the urn is beautifully made, but, like *Hyperion*, too much so. To build, the artist must enter and trod the "untrodden region" of his mind. On the urn, however, what's trodden can never grow back.

The urn is attractive but hollow. Like the sea's caves or Milton's live temple or Madeline's hollow lute, this is the shaped emptiness that is another characteristic of Keats's Special time—what Susan Wolfson calls "a field of absences": "absent certainties, about knowledge, about answers"; it elicits nothing so much as questions posed to and because of these absences by "a strength of intelligence."[5] The urn presents, finally, a stillness on the surface of blank plenitude. To be seen as beautiful, it must be interpreted as such, and interpretation, being a re-collective act, can take place only in time. The urn is seen, then, as a "cold pastoral." It will live; but those who view it will die.

Not that the urn is without value. It does delight us now, and will continue to delight others after time has wasted this generation. The poem again radically shifts tonal feeling; many thoughts and feelings come rushing at once. "Beauty is truth, truth beauty." Melos enacts meaning: being all the same, the accented long vowels in that phrase join beauty and truth emphatically. The assertion's sound confirms the assertion's validity.

Yet, as many readers have sensed, the equation of beauty and truth is not a very satisfactory way to conclude the poem. The dictum seems too easy, especially in light of what's come before. It is all we know on earth and all we need to know only in those moments when we can believe that beauty stands outside time, that what is true now is true always. Those moments, though real, pass. But in the context of the odes as a whole, the poem's end need not be a conclusion. Doubts about timelessness will propel the poet into another ode. In fact, he continues to question in the very line that appears to set aside questions. Béautў / ís trŭth, / trúth béautў. Both parts of that phrase involve metrical substitution, disrupting the language's iambic fabric. The artist's work makes itself clearly visible—or audible, rather: what the artist does is manipulate time; what the artwork does is participate in temporal patterns. The assertion's sound confirms but also challenges the assertions's validity. In the many-at-once-ness, the blank plenitude of Special time, we can, at the same moment and for the same reason, reject and want to believe in timeless truth.

"Ode on a Grecian Urn" challenges the made thing as well as the fixity and timelessness that it supposedly provides. Something hinted at in the expository region becomes overt: nature is itself a made thing. In "Ode to Psyche," it was a metaphor manufactured to describe that most desirable region of the mind. Located in a future that time would bring, that region also partook of a desire for timelessness: once that future becomes the present, it will not change. That future, in fact, can always be present *as* a future. Hope can provide a permanent prolonging of that season sheltered from a knowledge of the changing moons. Here, this stasis, as imaged by the fixity of the "natural" scenes on the urn, proves both unreliable and undesirable.

What about nature in itself—not the made thing but the found thing? This is what "Ode to a Nightingale" explores. In its opening lines, "Nightingale" locates art in the past. "My heart aches, and a drowsy numbness pains / My sense, as though of hemlock I had drunk / . . . one minute past." That "as though" belongs to figurative language, and figurative language, like an urn, is a made thing. As a poet, I combine. I put dissimilar things together to concretize a point. But I want to leave all that behind. A moment ago, when I contemplated the urn, I tried to do something like drinking hemlock: forgetting about time by means of the apparent permanence of art. It didn't work. The dryad of "Psyche" returns, changed: now awake, now singing, it pours forth its soul in "such an ecstasy"—an ex-stasis, a going-forth, a making palpable the passage of time with sounds that are musical but not quite music.

We have crossed a weak boundary within a region. Other ideas, feelings, and language come to the fore, but we remain in Special time, which is characterized by the breakdown of exclusivity. The poet's heart aches, but it does so because it is "too happy." The poet wishes to join in essence with the bird's song, and the act of trying to do so makes him ever more aware of himself, of his own happily aching heart. To go further into nature, it seems is to go further into the self, that is, to return to self with a difference. The poet now wants to believe that he is part of nature.

"Ăwáy! Ăwáy! Fŏr Í wĭll flý tŏ thée." Keats uses his "principle of melody in verse" here to effect an alternation between stressed long vowels and unstressed short vowels. Many at once: Special (and highly artificial) language leads to ordinary nature. The poet will fly toward the bird's song, not using "artificial" intoxication such as wine, but on "the viewless wings of Poesy" (33). In fact, he realizes, he is "already with thee!" The act of writing the poem has already allowed him to join the nightingale. This is a crucial moment in the poem, and in the ode sequence in general. The stanza pattern itself here seeks to distance this poem from the previous odes: its truncated eighth line is something new, whose brevity adds speed to the language. Confidence in the forward motion of time is renewed. But this remains in essence the ode stanza, and the ode itself, though it may seek to locate art in the past and reject artificial intoxication, remains a poem—the highly wrought utterance of a consciousness that hears art in nature, music in the noise made by a bird.

The opposition between made thing and found thing breaks down. Art is brought back from rejection "a minute past" to enter the poet's attention to nature; nature is brought back from not-made-ness to enter the poet's attention to art. Again, melos is meaning in this ode's Special language: Paul Fry has pointed out how contrast is undermined by repetition, as in "*leave* the world unseen" (19) and "[w]hat thou among the *leaves* hast never known" (22—emphasis added).[6] With sound, the poet joins his desires with the location of the nightingale's song. The made thing and the found thing are already joined by virtue of their both being objects of consciousness.

This move may join self and world, but it may also locate the world in the self—in which case, all beauty is as mortal as its perceiver. Retreating from this issue, the poem shifts radically. The poet leaves behind all the products of imagination, as well as all casting of imaginative light over nature (as in "The Queen Moon and all her starry fays"). He enters the realm of "the coming musk-rose, full of dewy wine." All is possibility. Nothing is made *or* found.

A way to preserve this state is to cease perceiving it. "Now more than ever seems it rich to die" (55). Beauty survives me: given that I "scarce espied" Psyche and Eros, it's likely that if I'd not espied them at all, they'd still be there, still beautiful. If my awareness ceases, then so will my sense of time's ravages, my vision of youth growing pale and "spectre-thin" and dying. But the nightingale's song, I feel sure, will go on. Time always moves forward. This forward motion is precisely the source of the song's beauty—and, in fact, its timelessness: though music must unfold over a certain duration, the song has survived down the course of the centuries. "The voice I hear this passing night was heard / In ancient days by emperor and clown" (63–64). Much as the music can appeal to opposed levels of society, thereby calling into question their opposition, so the music can appeal to both past and present, thereby calling into question *their* opposition. They become linked in one continuous flow.

But all the examples the poet gives of the song's history are just that: history, the made thing, the product of a consciousness that is, for the Romantic, fundamentally re-collective. Would the song exist if it weren't perceived? The poet and the song are both located in time, but where to locate time? Does the song "really" exist, or is it an object in the poet's imagination, merely a device for working out a poem?

There can be no going back to "Grecian Urn" now, no confidence about what is to happen when old age shall this generation waste. The poet's sense that the song would remain even if he died undermines itself. The song has always been beautiful because it has always been heard. It must, therefore, continue to be heard to be beautiful—or even to be. Unheard melodies are not sweeter after all. Beauty and mortality are one; a song *is* because it can end. "[T]hy plaintive anthem fades" (75). Vendler believes that this ode is Keats's response to the actual art of music.[7] This may be so, but it is also the case that, for this ode, all music, "natural," composed, or otherwise, is both made and found, both ideal and real. The poet's encounter with sound—be it the song of the nightingale or the making of a poem—provides an opportunity to interpret the passage of time as loss *and* beauty. Whether the song ended or relocated can't be known. What perhaps can be known is my response to having had this experience. I respond to music much as I respond to time: it attracts me because it is always falling away from me, always just beyond my reach.

I explore that response by re-collecting, which, as a poet, I do by writing re-collective poetry. "Forlorn! the very word is like a bell" (71). Language has power in itself. The word wrenches me back to me. Even the word's sound ("like a bell") does this; melos is re-collection. The poem's speaker is finally something that exists only in the poem. He comes back, changed, to where he began. The goal of "Psyche" has been reached: the poet exists in that region of his mind where poetry is made. But the intervening odes have thoroughly trodden that region. The poet wishes to produce the art that "Grecian Urn" explores, and also wishes to live (and to have his art live) in the "reality" that "Nightingale" explores. Yet both that self and that sense of reality depend on the act of writing. Composing poetry itself "tolls" the poet—calls him like musical sound, and makes him pay a price—when he returns

> . . . to my sole self!
> Adieu! The fancy cannot cheat so well
> As she is fam'd to do, deceiving elf.
>
> (72–74)

The poet has learned that world and self complicate each other, as do found and made, nature and art, time and timelessness. Clearly, they are not the same; just as clearly, they are not opposed. What then are they? The poet ends by declaring himself unsure. Negative Capability takes one only so far. The rhyme of "self" and "elf" joins those two ideas ironically. The self, though changed, reasserts itself over and against the imaginative, which seems now, in its apparent inability to provide insight for ordinary time, no different in essence from the sort of elfish things that Fancy provides. Unusual and Special consciousness, the fanciful and the truly imaginative, get confounded because both seem to stand at a remove, finally, from the needs of day-to-day life.

The casement from "Ode to Psyche" and "Ode on Indolence" appears again. Here, in this framing that is also an opening, may be a clue about how to resolve the relationship between the odes' tonalities. The poet must try to maintain as wide a perspective as possible, but he must also give that perspective a context. The imagination must awake, find its dream to be truth, and build a soul in order to create a finer tone unique to that identity. Stillinger points out that "Ode to a Nightingale" is the first ode to bring the speaker firmly back to reality.[8] He has gone as far as he can into the realm of Special consciousness. This return from imagination to ordinary consciousness is not a resolution but a crisis. "Fled is that music": music's ability to make loss meaningful is itself lost; Special time can't sustain itself. Now what? "Do I wake or sleep?" A passing question in "Psyche" now brings the entire flow of poetic logic to a halt, much as the reappearance of the four-note theme in its original key had halted development in the Beethoven movement. "Indolence" and "Psyche" must be returned to, but with a difference. The recapitulatory poems will attempt to work out this return, and to find a place for this difference.

14

The Recapitulatory Region

ODE to a Nightingale" mingled elements of the tonalities from "Ode to Psyche" and "Ode on Indolence" in realizing that the song's beauty exists because of time, yet in also wishing to freeze (or to die in) the moment of that realization. In Beethoven, the development's vigor led to an exhausted passage of a single sustained note repeated softly; similarly, Keats's intense re-collection of expository tonalities led less to resolution than to a stagnant and paralyzing synthesis: imagination as a fanciful cheat. Both fixity and radical indeterminacy had a place; but neither could sustain itself. Now comes a sudden burst of energy, a sure plunge back into the tonality of "Psyche."

We cross a strong boundary between regions when we leave "Nightingale" and enter "Ode on Melancholy." This ode has a powerful feeling of tonal stability—the strongest thus far in the sequence, and for several reasons. Its stanza is exactly the same shape as the stanzas in "Indolence" and "Grecian Urn"; the poet's attitude is sure, almost summary; and, as Stillinger points out, this is "the most logically constructed" of the odes. The first stanza shows how not to act; the second, how to act instead; and the third, the outcome of that action.[1]

"Melancholy" begins as a rejection of the rejection of memory, which amounts to an acceptance of process:

> No, no, go not to Lethe, neither twist
>   Wolf's-bane, tight-rooted, for its poisonous wine;
> Nor suffer thy pale forehead to be kiss'd
>   By nightshade, ruby grape of Proserpine;
> Make not your rosary of yew-berries,
>   Nor let the beetle, nor the death-moth be
>   Your mournful Psyche . . .

176

This was originally the second stanza. Keats cancelled a weak first stanza from his initial draft.[2] There, the poet warns that Melancholy, because it is always complicit with beauty and joy, cannot be relegated to locations and images traditionally associated with sadness. By beginning the poem with the above stanza, Keats shifts his emphasis—and connects this ode more closely with the other odes' concerns. The issue ceases to be where Melancholy cannot be located, and becomes that Melancholy cannot *not* be found everywhere. Don't do what the speaker in "Grecian Urn" and "Nightingale" wanted to do. We know now that these efforts don't work.

It is not clear whom this address is directed to—probably not a timeless entity. Notice that Psyche now is mournful. The soul is memory, and memory is mortality: what was once is now no more. A sense of time as running on and running out tempts the soul to desire forgetfulness; but that desire cannot be fulfilled. If not a timeless entity, then whom? Possibly some time-bound other, though the poet challenged in "Nightingale" the opposition between self and other. He is likely addressing himself as much as any possible other. To fly to nature is to employ the artificial wings of poesy; to go forth is to return. Thus he also rejects the forgetfulness offered by the developmental odes. Awareness is return with a difference. Notice that the poet does not reject the mournful Psyche. The soul itself remains. It neither waits for a future fane nor engages in fanciful feigning; instead, it locates itself here and now, full of beauty and sadness. The soul is nonforgetting, and nonforgetting is consciousness of both meaning and loss.

Rather than attempting, necessarily in vain, to forget sorrow, one should feast on it.

> But when the melancholy fit shall fall . . .
> Then glut thy sorrow on a morning rose,
> Or on the rainbow of the salt sand-wave . . .
> (11, 15–16)

To fail to acknowledge the inevitability of sorrow is to fail to take insight from imagination, thus to live in enthrallment to imagination. Every beginning contains an ending within it: flowers are "droop-headed," springtime is "an April shroud," a rose lasts only the morning. The wave in breaking breaks the rainbow, but its very transience is the cause of the rainbow.

> . . . if thy mistress some rich anger shows,
> Emprison her soft hand, and let her rave,
> And feed deep, deep upon her peerless eyes.
> (18–20)

I accept my lover in all her moments. Unless I do so, I will get none of her moments. What causes melancholy also causes hope and peace and joy.

The tonality of "Ode to Psyche" is recovered—with a difference. Time is forwardness, thus opportunity. It is also loss, and is so precisely because it is opportunity. Here is the insight generated by having passed through Special time's breakdown of exclusivity. Time makes beauty. The finer tone is an act of repetition, and repetition depends on original loss.

Recall how Beethoven handles this moment in his recapitulation. Even if we were to hear the exposition note for note again after the development, we would hear it differently. Now we have lived through a time when its stability was lost. Beethoven articulates our changed sense of these notes and chords and rhythms with changes in orchestration. The oboe "cadenza" especially suggests that here, at the heart of recovery, lies change—not despite, but because of this being a return. Tonal resolution can only come after tonal instability. The most precious things become so only when we realize they can be lost.

As Paul Ricoeur argues, time has meaning—is "deepened"—only when a consciousness mindful of its finitude participates within it.[3] "She dwells with Beauty—Beauty that must die" (21). Who is this "she"? Thy mistress? Melancholy? The female component of the poet's male soul? In a way, it doesn't matter. The mistress's beauty *is* melancholy. It—and she, and the poet, and the poem—live only because they can die.

The mature Keats has learned that a thing of beauty is *not* a joy forever. I cannot see time simply as the force that will someday somehow usher in the fane in the untrodden region of my mind. But neither can I see it simply as the ravager:

> . . . Joy, whose hand is ever at his lips
> Bidding adieu; and aching Pleasure nigh,
>   Turning to poison while the bee-mouth sips:
> Ay, in the very temple of Delight
>   Veil'd Melancholy has her sovran shrine . . .
>   (22–26)

I must write poems: structures of sound that begin, develop, and end. The shrine I should seek is not some timeless fane of imagination. Rather, it is

> seen of none save him whose strenuous tongue
> Can burst Joy's grape against his palate fine;
> His soul shall taste the sadness of her might,
> And be among her cloudy trophies hung.
>   (27–30)

Neither the priest of Fancy nor the pet lamb of poesy, the poet is the artist of the strenuous tongue, of language that shapes and is shaped by time.

The future tense from "Psyche" returns, but for a different purpose: time, in moving forward, will show that joy and sadness are inextricable. Like the storm at the end of "The Eve of St. Agnes," time is a boon because it is a threat. That poem had shuttled its resolution off into poetic and temporal distance. As such, it failed finally to clarify its own insights. The same might be said of the end of "Melancholy." The poet has deepened his sense of time as process. But he has yet to address the expository region's other tonality: that thirst for timelessness that arises directly out of the sense of process. Is there any alternative to the sense of time as moving inexorably forward? Must I give up all hope of happiness because I embrace the inextricability of beauty and process? If so, am I willing to give up beauty in order to be happy? The ending of "Melancholy" will not seem satisfactory, and the odes as a sequence will not be structurally complete, until the tonality of "Indolence" is felt in terms of the tonality of "Psyche." Time as process must somehow both preserve and transform time as stillness.

This act of preservation and transformation occurs in "To Autumn." We cross a weak boundary within a region. Though the specifics of the tonality change, the feel of tonal stability in "Autumn" remains as strong as in "Melancholy." We return with a difference to the expository region's second tonality. Like "Indolence," "Autumn" seeks timelessness, but its search is chastened by the experience of the developmental odes and "Melancholy." As in the expository region, the second set of materials emerges from the first. "Melancholy," in declaring useless all attempts at forgetfulness, suggested that life involves memory; going forth involves going back. "Autumn" follows up on that suggestion. A kind of timelessness is possible—not cessation, but re-collection: time moving forward to circle back on itself. The season sheltered from annoy is repeated in a finer tone.

It is no accident that this recursive motion sounds like the rhythm of the seasons. From the beginning of his career, Keats had been trying to find insight in nature—recall the sonnets "On the Grasshopper and the Cricket" and "On the Sea." As we've seen, those works were at once too general about what such an insight might be and too specific about where insight could occur. "Autumn" remedies that. As C. M. Bowra points out, Keats wants to show in the odes that imagination, neither an unsatisfied longing nor an end in itself, "stands in some essential relation to truth and reality." Keats fulfills that desire here. According to Bowra, in its imaginative contact with the ordinary world, "Autumn" avoids both longing for something unattainable, as in Poe, and disillusionment, as in Wordsworth.[4]

Actually, what "Autumn" is all about is disillusion—literally: both nature and the poet are dis-illusioned. Each becomes as fully as possible what it can be by enabling the other to become as fully as possible what it can be. Nature is neither opposed to consciousness nor identical with it; rather, it participates with consciousness in the creation, destruction, and re-creation of beauty.

In addition to explaining the poem's focus on seasonal change, this sense of participation also helps to account for the lack here, unlike in the prior odes, of a speaking "I." It's not necessary. Nothing is real until experienced; no self is real until it experiences. If the world is present, so is the self. That is, the world doesn't become "the world" until it's perceived, and the self doesn't become "the self" until it perceives. Like joy and grief, one makes the other possible. In addressing Autumn, the poet is apostrophizing as he'd done in the expository region; but he is also addressing himself—more specifically, his own sense of this moment of this season. Keats further weakens the boundaries between lyric, epic, and drama. The supposedly inner events of lyric and the supposedly outer events of drama and epic are inseparable. Note that this is the only ode that Keats doesn't title as such. It is simply "To Autumn." This poem is unique among the odes in another respect. One of the more appropriate accidents of textual history is that this is the only ode about which we know precisely when and where it was written. "To Autumn" is very much the utterance of a moment and a mind participating fully in each other.

That moment is a still and lovely landscape. But this is "Indolence" after "Grecian Urn," "Nightingale," and "Melancholy." As Andrew Welsh puts it, time is both passing and not passing here.[5] The manipulation of this complex temporality within the poem is one of Keats's greatest achievements. The first stanza is loaded and blessed with images of stillness, fullness, ripeness, readiness to begin what has not yet begun:

> To swell the gourd, and plump the hazel shells
>   With a sweet kernel; to set budding more,
> And still more, later flowers for the bees,
> Until they think warm days will never cease,
>   For summer has o'er-brimmed their clammy cells.
>
> (7–11)

With its high incidence of sound turning back on itself, the melos here is similar to that of the Spenserian stanza in "The Eve of St. Agnes"; the verse's sound at once re-collects literary history and Keats's past work. But here that dynamic of turning-back is given greater flexibility and a relevance specific to this poem, in such a way that the sound re-collects prior events in the ode sequence. Thus, "To Autumn" fulfills both that sequence and the criteria for Romantic melos (re-collection of what is prior for the art, the artist, and the artwork). Notice that the stanza in "To Autumn" is Keats's standard ode form except for one crucial difference: it contains an extra line. This line, penultimate in the stanza (and in the passage above), forms a couplet not with the final line but with the one preceding the penultimate line. This is not a witty epigram at the end but a chance to circle back even while reading on, to hold time still for a moment. Finally we proceed with a gathered momentum to the last line. This line rhymes with the stanza's seventh line, repeating on a broader scale the couplet's effect: we go back to go on. Sound re-collects itself, creates itself, and pushes itself into the past with one motion. Using not altogether attractive images like clammy and o'er-brimmed (emphasis added), Keats even lets a note of restiveness creep in. We have paused; we are ready to move again.

The second stanza shifts to images of harvest. With the same picture, time moves forward. The direct address of the expository poems is recovered with a difference, as is the high incidence of questions in the developmental region. Here we find a soft-core apostrophe, not to a deity, but to an unspecified figure that could just as easily be the poet poring over the loveliness of this day as the spirit of Autumn:

> Who hath not seen thee oft amid thy store?
>   Sometimes whoever seeks abroad may find
> Thee sitting careless on a granary floor,
>   Thy hair soft-lifted by the winnowing wind;
> Or on a half-reap'd furrow sound asleep . . .
>
>   (12–16)

"Half-reaped": like the poem at large, like time itself, the image moves forward toward full reaping and circles back toward not-yet-reaped. We are in midmoment, and in midpoem. The moment holds past, present, and future. What we call "now" is a moment in a duration, and is itself a duration, full of the past and liable to become past. The present is a location for the poet to become inspired, much as the stanza pauses to take a breath in its tenth line before plunging again toward expiration.

Another note of impatience creeps in: "Thou watchest the last oozings hours by hours" (22). The word "oozings" has a sticky feel to it, as if the poet is being held back from a desired shift of focus where sound is not asleep. That shift comes in the third stanza. Here the harvest is complete. Winter is impending. Arnold Davenport has shown how Keats very carefully creates this multidimensional temporality: the barred clouds *bloom* the soft-*dying* day; the wind *lives* or *dies;* the *small* gnats form a *choir* (i.e., a large group) that *sinks* and *rises;* the full-grown lambs (who are only called lambs when not full-grown) bleat *loudly* but in the *distance* (25–31, emphasis added).[6]

Again, sound becomes important. This is neither music as made nor music as found, but sound that becomes music by virtue of being perceived by the poet and organized into harmony in the poet's temporal experience. Here, finally, Keats has found a place for music as insight. As Richard Macksey argues, the songs of spring—the odes written in May of 1819—are displaced by music without words: the cricket's song, the lamb's bleating, the swallows' twittering. Macksey finds in "Autumn" not the "elusive grasping at experience and art vainly sought in the more feverish language and crisis rhetoric of the great poems that immediately preceded it," but "the serene tone of a new music."[7]

We can be more specific. The image of song is no longer necessary. Now we have words about music without words. This is an imaginative interpretation, embodied in and enacted by sound, of apparent emptiness in the ordinary world—a poetic response to life-in-time. "Autumn" re-collects the rhetorical music of the expository odes: the tuneless numbers of "Psyche," the pleasant and harmless throstle's lay of "Indolence," the declarative language of those poems. And it re-collects the Pythagorean music of the developmental odes: the ditties of no tone, the ecstatic, wordless melodies that inspire an urge to fly "Away! Away!," the questions and sudden shifts of those poems. In so doing, it arrives at the affective music of a consciousness that, because it has attended to and passed beyond the other kinds of music, becomes a new kind of ordinary consciousness. As Christopher Salvesen puts it, "Memory begins as (re)excitement or regret but ends as understanding and acceptance of the passage of time (which in turn leads to a calm, wisely passive release from time)."[8] With the seasons as its emblem, time moves forward but also circles back on itself. The harvest, in turning the fields from growth to stubble, makes way for new crops.

The final line confirms the poet's acceptance of timelessness-within-time: "gathering swallows twitter in the skies" (33). Present participle takes the place of past participle. The second tonality is placed in terms of the first. Even in stillness there is process. Death is not here, but it is coming, and its very impendingness makes this moment as beautiful and as precious as it is. "Where are the songs of spring? Ay, where are they?": memory is a cycle of question, affirmation, repeated but changed question. The forward motion of time presents an opportunity to go back, pause, re-collect, and then move on to more re-collections. Every moment is part of every other moment. Meaning is loss, loss meaning. That, in the end, is all you *can* know on earth.

When Beethoven's second theme is heard in C major, everything balances for a moment—a moment made of and by virtue of passing time. The sonata moves back in order to move forward toward its resolution. As "Autumn" shows, consciousness itself is no less re-collective. This is no gentle going into the good night, no simple resignation to loss. It is hard-won insight about how to live, how to face time in a way that neither insults intelligence nor belittles grief. Poetry, which is the process and product of secondary imagination, differs from consciousness, the process and product of primary imagination, only by degree. They merge when the mind employs language, actively and intensely, to search out the fullness of experience, the depth of time. We cannot remain where we are; but, since nothing in time is not available in this moment, we cannot and must not refrain from coming back, though changed, to where we were. Only by doing so can we write poetry. Moreover, only by doing so does life become meaningful. Autumn becomes music, time becomes beauty in any form of consciousness, poetic or musical or otherwise, that accepts that each moment is a liability leading to the silence of winter, thence to new and renewed songs of spring. The poet-physician, art as healer: poetry's specific value is that, in employing re-collective images, sound, and organization, it can both enact and guide that journey. It becomes, finally, the work that comments on the life.

"To Autumn" works, says Bate, like notes in music: "The present has meaning only in terms of what is past and what is to come."[9] Which is why this discussion must not end with the peace and acceptance of "To Autumn."

15

The Second Developmental Region

BEETHOVEN'S most important formal innovation was his tremendous expansion of the sonata's coda. As its name implies, a coda is usually a "tailpiece"—no more than a brief closing gesture like a dominant-to-tonic chord progression after the structural work of the music is complete. In the first movement of his Fifth Symphony, Beethoven undoes all that.

Repetition involves difference. Recall how the oboe "cadenza" opened a hole in the recapitulation. Beethoven uses the coda to widen that opening. If resolution depends on prior loss, why can't this resolution itself become lost, become prior to some future resolution? And what will keep that from being lost?

Thus, after bringing his movement to structural completeness, Beethoven writes nothing less than a second development section. This one is even longer than the first, involving a far greater degree of instability. The dot-dot-dot-dash motif does eventually return, not in C major as in the recapitulation, but in C minor, the key with which the entire movement started. By now, it's become almost a bad joke. We've finally recovered what we lost at the very beginning, and we should feel a greater sense of relief. But we experienced a tremendous shock the last time we felt that way. Too much has happened in the meantime; too much trust in resolution has already been violated. And, in fact, nothing happens at the end of the movement to indicate that yet another development isn't on the way. Despite the return of the opening key, the final cadence feels neither less nor more definitive than any other cadence in the piece. The music just cuts itself off. (Some conductors slow the music here to provide a stronger sense of closure. This move not only lacks a basis in Beethoven's meticulous dynamics; it also misses the point.)

Few artists, musical or poetic, were willing or able like Beethoven to put the idea of resolution as self-challenging into practice. How to manage this structural indefiniteness in an artwork without destroying the artwork? One solution, which Beethoven uses here, is to cut off the flow of time with an arbitrary gesture of closure like a sudden dominant-to-tonic cadence. Another is to appeal to that which supposedly transcends time, such as God, nature, the spirit of man. Still another is to declare the work a fragment; its beginnings and endings, though relevant to the work, cannot be contained within the work.

None of these fully confronts the central dilemma of Romantic time: the nowness of time is made of present and prior passing-away-ness. Consciousness is re-collection, equal measures of return and difference. Meaning arises when time circles back on itself, and time cannot circle back on itself without continuing to move forward. When resolution arises out of loss, a sense of past and potential loss will inform resolution. Insights that arise out of a temporal context necessarily fall back into that context. What time brings, time also takes away.

Beethoven lets everything fall apart for the sake of asking, what then? Keats, according to the terms he's set for himself, must do the same. For all its stillness, "To Autumn" never ceases being conscious of itself as a moment in time. In accepting that nothing lasts, it must also accept that even this acceptance will pass. The finer tone is, finally, the future's ordinary consciousness.

I maintain that Keats, in "What can I do to drive away," wrote a second development poem. Paul de Man has called this poem "the exact negative counterpart" of "Ode to a Nightingale."[1] Yes, but it's more: less the negative counterpart than the inevitable continuation of development. This poem brings back the tonal restlessness, the language full of questions and negations, even the images of the developmental odes. In struggling through an even more radically re-collective process, it returns us finally to the tonality where we began—and we end up, for that very reason, severely shaken.

Once more, time is a threat and timelessness is desired. Keats recovers the oppositions he'd disposed of in the developmental poems and parades them again across the poem. Now that he knows them to be impossible, he wants them more than ever. He's already found a moment of time when everything balanced, a moment equally full of past, present, and future. But the act of finding that moment was itself momentary. Now he's looking again:

> What can I do to drive away
> Remembrance from my eyes? for they have seen,

Aye, an hour ago, my brilliant queen!
Touch has a memory. O say, Love, say,
What can I do to kill it and be free
In my old liberty?
. . . .
How shall I do
To get anew
Those moulted feathers, and so mount once more
Above, above
The reach of fluttering Love,
And make him cower lowly while I soar?
(1–6, 18–23)

The poet knows that memory is neither freedom nor confinement. But since the moment of resolution has passed, he lacks other categories. Veering wildly between extremes he knows to be impossible, he wants to drive remembrance away, yet wants to do so in order to have a freedom available only in memory. Because he has seen the intimacy of time and resolution, he fears settling any issue. Resolution's been lost once; why not again? He is afraid even of setting up his ode stanza, using instead a couplet that breaks frequently, varies constantly in line length, and adds to the couplet tradition only an urge toward self-annihilation.

The poet rejects unusual but ordinary consciousness: "Shall I gulp wine? No, that is vulgarism." Yet he continues to seek the unusual but ordinary consciousness and language of conventional religion ("A heresy and schism / Foisted into the canon law of love"), of fanciful imagery, and of myth. He does so in a way that openly admits its own contradictoriness, its many-at-once-ness. He declares "monstrous" the region devoid of such mythic images—even though monsters do not exist apart from a perception conditioned by myth making. This region has dungeoned his friends, and himself as well, because of his inability to stop remembering that they are there.

Where shall I learn to get my peace again?
To banish thoughts of that most hateful land,
. . . .
Unown'd of any weedy-haired gods;
Whose winds, all zephyrless, hold scourging rods,
Iced in the great lakes, to afflict mankind;
Whose rank-grown forests, frosted, black, and blind,
Would fright a Dryad . . .
(30–31, 36–40)

These great lakes may be a reference to his brother George's ill fortune in America. But this region also describes the poet himself after the other odes. All is once more a pool of potential, though hardly pure, littered as it is with the ruins of the songs of spring: sordid urns, zephyrless winds, frightened dryads, birds who sing no sweet songs. Time has undone the insights of the recapitulatory region. All the poet can do is hang on to the wreckage of Special consciousness, at once hoping for and unable to trust insight.

In its steadfast refusal (or inability) to settle, "What can I do to drive away" enacts what "To Autumn" implied: the impossibility of the moment as lasting and lastingly identical with itself, of establishing meaning once and for all. Which makes the poem not only crucial to the odes sequence but crucial to an understanding of Keats's thought. It is hardly the "embarrassment" that Bate and Barnard feel it to be.[2] One of the last poems Keats wrote, it contains several features not seen before in Keats's work: a willingness to be intensely personal (therefore improper, if not vulgar, as Keats would have understood those qualities) in verse, and, more important, an awareness of a clearly self-reflexive other. This other is not a goddess or an urn or a personification, but a person, whose consciousness of time, though linked by love with the poet's own, must differ from the poet's. Romantic time, being the experience of the individual, has little room for such an other, since that other remains discrete from the self that explores otherness yet always returns, though changed, to self. That discreteness is the sadness (and sometimes the solace) of lovers.

But the poet seems not quite ready to explore these new complications. "Enough! Enough!" the poem concludes, "it is enough for me / To dream of thee!" A dominant-to-tonic cadence out of nowhere, a return to where we began, to a place where dreams are sufficient: the moment is hardly a comfort. As the odes sequence has more than shown, and as this poem itself has admitted, dreams and memories are never enough. Yet when reality, because of its liability to dissolve in time, is itself seen as something of a dream or memory, and not a very attractive one at that, then such an utterance becomes inevitable. As in Beethoven, the poem cannot resolve; it can only end. Both works do this by acknowledging, in a self-knowing and self-mocking way, their own inability to answer the questions they raise.

Beethoven articulates what's already there. His use of sonata form resists closure; but composers always seemed to feel that the sonata should be a first movement form. Questions about time that it raised could be further explored, or could be left behind in favor of other models of time, in later movements. Ultimately, this structural rhythm leaves open as many issues as it resolves, and, in fact, leaves them open *because* it resolves them. Like the sonata, the ode sequence works because it manages to heal, if only for a moment, a breech it creates. Tonal resolution depends on the prior creation of tonal instability, so the experience of tonal instability is, in a way, a setup. The answers that satisfy do so largely because they conditioned the question in the first place.

What other questions can be asked *now?* After all, re-collection never really allows the present to be, anymore than it ever really recovers the past. Since genuine absence is genuinely devastating, sometimes it's necessary to just let go. Usually one doesn't really learn this until one is older, or, like Keats, has faced great loss early. Wordsworth—the Wordsworth of "Surprised by Joy," learned it. But the ability to let go seems to have been almost more devastating than his daughter's death, the absence that made letting go necessary. Poetry for him was predicated on bringing things back though changed. Yet some things never come back. The loss of childhood, though painful enough, is nothing compared to the loss of a child. How then to write if poetry, which has always taken its origin from re-collection, now questions the relevance of that act?

Beethoven, too, knew about letting go, and, as always, sought to make it part of his art. He would come to be less satisfied with the sonata principle, with the idea of departure engineered specifically for the purpose of return. In the Fifth Symphony's later movements, especially in the blurring of divisions between those movements, he explores other ways of experiencing time. Many of his late works enter even more fully this "generative gap" (the phrase is Kramer's), courting those places where consciousness and language fail in an attempt to present within the work the disruptive origin of the work.[3] "Muss es sein?" Beethoven wrote atop a late score: Must it be this way? What else is there?

The Keats of "What can I do to drive away" was groping toward something similar—and at a much younger age. The early deaths of his parents and brother, and the possibility (so he seems to have begun suspecting in the fall of 1819) of his own early death: these surely taught him about what it means to lose irreparably. The language of this late poem parades its own inadequacies, shortcomings, contradictions, self-destructions, and reachings into silence in order to ask, here at the outermost bounds of what can be known and expressed, what comes next. What can consciousness do besides perceive, break down, and resolve exclusivity? What can time do besides return with a difference? What can art do besides express such a return? Like the Beethoven of the Fifth Symphony, Keats knew he had a long way to go; unlike Beethoven, he didn't get the chance to keep trying.

CONCLUSION

WHEN Romantic poets explore life-in-time, they often turn to music for a model and a vocabulary. As often, they find they cannot conclude without retreating, or at least without feeling a temptation to retreat, into speculative abstraction. God, nature, the One, society, even the imagination when hypostatized: any of these can set aside the difficulties and paradoxes of temporal experience. Keats seldom goes that way. Or rather, when he does, he knows it, owns up to it, and makes retreat itself an issue. Keats prefers to cut off a discussion rather than conclude it with a false resolution. As with Beethoven, a large portion of his career involves the search for what is not false resolution. Years might bring the philosophic mind; but the conditions that bring insight, Keats admits, also make insight questionable. Pain and wisdom, far from cancelling each other, arise out of each other. Part of being wise is recognizing that loss still hurts.

As Douglas Bush puts it, "Beauty is something beautiful" for Keats:[1] a thing or thought or feeling to be experienced in the fullness and transience of its joys and sorrows. Music was such an experience for Keats, and—as an idea, a prosodic model, and an organizing principle—a way of thinking through and writing about experience. His odes fulfill those efforts.

Questions inevitably remain. If Keats found his voice and vehicle in the melos of the ode stanza and the musical organization of the odes sequence, why did he continue to try other forms, especially those in which he'd had limited success? *Lamia, The Fall of Hyperion, Otho the Great:* these were probably written after most of the great odes. So were a number of sonnets. But, as I've argued, all great artists advance and retreat; sometimes, on trying again, they find success where once there was failure. Keats had done all he could do and needed to do with the ode stanza, and, as always, was casting about for new directions, even while looking to see what else the old still might offer. That too is the sign of a great artist.

If the odes really do have a structural rhythm cognate with the sonata in music, why didn't Keats just write one long poem? Perhaps if he had set out to do so, it would have been another *Hyperion*. Chopin and Schumann wrote labored, self-consciously "important" works in which their own voices, so wonderfully audible in other pieces, can hardly be heard. The same seems true of Keats. His ideas of epic and drama led him only to brilliant failures. By focusing on one relatively short poem at a time, he freed himself from confining expectations, and was able to achieve, by essentially lyric means, the odes' dramatic tension and postponement of resolution as well as their quasi-epic scope and concerns. Perhaps more important, Keats fully lived, and fully believed in, each ode as it was being written. The act of writing poetry becomes an act of discovery about life: I return to my experience of time with the difference that I now use image, sound, and form to transform time into meaning. The poetry's axioms were proved on the poet's pulses. These odes, it seems, came like leaves to a tree: at once the cause and the result of a life full of growth and change.

The form of the poetic sequence also allows for an end run around many of the difficulties Romantic theory sets for itself. With its freedom of design and utterance, and with its flexibility of sonic shape, the tonal sequence can re-collect tradition—lyric, epic, and dramatic—without being bound by its strictures. The ode sequence re-collects the poet's own work in such a way that previous poems are not only relevant to present ones but become part of them by virtue of the individual poem's giving itself over to a larger utterance. And the poetry here re-collects itself without consuming itself. Because each ode is part of a sequence, the poem ends and continues in the next poem, almost as if it's one poem being written over and over, ever the same, ever new. Therefore its form can be re-used, albeit with modifications that articulate at once its repetition of and difference from previous poems. Some of Keats's greatest difficulties as an artist arose from his sense that the best poetry had already been written.[2] With the extended tonal organization, Keats finds a way to renew the past by writing poetry that renews itself.

All of which assumes, of course, that the odes ought to be read as a sequence. Whether Keats consciously intended this, such an argument can be made. The odes were all written around the same time and share a range of concerns. Those concerns are organized similarly to the ways in which music organizes its concerns. Part of what makes these poems great is that, though richest when read all together and in order, each is a good enough poem to be read on its own. In that sense, and in that sense only, the odes may more nearly resemble a multimovement work like a Schubert song cycle or the Chopin preludes than they do the sonata. No such cycle exists, however, involving the kind of tonal planning that, as many readers have sensed and as I've tried to explain, allows the odes to become a coherent whole.[3]

If that is the case, is Beethoven the most appropriate composer with which to compare Keats? Some readers may sense that other composers have written in a more Keatsian mood. But mood is a very misty notion, offering little for extended, detailed analysis. More to the point, no work by, say, Schubert or Chopin presents the precise structural rhythm that Beethoven's does—a rhythm that is, I believe, cognate with the odes' unfolding. The first movement of Beethoven's Fifth Symphony is not "how the odes would sound if they were music"; it is an artwork organized, like the ode sequence, with expository, developmental, recapitulatory, and second developmental regions. This organization allows both works to raise and address highly similar questions about time and meaning in highly similar ways and at highly similar paces. Given his goals, Keats might possibly have written a work that achieves, like *The Prelude,* a Beethovenian grandeur, though the odes are not without that quality, albeit on another scale. In the end, though, Keats and Beethoven (or Chopin or Schubert or whoever) must part company—in mood, and in everything else. Before they do, they have a chance to show us how what is important and clear in one art can help us understand what is no less important but perhaps not as clear in another art. The temporal and tonal organization of longer lyrics is such a crucial, but not altogether understood, poetic phenomenon. Interestingly, M. L. Rosenthal, whose ideas about poetry's musiclike tonality proved helpful, is one of the few critics to have written at length about the poetic sequence.[4] More work needs to be done. Music can help.

Could a reading of the odes that does not use music find the structural rhythm we've had to use music to find? Probably. But that's the point. This structural rhythm informs poetry no less than it informs music. The sonata as an analytical model should do no more than enable us to understand better this poetic rhythm, and to locate it in a wider artistic and cultural context. Music makes us better critics. It helps us read the poetry of an age that often saw music as the model for all the arts. Bad Romantic poetry tries to imitate music. Good Romantic poetry discovers within the means of poetry ways for combination to cogovern with reference in verbal language—that is, ways in which the unfolding of time can be as palpable and as powerful in a poem as in a musical composition. A sensitive and intelligent reader will see this; a musically informed reader will see it more easily.

We've built, with music's help, a model of time that is useful only insofar as it can suggest ways of reading that clarify and enrich our experience of particular poems, or can explain how such readings have occurred. Like any critical method, sometimes it works, sometimes it doesn't. This study has tried to illuminate where the intuition that says "use music" comes from, to clarify some of the methodology that follows from that intuition, and to demonstrate the kinds of readings such a method makes possible. As I've argued, when we ask, What is Romanticism? we confront a range of issues that we also confront when we ask, What is the relation between poetry and music? We come to a consideration of the pattern of Romantic time, a pattern informing poetry no less than music in the late eighteenth and early nineteenth centuries.

Our speculations about time, music, and language might also be applied fruitfully to much literature since Keats's day. We may accept or reject Romanticism's view that meaning is loss, loss meaning. But we cannot ignore it, since it is an attitude that for good or bad continues to shape our thinking. Arguably, Romanticism is a basic way of understanding experience—not one way of two, the other typically being classicism, but one of many. With music's help, Romanticism provides one perspective on why the past can have such an inescapable presence in our lives. Joyce, Faulkner, Yeats, Eliot, Merrill, Proust: the organization of time and memory is essential to each of these writers, whether they've worked in poetry or prose. For each, then, music might be a useful critical tool, much as music seemed useful in one way or another to these writers. In fact, Alex Aronson, Robert Wallace, and Joseph W. Reed have shown some interesting possibilities for understanding music's relation with fiction.[5]

The danger lies in applying critical criteria where they don't belong. To be sure, neither the sonata principle, nor the idea of re-collection, nor music in general has everything we need as critics—even for Romanticism itself. It's difficult to imagine a reading of, say, Don Juan that would find music useful. In that poem, irony is the driving force, a process of endless building up and tearing down over time. Byron's language makes temporality palpable; and Byron steers in the direction of constant development. These characteristics he shares with music. But they share little more. Given that constant development can proceed in virtually limitless directions according to the needs of the artist and the exigencies of the artistic material, poet and composer (or for that matter, poet and poet) will likely diverge very soon when it comes to the specifics of their respective unfoldings.[6]

The good musician has a wide repertoire; the good reader should aim for no less with respect to critical techniques. Even the best readings are liable to become the past, and nothing—*nothing*—is more dated than dated literary criticism. As long as we ally ourselves with a single system (and, what is even more numbing, a single set of oft-repeated critical terms), we'll miss anything that the system either can't account for or insists is of little value—usually *because* the system can't account for it. In more recent criticism, we've glimpsed a much wider world. Yet we're also busy committing the characteristic sins of academic endeavor: institutionalizing the paths of access to that world, thus making art tame enough (or lame enough) for classrooms and journals. What Andrew Cooper calls "the new critical orthodoxy"[7] is something of a sleek F-16 to formalism's clunky but reliable DC-3. Having resurrected ambiguity as indeterminacy, we can maneuver with ease at tremendous speeds, and can shoot down anything else that tries to fly, but we've adopted a vehicle with narrow applications, and the principles that get us off the ground have been around for decades.

This is not to dismiss the usefulness of all that goes under the rubric of theory. Recent years have seen the development of much-needed attention to literature's relation to society, to gender and race, to the writer's life, to political issues, to language—and to the other arts. Why stop now? If Keats teaches us anything, it is that varying temporal circumstances require not only varying interpretations but also varying interpretive methods. Criticism, too, is a many-chambered mansion. In those chambers there is room for virtually any response—except the one that purports to be exhaustive. We need to be thieves and pack rats, to borrow and steal and plunder whatever seems useful. We need standards; but we also need to be open, to resist the urge to do something we do, alas, very well: align ourselves with one system, one vocabulary, one set of values, one academic discipline, and one metaphysics (or, what is much the same, one way of deconstructing metaphysics). Time shapes criticism no less than it shapes poetry. There is (speaking of thievery) more day to dawn.

Music—the structure and beauty of the passing moment—can help us come to grips with the ways time shapes us, no less than it can help us read the Romantics. Music is one way, but one way only, for us to understand better what is a central Romantic insight: we can feel, equally strongly, in the same moment, and for the same reasons, that we are both eminently unbuildable and "continuous selves in a continuous world."[8] Every moment is part of every other moment. Nowness and passing-away exist within and because of each other in music, and in poetry, and in life.

Music showed Keats this, and many other things, even at the end. After the age of twenty-four, he went nowhere as a poet. Instead he went to Rome. There he found music, though not the kind he wanted: a street below his window "pester'd with cries, ballad singers, and street music" (L384). But then there was Joseph Severn playing the piano for him. "This Haydn is like a child," Keats remarked after one such session, "for there is no knowing what he will do next."[9] Another point a composer and a poet have in common: Keats forever young, and there is no knowing what he would have done next.

He'd watched his mother and brother go this way. And he was a surgeon. He knew it was tuberculosis, knew what was happening to him.[10] His delight in Haydn there on his deathbed suggests that his native curiosity, so powerful that it is indistinguishable from both courage and honesty, would have continued to inform his work and his life, and that music would have continued to play an important role.

Important, yet probably different: Keats's greatest poems, the odes, follow a structural rhythm cognate with the sonata principle—a first movement form. What would Keats's "later movements" have been? Opinion is divided. Christopher Ricks says that what is best in Keats is often the insight most readily available to the perceptive adolescent; thus, we can only guess at the direction of his mature thought.[11] This is certainly true of his early work (though compared with what almost any other major poet in the language wrote at age twenty or twenty-one, that work doesn't seem so unaccomplished), and even the late poems contain much that belongs to what Keats called in his preface to *Endymion* "a space of life between" childhood and adult imagination "in which the soul is in a ferment." His late works also show him to be, as Fry puts it, in "the last stages of a brilliant apprenticeship still in progress." On the other hand, Robert Gittings makes a good case for Keats being finished as a poet by the end of 1819, although Perkins sees in Keats "a range of concerns which subsumes much of Wordsworth and almost all of Shelley, and which, at least in some directions, may have carried him further than either Wordsworth or Shelley were able to go."[12]

Little agreement here. Nor should there be. For one thing, the body of evidence will always be incomplete. For another, some of that evidence is great art, and great art is so because it is vital. Even while providing us with criteria for interpretation, it demands of us that we keep our minds open, our sense of life dynamic. Clearly, Keats's quality of intelligence, though very much at home in its age, was unlike that of any other major Romantic poet's. Just as clearly, we'll never know exactly where it would have led him, and we are the poorer for that. Like the poet of "What can I do to drive away," we're left surveying the ruin, remembering the magnificence that once stood, and, with equal measures of dread and wonder, trying to imagine what could possibly come next.

Perhaps we're confining ourselves to the realm of ordinary time by dwelling on an exclusivity between what has been and what can never be. Keats's unwritten movements will tantalize us for as long as we read his poetry. But we read his poetry only in time, and in time, all moments are part of one another. If one moment we wish for what we can never have, another moment we realize that our wish arises out of what we do have. John Keats, who left us the silence of winter, also left us the songs of spring, the music of autumn.

And isn't silence part of any music?

And doesn't silence have its music too?

NOTES

References to Keats's poems appear in the text parenthetically by line number or, where appropriate, by book and line number. The texts of Keats's poems are taken from *Complete Poems*, ed. Jack Stillinger (Cambridge: Harvard UP, 1982), which is referred to in the notes as *CP* plus page number.

References to Keats's letters appear in the notes and parenthetically in the text as L plus page number. All quotes preserve his spelling and punctuation, and are taken from *Letters of John Keats*, ed. Robert Gittings (Oxford: Oxford UP, 1975), a more recent and accurate edition than the standard H. E. Rollins edition (Cambridge: Harvard UP, 1958).

Quotations from William Wordsworth's *The Prelude* are taken from the Norton Critical Edition, ed. Jonathan Wordsworth et al. (New York: Norton, 1979), which is referred to in the notes as Norton plus page number. Unless otherwise indicated, the quotations follow the 1805 version as being most representative of the poet's thought when he was doing his finest work.

Except as detailed in the notes, the texts of all other Romantic poems and prose works are taken from *Major British Romantic Poets*, ed. William Heath (New York: Macmillan, 1975), which is referred to in the notes as Heath plus page number. The poets' spelling and punctuation have been preserved.

The notes give authors and, if necessary, short titles. Full citations appear in the bibliography.

PREFACE

1. See note above on primary sources and references.
2. For a very different approach, see Knapp, especially the introduction.
3. Butler 185.

INTRODUCTION

1. Barricelli 2.
2. Wasserman 3.
3. Barricelli 1.

4. Blackstone xiv.

5. Being a composer and poet himself, Kramer understands aspects of the creative process that most critics can only observe from a distance.

6. Calvin S. Brown 176; Wellek and Warren 119, 126. See also Barricelli and Gibaldi (both titles) and Springer.

7. Geoffrey R. Russom has pointed out—one of countless ideas he has shared with me—how skaldic poetry often creates a literary counterpoint by using interwoven sentence fragments to embody its complex metaphor structure.

8. Frye, "Lexis and Melos" in Frye, Sound and Poetry x–xiii.

9. Frye, Anatomy of Criticism 255. For a contrasting view on consonance (and fallacies following from it) see Raymond.

10. Cooke 14–24.

11. Lerdahl and Jackendoff 5–6; Meyer 28.

12. Winn 266ff.

13. Meyer 28; Cooke 21.

14. Langer 24ff. For a more clinical treatment, see Sloboda, esp. 17–23.

15. Treitler 11.

16. Jakobsen 115; La Drière, "Structure, Sound, and Meaning" in Frye, Sound and Poetry 93.

17. Kramer 5–7.

18. Pater 55.

19. Kramer 5.

20. Kramer 4.

21. Barricelli 74; Wolfson 17–18.

22. Whitrow 4, 183ff.

23. Whitrow 179.

24. MacFarland 249, 10.

25. "The Rhetoric of Temporality" in de Man, Blindness and Insight 222–23.

26. Abrams, "The Greater Romantic Lyric" in Bloom, Romanticism and Consciousness 201.

27. Quoted in Matthews 223–24. Though verbatim accuracy is debatable here, the quote is "consistent with reliable information . . . [Beethoven] often worked on compositions over a span of years [and] extensively revised his themes (to be sure, not in his head, but on paper) . . ." See Maynard Solomon, "On Beethoven's Creative Process: A Two-Part Invention" in Music and Letters 61 (1980): 272–83.

28. William Wordsworth, preface, Lyrical Ballads, Heath 406.

29. Wordsworth, preface, Heath 402.

30. Wordsworth, "Lines Composed a Few Miles Above Tintern Abbey" 84–96, Heath 203.

31. Wordsworth, preface, Heath 402.

32. Percy Bysshe Shelley, "A Defense of Poetry," Heath 987.

33. Shelley, "Defense," Heath 987.

34. Salvesen 34; Robinson 107.

35. Hoffmann, "Beethoven's Instrumental Music" in Strunk 777–78.

36. Treitler 176ff.

37. Wordsworth, preface, Heath 402.

38. Wordsworth, The Prelude 11.257–78, Norton 428–30.

39. Wordsworth et al. 175.

40. Samuel Taylor Coleridge, Biographia Literaria ch. 13, Heath 516.

41. Coleridge, Biographia ch. 14, Heath 519.

42. Abrams, *Natural Supernaturalism* 141ff.

43. In a field dominated by discussions of chemical reactions and the like, Bolles's work provides a welcome alternative, incorporating the neurological aspects of memory into an extensive yet highly accessible treatment of its interpretive functions.

44. Wallace, *Emily Brontë and Beethoven*. Highly recommended.

45. Whitrow 11, 12; Whitrow 6. This typically occurs around age two. For more on the related acquisitions of selfhood, language, and a temporal sense, see Stern 111–27; see also the suggestions for further reading listed in Stern 162–63.

46. Neubauer 31.

47. Thomas MacFarland, "Wordsworth's Hedgerows: The Infrastructure of the Longer Romantic Lyric" in Johnston and Ruoff 241–42.

48. Andrew M. Cooper 33.

THE VARIETIES OF MUSICAL EXPERIENCE

1. CP xvi–xvii.
2. Abrams, *The Mirror and the Lamp* 92–93. See also Coffmann.
3. Abrams, *The Mirror* 50–51, 94.
4. Winn 261–69. Required reading.
5. Winn 284. See also Stein.
6. Neubauer 2, 4, 10. See also Winn 20, 55.
7. Conrad 143.
8. Schmidgall 69.
9. Barlow does, however, bring together much useful biographical information.
10. Abrams, *The Mirror* 93; Winn 259ff.
11. Neubauer 60.
12. Neubauer 108.
13. Neubauer 80, 77.
14. Neubauer 119–20, 182ff.
15. Neubauer 101, 182.
16. Neubauer 199; see Neubauer 175 and Wellek 318.
17. And also with laudanum, but only toward the end of his life when he was in physical and emotional distress. See Bate, *John Keats* 463ff., 658.
18. Ronga 85–86.
19. Wellek 131.
20. Neubauer 158; Abrams, *The Mirror* 93.
21. Neubauer 74–75.
22. Barry 123, 16.

IMAGE AS STRUCTURE

1. Andrew M. Cooper 190.
2. See Hollander, *The Untuning of the Sky* and *Images of Voice*; see also Mellers.
3. Shelley, "Defense," Heath 975.
4. Milton 71.
5. See Hammond and Scullard s.v. "Delos."
6. Pack 147.
7. Andrew M. Cooper 106.
8. Wolfson 297ff.

WORDS, MUSIC, AND INTERPRETATION

1. "A Chapter on Ears" in Lamb 273–74.
2. "On Ears" in Lamb 273.
3. Neubauer 205.
4. Shelley, "Defense," Heath 977.
5. Shelley, "Defense," Heath 977; Wellek 323. But see also Tetreault.
6. Shelley, "Defense," Heath 978.
7. Shelley, "Defense," Heath 977.
8. Shelley, "When the Lamp is Shattered" 5–6, 9–12, Heath 962; Shelley, "Music When Sweet Voices Die" 1–4, Heath 958.
9. Shelley, "Defense," Heath 975.
10. Fairchild 5.
11. Langer 154; see also Booth for an extremely thorough and unusually sensible discussion of why songs need to be regarded as something more than words set to music. For a more conventional approach, see Ivey.
12. Wellek 40; Barry 66ff.
13. Neubauer 97, 134.
14. Shelley, "Defense," Heath 975.
15. Shelley, "Defense," Heath 976, 978, 988.
16. Shelley, "Defense," Heath 976, 977.
17. Wellek 84; Barry 10, 181.
18. Quoted in Barry 61.
19. Barry 101, 104.
20. Barry 12, 11.
21. Barry 97.
22. Barry 131, 182, 178.
23. Barry 131.
24. Wordsworth, "Tintern Abbey" 40–50, Heath 203.
25. Barry 51.
26. Wordsworth, *Prelude* 1.372ff., Norton 48ff.; 6.453ff., Norton 212ff.; 13.52ff., Norton 460.
27. Barry 127.
28. Barry 12–13, 16.
29. Wellek and Warren 127.

"THE EVE OF ST. AGNES"

1. Bartlett 175–80.
2. For sources see CP 453–54.
3. Adelman, "The Dangers of Enthrallment" in Danzig 101.
4. Stillinger, "The Hoodwinking of Madeline" in Abrams, *English Romantic Poets* 448ff.; Wolfson 288.
5. Bloom and Trilling 524.
6. Adelman, "The Dangers" 108.
7. Bate, *John Keats* 449.
8. CP 457.
9. CP 457; Bate, *John Keats* 447.
10. Wasserman 97ff., 116.

MELOS AND MEANING

1. Frye, "Lexis" in Frye, *Sound and Poetry* xxi.
2. Pettet 81.
3. Zaenker 521–22.
4. Conrad 5; see Harding 86 and List passim.
5. Alexander Pope, "Essay on Criticism" 318, 348–49, Williams 46, 47. All quotes from this poem are taken from Williams and preserve the original emphases and spelling.
6. Pope, "Essay" 365–69, Williams 47.
7. Pope, "Essay" 154–57, Williams 42.
8. Pope, "Essay" 143–44, Williams 42.
9. Pope, "Essay" 341–43, Williams 47.
10. Winn 260; Boswell 305.
11. See "The Rambler" nos. 92 and 94 in Johnson 224–33, 240–47.
12. See Myers and Simms s.v. "melos" and "sound system." See also Kumbier.
13. Fairchild 43. Fairchild's is an outstanding discussion of the relation between poetic meter and musicality. See also Goss and Sosnowski.
14. Fairchild 43.
15. Fairchild 36.
16. Hollander, "Romantic Verse Form and the Metrical Contract" in Bloom, *Romanticism and Consciousness* 182–85; Fairchild 34. Cf. Wordsworth's notion of "formal engagement" as discussed in chapter 7 below.
17. See Kinsley passim and Woods passim. Nor does Keats seem to be using a form employed by any of his contemporaries who were also imitating and varying the ballad stanza. See Heath passim and Bloom and Trilling passim.
18. See Lucas 27–28; see also Chaucer lii–liii.
19. MacFarland 383–87, 400–401.

THE ROMANTIC USES OF SOUND

1. Rosen, *Classical Style* 23. For deep background, see Martin Cooper, Crocker, and Pauley.
2. See Sadie s.v. "French overture." Mozart's use of the triad as motivic fodder in this movement is linked to the opera's Masonic symbolism, but this is secondary to its ability to provide strictly musical coherence. On this symbolism, see Nettl.
3. Mathews 64ff.
4. Wordsworth, preface, Heath 401.
5. Wordsworth, preface, Heath 399, 405.
6. Wordsworth, preface, Heath 399.
7. Wordsworth, preface, Heath 405, 403, 404, 402.
8. Wordsworth, preface as appears in Abrams, *Norton Anthology* 160.
9. Abrams, *The Mirror* 102.
10. Abrams, *The Mirror* 116.
11. Wordsworth, preface, Heath 399, 406.
12. Wordsworth, preface, Heath 405.
13. Wordsworth, preface, Heath 402, 405.
14. Wordsworth, preface, Heath 406.
15. Wordsworth, preface, Heath 399.
16. Wordsworth, "Tintern Abbey" 52–58, Heath 203.

17. Wordsworth, preface, Heath 405.
18. Wordsworth, preface, Heath 403.
19. Coleridge, *Biographia* ch. 14, Heath 518.
20. Coleridge, *Biographia* ch. 14, Heath 518.
21. Barry 157; Sapir 224.
22. Wellek 170.
23. Coleridge, *Biographia*, Heath 518–19.
24. Coleridge, *Biographia*, Heath 518.
25. Coleridge, *Biographia*, Heath 517.
26. Coleridge, *Biographia*, Heath 518, 519.
27. Bloom, "The Unpastured Sea: An Introduction to Shelley" in Bloom, *Romanticism and Consciousness* 376; Wellek 204, 53.
28. Shelley, "Defense," Heath 977.
29. Shelley, "Defense," Heath 976.
30. Shelley, "Defense," Heath 989, emphasis added.
31. Shelley, "Defense," Heath 977, 986.
32. Shelley, "Defense," Heath 987.
33. Shelley, "Defense," Heath 977.
34. Shelley, "Defense," Heath 977.
35. Coleridge, "The Rime of the Ancient Mariner" 363–66, Heath 453.
36. Coleridge, "Frost at Midnight" 28–33, Heath 464.
37. Wordsworth, "Tintern Abbey" 76–78, Heath 203.
38. Wordsworth, *Prelude* 13.40ff., Norton 460. See also Bartlett and Miyagawa.
39. Quoted in Holmes 230; Shelley, "Mont Blanc: Lines Written in the Vale of Chamouni" 142–44, Heath 800.
40. Wordsworth, *Prelude* 1.67–68 (1799), Norton 3; 1.351–52 (1805), Norton 46; 1.340–41 (1850), Norton 47.
41. See OED s.v. "harmony."
42. Shelley, "To a Skylark" 101–05, Heath 913.
43. Shelley, "Ode to the West Wind" 14, 57–60, Heath 904.
44. Shelley, "Hymn to Intellectual Beauty" 8–10, Heath 797. See also O'Malley.
45. See Kramer ch. 4, esp. 95–99.
46. Bate, *John Keats* 95. See also L162, L180; Barlow chs. 1, 2.
47. Ward 148. See also L45.
48. Ricks 10.
49. Woodring 4; Bush, "Keats" in Bate, *Keats: A Collection* 16; Bate, *Stylistic Development* 132–33; Masson, "The Keatsian Incantation" in Muir 160.
50. Ricks 72.
51. Pettet 366–67.
52. Bate, *John Keats* 413–17.
53. Bate, *John Keats* 414.
54. Bate, *John Keats* 417.

THE VERSE PARAGRAPH

1. See Wolfson passim.
2. Bate, *John Keats* 270.
3. Bate, *Stylistic Development* 67ff.
4. Bate, *John Keats* 356–74.

5. CP 92, L194.
6. On the meter being determined by the word rhythm, see Kiparsky 224.
7. Bate, *John Keats* 454–56.

THE STANZA

1. Milton 210.
2. Bate, *Stylistic Development* 91–92.
3. Adelman, "The Dangers" in Danzig 110.
4. Bate, *John Keats* 665.
5. Bate, *John Keats* 312, 314.
6. CP 417, 436, 439.

THE ODE STANZA

1. See Bush 126.
2. Bate, *John Keats* 601.
3. Shelley, "Defense," Heath 978.
4. See Kramer, esp. 18ff. See also (as Kramer advises) Marshall Brown.
5. Welsh 190ff.
6. See Preminger s.v. "ode."
7. CP 427.
8. Fry 10.
9. Bate, *John Keats* 495ff., 40–42.
10. CP 423; Bate, *John Keats* 120ff., 142.
11. Bate, *John Keats* 297, 496.
12. Bate, *John Keats* 299.
13. Bate, *John Keats* 496.
14. For an interesting discussion of this poem's sonic effect, see Hollander, *Melodious Guile* 93–96.
15. Bate, *John Keats* 293.
16. Bate, *John Keats* 297.
17. Bate, *John Keats* 497–98.

THE EXTENDED TONAL ORGANIZATION

1. MacFarland 237.
2. Robinson 101.
3. Fry 2.
4. Vendler 6.
5. Blackstone 318.
6. Barlow 144ff.
7. Hertz 4ff.
8. Berry 313 and 184ff.
9. Possibly the most enlightening, and certainly the most entertaining, description of this movement's effect is Peter Schickele's "New Horizons in Music Appreciation," where the music is "called" like a football game.   For a more sober discussion of the age's

tremendously varied approach to composition in the sonata, see Rosen, *Sonata Forms*. The plural in Rosen's title is worth noting.

10. See Weekley s.v. "sonata" (the past participle of the Italian verb *sonare*, "to sound," i.e., a sounded or instrumental composition) and s.v. "sonnet" (from the French, itself from the diminutive of the Italian noun *suono*, "sound," i.e., a small sound or short poem).

11. Neubauer 41; Calvin S. Brown 177, 176.

12. Frye, "Lexis" in Frye, *Sound and Poetry* xvi.

13. Perkins 271; Black 166.

14. Black 166; Scher vii.

15. Rosenthal 97. See also Yost.

16. Hertz 23; Harding 100.

17. Kramer 10.

18. "Imagination and Reality in the Odes" in Stillinger, *The Hoodwinking of Madeline* 104. For more extensive discussion see Stillinger, *Texts of Keats's Poems*.

THE EXPOSITORY REGION

1. Perkins 201ff.; Salvesen 7; Barnard 98ff.

2. Bate, *Stylistic Development* 133ff., 140.

3. Wigod 180.

4. Sutherland 116. Refreshingly different.

5. CP 467.

6. Perkins 202, 213.

7. Adelman, "The Dangers" in Danzig 99.

THE DEVELOPMENTAL REGION

1. Perkins 298.

2. Coleridge, *Biographia* ch. 13, Heath 516.

3. Baker 147; Wasserman 17.

4. Wasserman 34.

5. Wolfson 231.

6. Frye 240.

7. Vendler 71ff.

8. Stillinger, *The Hoodwinking* 106.

THE RECAPITULATORY REGION

1. CP 470.

2. CP 471.

3. Kee 52–58.

4. Bowra 5, 273.

5. Welsh 115ff.

6. Davenport, "A Note on 'To Autumn'" in Abrams, *English Romantic Poets* 443.

7. Macksey, "'To Autumn' and the Music of Mortality: Pure Rhetoric of a Language Without Words" in Arden Reed 304, 266, 265.

8. Salvesen 167–68.
9. Bate, *Stylistic Development* 47–48.

SECOND DEVELOPMENTAL REGION

1. de Man, *Selected Poetry of Keats* xxvii.
2. Bate, *Stylistic Development* 186; Barnard 150–51.
3. Kramer 59, 87.

CONCLUSION

1. Bush, "Keats" in Bate, *Keats: A Collection* 26.
2. Bate, *John Keats* viii.
3. On the very different tonal planning of a song cycle see Komar 77ff.
4. See Rosenthal and Gaul passim.
5. See Aronson, Cluck, Joseph W. Reed, and Wallace (both titles).
6. But see Stevenson passim.
7. Andrew M. Cooper 2.
8. Kramer 241.
9. Bate, *John Keats* 677.
10. Aileen Ward's account is particularly moving, and redeems much of her would-be psychoanalysis. See 399ff.
11. Ricks 11–12.
12. Fry 219; Gittings 199; Perkins 55.

BIBLIOGRAPHY

Abrams, M. H., ed. *English Romantic Poets*. 2nd ed. London: Oxford UP, 1975.

——— . *The Mirror and the Lamp: Romantic Theory and the Critical Tradition*. London: Oxford UP, 1953.

——— . *Natural Supernaturalism: Tradition and Revolution in Romantic Literature*. New York: Norton, 1971.

——— , et al., eds. *The Norton Anthology of English Literature*. Vol. 2. 5th ed. New York: Norton, 1986.

Aronson, Alex. *Music and the Novel: A Study in Twentieth Century Fiction*. Totowa, NJ: Barnes, 1980.

Baker, Jeffrey. *Time and Mind in Wordsworth's Poetry*. Detroit, MI: Wayne State UP, 1980.

Barlow, Linda Kay. "Musical Allusions in the Poetry of Keats." Diss. U of North Carolina, 1984.

Barnard, John. *John Keats*. British and Irish Authors Introductory Critical Ser. Cambridge: Cambridge UP, 1987.

Barricelli, Jean-Pierre. *Melopoiesis: Approaches to the Study of Literature and Music*. New York: New York UP, 1988.

Barricelli, John-Pierre, and Joseph Gibaldi, eds. *Interrelations of Literature*. New York: MLA, 1982.

——— , eds. *Teaching Literature and the Other Arts*. New York: MLA, 1990.

Barry, Kevin. *Language, Music, and the Sign: A Study in Aesthetics, Poetics, and Poetic Practice from Collins to Coleridge*. Cambridge: Cambridge UP, 1987.

Bartlett, Brian. "Inscrutable Workmanship: Music and Metaphors of Music in *The Prelude* and *The Excursion*." *Wordsworth Circle* 17.3 (Summer 1986): 175–80.

Bate, W. Jackson. *John Keats*. Cambridge, MA: Harvard UP, 1963.

——— . *Stylistic Development of Keats*. New York: Humanities, 1946.

——— , ed. *Keats: A Collection of Critical Essays*. Englewood Cliffs, NJ: Prentice, 1964.

Berry, Wallace. *Structural Functions in Music*. New York: Dover, 1987.

Black, Michael. *Poetic Drama as a Mirror of the Will*. New York: Barnes, 1977.

Blackstone, Bernard. *The Consecrated Urn: An Interpretation of Keats in Terms of Growth and Form*. London: Longmans, 1959.

Bloom, Harold, ed. *Romanticism and Consciousness*. New York: Norton, 1970.

Bloom, Harold, and Calvin Trilling, eds. *Romantic Poetry and Prose*. Vol. 4 of *Oxford Anthology of English Literature*. New York: Oxford UP, 1973.

Bolles, Claude Blair. *Remembering and Forgetting: An Inquiry into the Nature of Memory.* New York: Walker, 1988.

Booth, Mark W. *The Experience of Songs.* New Haven, CT: Yale UP, 1981.

Boswell, James. *The Journal of a Tour to the Hebrides.* New York: Literary Guild, 1936.

Bowra, C. M. *The Romantic Imagination.* London: Oxford UP, 1949.

Brown, Calvin S. *Music and Literature: A Comparison of the Arts.* Athens: U of Georgia P, 1948.

Brown, Marshall. "The Pre-Romantic Discovery of Consciousness." *Studies in Romanticism* 17 (1978): 387–412.

Bush, Douglas. *John Keats: His Life and Writings.* London: Collier, 1966.

Butler, Marilyn. *Romantics, Rebels, and Reactionaries: English Literature and Its Background 1760–1830.* New York: Oxford UP, 1982.

Chaucer, Geoffrey. *Complete Works of Geoffrey Chaucer.* Supp. vol. Oxford: Clarendon, 1897.

Cluck, Nancy Ann, ed. *Music and Literature: Essays on Form.* Provo, UT: Brigham Young UP, 1981.

Coffmann, Sue E. *Music in a Finer Tone: Musical Imagery of the Major Romantic Poets.* Salzburg: Institut für Anglistik und Amerikanstik, 1979.

Conrad, Peter. *Romantic Opera and Literary Form.* Berkeley: U of California P, 1977.

Cooke, Deryck. *The Language of Music.* London: Oxford UP, 1959.

Cooper, Andrew M. *Doubt and Identity in Romantic Poetry.* New Haven, CT: Yale UP, 1988.

Cooper, Martin. *Ideas and Music.* Philadelphia: Chilton, 1965.

Crocker, Richard. *A History of Musical Style.* New York: McGraw, 1966.

Danzig, Allan, ed. *Twentieth Century Interpretations of "The Eve of St. Agnes."* Englewood Cliffs, NJ: Prentice, 1971.

de Man, Paul. *Blindness and Insight: Essays on the Rhetoric of Contemporary Criticism.* 2nd rev. ed. Theory and History of Literature Vol. 7. Minneapolis: U of Minnesota P, 1983.

———. Introduction. *Selected Poetry of Keats.* Ed. Paul de Man. New York: Signet, 1966.

Fairchild, B. H. *Such Holy Song: Music as Idea, Form, and Image in the Poetry of William Blake.* Kent, OH: Kent State UP, 1980.

Fry, Paul H. *The Poet's Calling in the English Ode.* New Haven, CT: Yale UP, 1980.

Frye, Northrop. *Anatomy of Criticism: Four Essays.* Princeton, NJ: Princeton UP, 1957.

———, ed. *Sound and Poetry.* English Institute Essays 1956. New York: Columbia UP, 1957.

Gittings, Robert. *John Keats: The Living Year 21 September 1818 to 21 September 1819.* Cambridge, MA: Harvard UP, 1954.

Goss, Fred. "Sound the Voice of the Bard: Reading Blake Aloud." *Sparks of Fire: Blake in a New Age.* Ed. James Bogan and Fred Goss. Richmond, CA: North Atlantic, 1982. 96–99.

Hammond, N. G. L., and H. H. Scullard. *The Oxford Classical Dictionary.* 2nd ed. Oxford: Clarendon, 1970.

Harding, D. W. *Words Into Rhythm: English Speech Rhythm in Verse and Prose.* Cambridge: Cambridge UP, 1976.

Hertz, David Michael. *The Tuning of the Word: The Musico-Literary Poetics of the Symbolist Movement.* Carbondale: Southern Illinois UP, 1987.

Hollander, John. *Images of Voice: Music and Sound in Romantic Poetry.* Cambridge: Heffer, 1970.

————. *Melodious Guile: Fictive Pattern in Poetic Language.* New Haven, CT: Yale UP, 1988.

————. *The Untuning of the Sky: Ideas of Music in English Poetry, 1500–1700.* Princeton, NJ: Princeton UP, 1961.

Holmes, Richard. *Coleridge: Early Visions.* New York: Viking, 1990.

Ivey, Donald. *Song: Anatomy, Imagery, and Styles.* New York: Free Press, 1970.

Jakobsen, Roman. *Six Lectures on Sound and Meaning.* Trans. John Mepham. Cambridge, MA: MIT P, 1978.

Johnson, Samuel. *The Works of Samuel Johnson.* Vol 2. Troy, NY: Pafraets, 1903.

Johnston, Kenneth, and Gene W. Ruoff, eds. *The Age of William Wordsworth: Critical Essays on the Romantic Tradition.* New Brunswick, NJ: Rutgers UP, 1987.

Kee, James M. "Narrative Time and Participating Consciousness: A Heideggerian Supplement to McGann's *Romantic Ideology.*" *Romanticism Past and Present* 9.2 (Summer 1985): 51–63.

Kinsley, James, ed. *The Oxford Book of Ballads.* Oxford: Clarendon, 1970.

Kiparsky, Paul. "The Rhythmic Structure of English Verse." *Linguistic Inquiry* 8.2 (Spring 1977): 189–247.

Knapp, Bettina. *Music, Archetype, and the Writer: A Jungian View.* University Park: Pennsylvania State UP, 1988.

Komar, Arthur, ed. *Dichterliebe: An Authoritative Score, Historical Background, Essays in Analysis, Views and Comments.* New York: Norton, 1971.

Kramer, Lawrence. *Music and Poetry: The Nineteenth Century and After.* Berkeley: U of California P, 1984.

Kumbier, William Allan. "Sound, Form, and Signification: Studies in Blake, Smart, and Rousseau." *DAI* 43 (1982): 164A.

Lamb, Charles. *The Portable Charles Lamb.* Ed. John Mason Brown. New York: Penguin, 1980.

Langer, Susanne. *Feeling and Form: A Theory of Art.* New York: Scribner's, 1953.

Lerdahl, Fred, and Ray Jackendoff. *A Generative Theory of Tonal Music.* Cambridge, MA: MIT P, 1985.

List, George. "The Boundaries of Speech and Song." *Ethnomusicology* 7 (1963): 1–16.

Lucas, St. John, ed. *The Oxford Book of French Verse, XIII–XX Centuries.* Oxford: Clarendon, 1957.

MacFarland, Thomas. *Romanticism and the Forms of Ruin: Wordsworth, Coleridge, and Modalities of Fragmentation.* Princeton, NJ: Princeton UP, 1981.

Matthews, Denis. *Beethoven.* Vintage Mater Musicians. New York: Vintage, 1988.

Mellers, Wilfrid. *Harmonious Meeting: A Study of the Relations Between English Music, Poetry, and Theatre c. 1600–1900.* London: Dobson, 1965.

Meyer, Leonard. *Emotion and Meaning in Music.* Chicago: U of Chicago P, 1956.

Milton, John. *Complete Poems and Major Prose.* Ed. Merritt Y. Hughes. New York: Macmillan, 1985.

Miyagawa, Kiyoshi. "Sound and Vision in Wordsworth's Poetry." *Studies in English Literature (Tokyo)* (1981): 25–42.

Muir, Kenneth, ed. *John Keats: A Reassessment.* Liverpool English Texts and Studies 5. Liverpool: Liverpool UP, 1958.

Myers, Jack, and Michael Simms, eds. *The Longman Dictionary of Poetic Terms.* New York: Longman, 1989.

Nettl, Paul. *Mozart and Masonry.* New York: Dorset, 1987.

Neubauer, John. *The Emancipation of Music from Language: Departures from Mimesis in Eighteenth-Century Aesthetics.* New Haven, CT: Yale UP, 1986.

O'Malley, Glenn. *Shelley and Synesthesia*. Evanston, IL: Northwestern UP, 1964.

Pack, Robert. *Affirming Limits: Essays on Mortality, Choice, and Poetic Form*. Amherst: U of Massachusetts P, 1985.

Pater, Walter. *Selected Writings of Walter Pater*. Ed. Harold Bloom. New York: Columbia UP, 1974.

Pauly, Reinhard. *Music in the Classical Period*. 2nd ed. Prentice Hall History of Music Ser. Englewood Cliffs, NJ: Prentice, 1973.

Perkins, David. *The Quest for Permanence: The Symbolism of Wordsworth, Shelley, and Keats*. Cambridge: Harvard UP, 1959.

Pettet, E. C. *On the Poetry of Keats*. 1957. Cambridge: Cambridge UP, 1970.

Preminger, Alex, et al., eds. *Princeton Encyclopedia of Poetry and Poetics*. Enl. ed. Princeton, NJ: Princeton UP, 1974.

Raymond, George Lansing. *Rhythm and Harmony in Poetry and Music*. New York: Putnam, 1920.

Reed, Arden, ed. *Romanticism and Language*. Ithaca, NY: Cornell UP, 1984.

Reed, Joseph W. *Three American Originals: John Ford, William Faulkner, Charles Ives*. Middletown, CT: Wesleyan UP, 1984.

Ricks, Christopher. *Keats and Embarrassment*. Oxford: Clarendon, 1974.

Robinson, Paul. *Opera and Ideas*. New York: Harper, 1985.

Ronga, Luigi. *The Meeting of Poetry and Music*. Trans. Elio Gianturco and Caro Rosanti. New York: Merlin, n.d.

Rosen, Charles. *The Classical Style: Haydn, Mozart, Beethoven*. New York: Norton, 1972.

——— . *Sonata Forms*. New York: Norton, 1980.

Rosenthal, M. L. *The Poet's Art*. New York: Norton, 1987.

Rosenthal, M. L., and Sally Gaul. *The Modern Poetic Sequence*. New York: Oxford UP, 1983.

Sadie, Stanley, ed. *The Norton/Grove Concise Encyclopedia of Music and Musicians*. New York: Norton, 1988.

Salvesen, Christopher. *The Landscape of Memory*. London: Arnold, 1965.

Sapir, Edward W. "The Musical Foundations of Verse." *Journal of English and Germanic Philology* 20.2 (1921): 213–28.

Scher, Steven Paul. *Verbal Music in German Literature*. New Haven, CT: Yale UP, 1968.

Schickele, Peter. "New Horizons in Music Appreciation." *The Wurst of P. D. Q. Bach*. Vanguard Records VSD 719/20, 1971 (sound recording).

Schmidgall, Gary. *Literature as Opera*. New York: Oxford UP, 1977.

Sloboda, John A. *The Musical Mind: The Cognitive Psychology of Music*. Oxford Psychological Ser. 5. Oxford: Clarendon, 1985.

Sosnowski, Terry Ford. "Music of an Angel's Tongue: Meter and Prosodic Devices in the Lyrics of William Blake." *DAI* 44 (1983): 494A.

Springer, George. "Language and Music—Parallels and Divergencies." *For Roman Jakobsen: Essays on the Occasion of His 60th Birthday*. Ed. Morris Halle. The Hague: Mouton, 1956. 504–17.

Stein, Jack M. *Richard Wagner and the Synthesis of the Arts*. Detroit, MI: Wayne State UP, 1960.

Stern, Daniel N., M.D. *Diary of a Baby*. New York: Basic, 1990.

Stevenson, Ronald. "Byron as Lyricist: The Poet Among the Musicians." *Byron: Wrath and Rhyme*. Ed. Alan Bold. Totowa, NJ: Barnes, 1983. 78–99.

Stillinger, Jack. *The Hoodwinking of Madeline and Other Essays on Keats's Poems*. Urbana: U of Illinois P, 1971.

——— . *The Texts of Keats's Poems*. Cambridge, MA: Harvard UP, 1974.

Strunk, Oliver, ed. *Source Readings in Music History*. New York: Norton, 1950.
Sutherland, Donald. *On Romanticism*. New York: New York UP, 1971.
Tetreault, Ronald. "Shelley at the Opera." *Journal of English Literary History* 48.1 (1981): 144–71.
Treitler, Leo. *Music and the Historical Imagination*. Cambridge, MA: Harvard UP, 1989.
Vendler, Helen. *The Odes of John Keats*. Cambridge, MA: Harvard UP, 1983.
Wallace, Robert K. *Emily Brontë and Beethoven: Romantic Equilibrium in Fiction and Music*. Athens: U of Georgia P, 1986.
———. *Jane Austen and Mozart: Classical Equilibrium in Fiction and Music*. Athens: U of Georgia P, 1983.
Ward, Aileen, *John Keats: The Making of a Poet*. New York: Farrar, 1963.
Wasserman, Earl. *The Finer Tone: Keats's Major Poems*. Baltimore, MD: Johns Hopkins UP, 1953.
Weekley, Ernest. *An Etymological Dictionary of Modern English*. New York: Dover, 1967.
Wellek, René. *A History of Modern Criticism 1750–1950, Vol. 2: The Romantic Age*. New Haven, CT: Yale UP, 1955.
Wellek, René, and Austin Warren. *Theory of Literature*. New York: Harcourt, 1942.
Welsh, Andrew. *The Roots of Lyric: Primitive Poetry and Modern Poetics*. Princeton, NJ: Princeton UP, 1978.
Whitrow, G. J. *Time in History: The Evolution of Our General Awareness of Time and Temporal Perspective*. Oxford: Oxford UP, 1988.
Wigod, Jacob. *The Darkening Chamber: The Growth of Tragic Consciousness in Keats*. Salzburg Studies in English Literature 22. Salzburg: Institut für Englische Sprache und Literatur, 1972.
Williams, Aubrey, ed. *Poetry and Prose of Alexander Pope*. New York: Houghton, 1969.
Winn, James Anderson. *Unsuspected Eloquence: A History of the Relations Between Poetry and Music*. New Haven, CT: Yale UP, 1981.
Wolfson Susan J. *The Questioning Presence: Wordsworth, Keats, and the Interrogative Mode in Romantic Poetry*. Ithaca, NY: Cornell UP, 1986.
Woodring, Carl. *Politics and English Romantic Poetry*. Cambridge, MA: Harvard UP, 1970.
Woods, Frederick, ed. *The Oxford Book of English Traditional Verse*. New York: Oxford UP, 1983.
Wordsworth, Jonathan, et al. *William Wordsworth and the Age of English Romanticism*. New Brunswick, NJ: Rutgers UP, 1987.
Yost, George. "Keats's Tonal Development." *Studies in English Literature* 23.4 (1983): 561–78.
Zaenker, Karl A. "String Quartets in Prose." *Canadian Review of Comparative Literature* 8.4 (1981): 521–22.

INDEX

Alphabetization is letter by letter. First lines of poems are distinguished from titles by the absence of any but initial capital letters. Titles otherwise unidentified are Keats's.

WORD LIKE A BELL
was composed in 10/12 Sabon
on a Xyvision system with Linotron 202 output
by BookMasters, Inc.;
printed by sheetfed offset
on 60-pound Glatfelter Natural acid-free stock,
Smyth sewn and bound over .088″ binders boards
in Holliston Roxite B grade cloth
by Braun-Brumfield, Inc.;
text designed by Will Underwood;
dustjacket designed by Diana Gordy;
and published by
THE KENT STATE UNIVERSITY PRESS
Kent, Ohio 44242